Social Media in Society

Jonathon Hutchinson • Fiona Suwana
Cameron McTernan

# Social Media in Society

palgrave
macmillan

Jonathon Hutchinson
University of Sydney
Camperdown, NSW, Australia

Fiona Suwana
University of South Australia
Magill, SA, Australia

Cameron McTernan
University of South Australia
Adelaide, SA, Australia

ISBN 978-3-031-66359-8        ISBN 978-3-031-66360-4   (eBook)
https://doi.org/10.1007/978-3-031-66360-4

This Palgrave Macmillan imprint is published by the registered company Springer Nature Switzerland AG.
The registered company address is: Gewerbestrasse 11, 6330 Cham, Switzerland

If disposing of this product, please recycle the paper.

# ACKNOWLEDGEMENTS

The process of writing this book has been undertaken over an extended couple of years, and we are proud to finally see this manuscript in its final form. Conceived in early 2017, this book came out of a need for a teaching resource that draws on our most up-to-the-minute field research and includes the years of close research within social media. This book draws on interviews with online content creators, creative agencies, brands and government representatives, and spans beyond ten different countries. Our hope is that we can contribute what might be the closing comments on the communication field we have explored for over a decade, social media.

To that end, this book would never have been conceived if it wasn't for the early work of Damien Spry. Without him, as a field-leading thinker, and visionary in many ways, this book would not have been possible. From his early conception of this book, and the time he spent in its early formation, I and the other two authors have been able to introduce our work into a frame that covers the span of the good and bad of social media. Thank you, Damien, for your input, drive and overall love of this area that inspired us to keep pushing when the work would become too much.

As with most books of this moment, we were severely interrupted with the lockdowns of COVID-19. Not only did this interrupt the field work and writing of this book, but it also changed the author line-up. Twice. I'd like to thank my co-authors for coming on when needed and bringing their best academic skills and voice to his project. If we (I) didn't have your energy throughout this writing project, I'm not sure this manuscript would have seen the light of day. Thank you for the conversations, the aha moments, and for pushing through the grind with me as we came towards the finishing line.

The evolving writer line-up was part of the back-stage process, and in the front-of-house space, we also received an enormous amount of support to complete this book. We'd like to thank Alice and our publishing team at Palgrave Macmillan for their continued support of our work, the changing author line-up and the space for us to turn our ideas into logical and meaning-ful chapters of knowledge. Thank you, it has been amazing working with you.

We'd also like to thank our many colleagues who have listened to ideas about this book, have contributed sound arguments and robust debate with us about the concepts in this book, and have been listening to colleagues as we work through this process. These projects never just appear; they are the work of the authors and their professional communities who consistently engage with them on scholarly pursuits of excellence. Thank you to our colleagues at the University of Sydney, and the University of South Australia (UniSA) espe-cially, and to our colleagues located all around the world who engage with our work.

Jonathon: I'd like personally to thank my family who continually provide me the space to work in my professional world and dream big. We're at the point in life where everyone is growing into the next phase of our big family, and that comes with so many challenges. It is incredibly assuring to know that I have the support and love of my family with me in whatever I do, be that personal or professional, Thank you Leisa, Henry, Otto and Gus for being the most inter-esting and loving humans on the planet. I'd also like to thank my colleagues I work with the University of Sydney. Without you all and your support to achieve great things, undertaking a book like this would not be possible. Thanks for the chats, the debates and the scholarly good times!

Fiona: First, I would like to thank my Lord Jesus Christ for helping me to thrive in this academic journey—faith to faith! I am truly grateful for His end-less love, blessings, and grace. I want to express my deep appreciation to Dr Damien Spry for accepting and collaborating with me since beginning ADL teaching, research, and publication—and to Jonathon and Cameron, the pow-erhouse co-authors, for fully trusting me and finishing this book together with a fantastic friendship, knowledge and experience that I treasured. Prof Terry Flew constantly mentored and inspired me in academics. I profoundly thank my UniSA colleagues, Prof Susan Luckman, Bec, Fae, Sally, and the 2024 ECR leaders and group for your endless support and direction—I am incredibly blessed to be in the best teaching and research team. Also, I'm forever grateful to my personal mentors/coaches (SRGDN), who always speak life and sow to me.

This book is a testament to the unwavering love and support of my beloved family. My diamond husband, Jay Tjhia, has been my champion leader, show-ing and inspiring unconditional love, care, patience, creativity and countless sacrifices + my beautiful daughter, Elora Quinn Tjhia, has been a precious love, light, sweet courage and pure joy that I want to inspire her to become an inventor, groundbreaker and big dreamer so let's create great legacies and achieve our next big dreams together as #TeamTjhia. I am deeply thankful to my Papi, Mami, Koko, Aso, A&A (Suwana Fam), Mama, Bro-in-laws, Sis-in-laws (Tjhia Fam), and incredible friends become my Indonesian fam and

Australian fam (esp. Futures Church in Adelaide) for their exceptional love, care and prayers, which have become strength to me. I would only have reached this book milestone because of You and you all—glory to glory!

Cameron: I want to thank my wonderful fiancé, Riley. Thank you for being a sounding board for this book and listening to my endless chatter in the car. Also, Adrian and Terry, thank you for allowing me the time to work on this even given all my other commitments. Damien, we can add this book to the now extensive list of opportunities you've given me. Finally, Chrisanthi, thank you for making the time to provide such kind and valuable feedback.

# CONTENTS

# LIST OF FIGURES

# LIST OF TABLES

## CHAPTER 1

# Introduction: Social Media Histories, Contexts, Development

This chapter introduces the key themes relating to the role of social media in contemporary society. Using the seminal question from media studies stalwart Harold Lasswell (1948) and his *5 W's* rubric, 'Who says what to whom, through which channel and with what effect', the chapter gives a concise overview of the key features of social media, including:

- the people who use, create, and control social media, as well as social media users and content creators (who, and to whom);
- the content and social media practices, including social games, engagement activities, memes and other images (what);
- the technologies, including platform interfaces, affordances and algorithms (through which channel); and
- impacts, effects and affects of social media, including those from the level of the individual, the social/community, the nation and the global, and the contexts which shape social media impacts.

The five W's are introduced with reference to examples from case studies and are used to acquaint the reader with the various ways of approaching the study of social media, and its impacts on society. In this way, this first section forms an overview of the book's topics, themes and approaches, as well as the topics that subsequent chapters will explore at greater depth. These key topics include:

- User-generated content and 'produsage'
- Networked media systems and infrastructures contrasted with broadcast and mass media models
- Social media practices understood as participation, engagement, influence and conflict

J. Hutchinson et al., *Social Media in Society*, https://doi.org/10.1007/978-3-031-66360-4_1

- Privacy/Surveillance and the personal/political
- Capitalism and Freedom as ideologies of the social media

This chapter considers the development of social media in the context of theories of techno-social change, such as diffusions of innovation and moral panics. It includes pre-digital forms of media that emphasise sociality on a personal level (such as the sharing of letters) and for political purposes at the level of the state (such as graffiti and leaf letting) (Standage, 2013). The contrast, continuities and overlaps with mass media forms the thematic underpinning for the more recent history of social media, from the late twentieth-century Internet-based immediate antecedents to the present-day platforms. Throughout this history, technological developments will be introduced in the context of their socio-cultural environs and their political and economic circumstances. This section also maps the rest of the book and introduces some key ideas about the research and study of social media, in preparation for Chap. 2.

## Introducing Social Media in Society

Social media has been popular, although experiencing a pushback or decrease in interest of late, because of the ubiquitousness of platforms for everyday users with a particular focus on Facebook, Instagram, TikTok, LinkedIn, Snapchat and Twitter, that will be referred to by its new name under the Musk era, X. While these platforms have dominated the last ten years especially, and in fear of providing the reader with a vast shopping list, there are also other significant players such as Reddit, WeChat, YouTube and many others along the way that have risen and fallen—or been purchased by the larger platforms— that contribute to our contemporary understanding of social media. While social media has been the focus of many scholars during this period, there are a few key academics that enable us to provide a conceptual understanding of social media while also introducing some of the key terms.

danah boyd and Nicole Ellison (2007) defined social media or social network sites as web-based services that allow individuals to (1) construct a public or semi-public profile within a bounded system, (2) articulate a list of other users with whom they share a connection, and (3) view and traverse their list of connections and those made by others within the system. The nature and nomenclature of these connections may vary from site to site. Zizi Papacharissi (2015) laments the widely used but rarely defined term 'social media', arguing that media has always been a social endeavour. Another scholar, Tom Standage (2013) affirms that the notion of media is always social. Standage (2013) also shared that in the early use of papyrus scrolls, people would often copy, share and quote letters with new commentary added as letters were passed along. It would appear then that this term is somewhat amorphous, yet it is still regularly used by scholars, writers, and the general public. While most of us *know* what other people mean when we talk about social media, we run into complex meanings when we unpack and begin to define it more holistically.

YouTube, among other social networks, is commonly referred to as a social media *platform*, further adding to how we understand and experience our social media. But how much does it have in common with other platforms like Facebook, TikTok or X? Science and Technology Studies scholar, Tarlton Gillespie published a seminal article in 2010, *The Politics of Platforms*, that shifted our thinking away from networks alone and towards social media in the form of a platform to encapsulate the role these technologies embody. Platforms, he notes, is 'an increasingly familiar term in the description of the online services of content intermediaries, both in their self-characterizations and in the broader public discourse of users, the press, and commentators' (p. 348). In this light, Gillespie reminds us of the intermediary role social media is performing as a communication space, but also as an advertising, political and regulatory. We return to this concept in Chap. 4, but it is worth noting the shift of what we broadly conceive as *social media* is significantly broader and complex than first understood.

To add to the rise of recent communication practices (Newman et al., 2023) instant messaging services, such as WeChat, WhatsApp, and Messenger, have become a significant component of what we call social media. Perhaps, we use instant messaging services as a digital one-to-one/many-to-many version of mass media that predated the Internet in what has been argued as a characteristically un-social period of media history. However, all media are social in the form of a social institute that creates, translates and conveys meaning from individuals to individuals, individuals to many, many to many—media concepts we unpack further below. Traditional media, such as newspapers, books, radio and television are heavily institutionalised (Lüders, 2008), with only a tiny segment of the public given the power on these platforms by which to voice their opinions or share information. Social media certainly challenged this institutionalised approach towards communication.

A recent meta-analysis attempted to clarify the meaning of the term social media by reviewing 88 papers defining the term. Aichner et al. (2021, p. 215) note that the label has been applied to a broad range of media and communication technologies, including "blogs, business networks, collaborative projects, enterprise social networks (SN), forums, microblogs, photo sharing, products review, social bookmarking, social gaming, SN, video sharing, and virtual worlds". Their results also show a history of definitions spanning more than 25 years of scholars using the term synonymously with social networks and virtual communities. Among the most cited is boyd and Ellison's (2007, p. 211) definition of social networking sites. Nevertheless, YouTube could be a better platform for all those things, and their definition does nothing to account for user-generated content. One of the problems with synonymising social networking sites with social media is it firmly locates the concept within the technology and their websites. As such, it mostly ignores culture as a contributing factor to the role in defining this paradigm—problematic and determinist. In this grand narrative of social media, it's also important to note that boyd and Ellison's definition arrived in 2007, the same year as the release of the iPhone and as such, predates the app-ification of our digital media lives that Goggin (2021, p. 3) highlights. Goggin notes apps are a two-handed approach to the sociotechnical approach towards communication:

> *On the one hand, there are the visions and realities of the mobile, cyber and online societies which people envisaged from the late 1980s through to the early 00s. On the other hand, there are the imaginaries and materialities of the pervasive media and immersive digital societies, which emerged internationally in the 2010s and onwards, in all their different forms and inequalities.*

In this context, we begin to unpack the relationship between users, technologies and cultures of use, and the ways in which inequalities are introduced and amplified within social media. Social media and its ubiquity suggest understanding how users engage with networks, platforms and apps as part of the entire ecosystem which extends beyond the content or media alone. Here, we begin to introduce politics as a key aspect of social media including data and privacy [cite], the continual and ever-present processes that turn our lives in data through datafication (Majias & Couldry, 2019), and surveillance capitalism (Zuboff, 2019) that we have now come to associate with social media platforms and smartphones. These few aspects alone introduce not only the surveillance aspects of using social media, but also the burgeoning data markets that emerged during the 2000s and 2010s, and significantly how these data had significant and consequential impact on our information and political systems.

The use-case for the term social media is context-dependent, and as such, the criteria for what it is and is not might change depending on its application. For instance, in a media industries framework, we might designate a platform as social if it emerges from the paradigms of Silicon Valley and Big Tech. But where do platforms, or technology companies as most refer to themselves as, from outside of the United States, for example BeReal or Douyin, position themselves? We might also look to theories of democracy and consider platforms where access is de-institutionalised, but we also continue to see online communities discussed alongside Instagram, where its community building constitutes an essential social media communication and connection that becomes commercialised, such as in fitness, food, travel, lifestyle, and other topics. Moreover, in the context of this book, we should consider moving away from designating specific platforms as social media and instead consider social media as something closer to a cultural moment: a shift known as a period when one trend dies, and another emerges (Mauran, 2022). Or perhaps as a zeitgeist—a moment in time when the audience has become the centre of attention and the technologies, industries and culture which have aligned to promote and capitalise upon it.

This conceptualisation of social media as a contemporary historical paradigm for mass communication provides more latitude to consider the broader context by which social media technology and culture emerge. This approach recognises that there is a trajectory to social media and that there is no clear starting point to locate the movement. Instead, gradual technological steps such as the development of the Internet, Web 2.0, platforms, smartphones and apps have all nudged us to arrive at this moment. This is a moment that doesn't emerge in a technology, regulatory or user bubble alone, but instead incorporates cultural innovations such as blogging, memes and influencers who have helped to arrive in this social media epoch.

## THE TECHNOLOGICAL, INDUSTRIAL, POLITICAL AND CULTURAL DRIVERS OF TRANSFORMATION

### From a One-to-Many Towards Many-to-Many Model

Mass communication theory, especially that of Denis McQuail (2010), describes the traditional types of communication that embraced the one-to-many model. In this approach, communication holds an incredibly powerful position in that the message that is crafted by a few is disseminated to the masses to influence how they think, act, and build a sense of society. Here, media is certainly not a passive activity where the media, and thereby meaning is being beamed into every loungeroom around the country, at every news-stand at every train station, and on every radio in a city's car system. It is the basis on which our communication model was built from early Aristotle modes of communication, through to our more recent broadcast radio and television models. This, of course was challenged with the introduction of social media, most specifically how the opportunity of discourse and its implementation was designed and mobilised among audiences.

In early media studies, social theorist Jürgen Habermas (1991) stated that the public sphere in coffee house discussions was a proactive tool for a new social class to wield, assert or discuss their political, social and economic rights to their states through communication techniques. This is an underground/do-it-yourself approach to democracy that circumvents the existing traditional media avenues to address the underrepresented, the marginalised and to some extent those without political voice. It was a theory that examines how alternative public interests are brought to the table when politicians, and their media avenues, seek to avoid specific issues. Here we see the voice of the people emerge and gain attention through alternative modes of communication. It is the establishment of flows of communication beyond the trusted channels, often dominated by state and market, towards a more citizen-centred model—the emergence of a many-to-many communication model.

Along the way, social media, like the coffee-house contestations and the one-to-many early media, consolidate and integrate many-to-many communication flows with other media amidst pressures from public spheres (Jensen, 2015; Staab & Thiel, 2022). Multi stakeholders like markets, states, and civil societies worldwide utilise and apply social media for their interests, occasionally for complementary but also for conflicting purposes (Jensen, 2015). Social media has become so important for the development of the democratic public sphere as it can be broadcast many to many to their audience. As such, we experienced the establishment of a kind of public that was enabled through social media participation in networked and event publics. Again, these are unpacked in detail below.

A core consideration of this section is that social media enables multiple forms of communication among its users: one-way, two-way, multiple voices of communication with an audience beyond any specific recipient. This form of communication falls under the term many-to-many communication (Shirky, 2009; Rafaeli & LaRose, 1993), which has been used to describe the nature of interaction on listservs, blogs, and chatting (Hogan & Quan-Haase, 2010). Social media that afford many-to-many communication can broadcast messages to a broader audience that can then exchange perspectives, additional input and further knowledge—the social affordance of a two-way audience. Social media is not unidirectional (one-to-many) in the classical mass media of the twentieth century, while the recipients of the information in social media are also senders of communication (Staab & Thiel, 2022). Social media is multidirectional and broadcasts many to many. Like Zuboff (2019) argued, social media is the multi-directionality of communication (many-to-many communication, user-generated content, etc.) and is analytically reversed by the insight that the actual contact generates observational data as a mediating platform uses, which creates a strong vested interest in developing the communication.

Social media have evolved by their abilities to broadcast to many-to-many communication, drawing on and feeding into networks of one-to-one and one-to-many communication (Jensen & Helles, 2011). Like other new media, their definition of communication technologies and social action resources continues to be negotiated in theory and practice. As digital media technologies, social media are grounded in the principles of communication and digital media, alongside cultural and science and technology studies. The computer is a meta-medium (Kay & Goldberg, 1999) that hosts a range of newly born and old-adopted media that becomes part of circuit of culture (du Gay et al., 2013) that both enables informs and is guided by cultural uses.

### *Communities, Networks and Publics*

Social media has expanded beyond perpetual new social networks and numerous platforms; social networking is increasing online use, and new communities are being created and recreated on this connection and further for public participation. Tierney (2013) argued that social media generally enables categorical identities more than the dense, multiplex, and organised sites of relationships connected with the term network. Tierney also stated that the terms networks, community, and public sphere for social media can be misleading partially because of the political and social dimensions (Tierney, 2013). In the context of social media, it is helpful to breakdown each of these terms to understand not only what they are, but how they function and operate in digital mediated environments.

Community is a contested term that offers one way of understanding how individuals group together, often for positive purposes, but also in formations that embody exclusionary practices. Cohen (1985, p. 9) suggests community "is symbolically constructed, as a system of values, norms, and moral codes which provides a sense of identity within a bounded whole to its members". Using Cohen as an approach also aligns with the earlier community conception of Barth and Bergen (1969), who suggest community is merely a boundary construction that separates people from what they are not. Cultural sociology suggests objects and symbols indicate a sense of belonging, or difference, and constructs environments to define 'us' and 'them'. Similarly, cultural sociology also suggests a symbol exposes one meaning but also expresses a secondary connotation for those attuned to its significance (Cohen, 1985). Therefore, a combination of symbols constitutes a style, defining boundaries for individuals who belong to a community, enabling individuals to construct their own identities by aligning with the community conventions. Alternatively, as Barth and Bergen (1969) suggest, boundaries are constructed as a means of understanding what the community members are not—"signs of forbidden identity" (Hebdige, 1979: 18). Using the subculture lens of Hebdige enables the examination of how community is constructed, while the shared conventions of subculture are also useful for identifying the markers of a community.

Wellman et al. (1996, p. 214) identify computer-supported social networks (CSSNs) as a mechanism between "people as well as machines" to "link globally with kindred souls for companionship, information, and social support from their homes". These scholars attempted to understand what online communities would look like and how they would operate given their limited social presence and geographical proximity. This was the precursor for understanding the larger societal impact of online communities, or virtual communities, through increased connectivity afforded by information and communication technologies (Wellman & Gulia, 1999). As communities extend beyond their localised versions where individuals are born into their networks, individuals begin to choose who is in their networks. Here we see the emergence of "personal community networks: fragmented multiple social networks connected only by the person (or the household) at the centre" (Wellman et al., 2005, p. 163). Simply put, networks describe a mode of connection between smaller clusters of individuals, rather than the larger cluster, which provides "diversity, choice, and manoeuvrability at the probable cost of cohesion and long-term trust" (ibid.: 164).

Publics are a formation of individuals that come together for a specific purpose, but often are defined by time, for example through an event. They are, however, representative of how individuals have progressed from communities and networks to sophisticated forms of gatherings of individuals that are enabled through digital technologies. boyd (2014, p. 40) brings these ideas together through the concept of *networked publics,* where she notes they are the mediated ways in which publics gather:

> Networked publics are publics that are restructured by networked technologies. As such, they are simultaneously (1) the space constructed through networked technologies and (2) the imagined collective that emerges as a result of the intersection of people, technology, and practice. Networked publics serve many of the same functions as other types of publics—they allow people to gather for social, cultural, and civic purposes, and they help people connect with a world beyond their close friends and family.

In each of these groupings of individuals through communication technologies, or digital intermediation, they are reflective of the cultural uses of digital communication to enable a variety of practices. These technologies simply do not emerge and enable cultures but are instead reflective of the sociotechnical arrangements that continually evolve and shift how we connect and communicate as humans. As this book progresses, we will observe how a variety of combinations—communities, networks and publics—engage in social media for a variety of activities.

## Chapter Breakdown

Building on this introductory chapter, Chap. 2 begins to unpack our contemporary social media ecology is based on the developing infrastructures that have emerged during the past 20 years of information and communication technologies. Developing from earlier versions of networked communication systems built across the Internet, our contemporary social media system inherently embodies the ethos of the World Wide Web (www) as envisioned by Sir Tim Burners-Lee: one that enables the collaborative and collective practices of its users to create, share and distribute information and knowledge. However, we have seen this earlier vision of the utopian social media epoch pass as its infrastructures and technologies have become powerful data brokers for the technology companies that build and support them. Our current social media environment is now a complex ecosystem of infrastructures, technologies, automation, artificial intelligence and machine learning, all of which are significantly controlled by the (mostly) Silicon Valley–based technology giants of our time. In this context, the need to better understand how social media operates, and influences societies, is crucial. This raises the questions: how can we study social media's role in society? How can we do research into social media, its operations and implications, its roles and functions? What research methods are used to explore social media and its uses? Also, how can we make sense of social media: what theories and approaches to social media studies are available to help us think about and understand how social media affects us and our social worlds?

Chapter 2 makes visible the infrastructures of our social media environments. By leaning on our earlier media and technology studies literature (McLuhan, Kittler, Williams), science and technology studies (Rositer), computational science and digital cultures (Goffman, Senft, Marwick, boyd), this chapter maps out the production of social media data and how that data is used, managed, moved and monetised across networks. Specifically, it explores the shifting public sphere towards the digital sphere, legal and regulatory implications of social media, the political economy of social media, networks and the users within these spaces. The final section of this chapter introduces and discusses some of the limits and considerations of the study of social media, including the restricted access to data imposed by the social media companies and—paradoxically—the virtually unrestricted access to personal, identifiable social media content. Issues of access, privacy and consent are therefore foregrounded as vitally important ethical considerations for social media studies.

Chapter 3 includes case studies on the major social media platforms, including the Facebook stable—Facebook, Messenger, Instagram and WhatsApp—Twitter, YouTube, Snapchat, TikTok, LinkedIn, Reddit, Line, Medium, WeChat, Sina Weibo and QQ. For the major US-based companies, this chapter foregrounds the foundation histories (and creation myths) and the ideological and philosophical underpinnings of the entrepreneurial and hacker communities from whence many social media companies emerged. This section acts as a biographical account of the platforms themselves—their structures, features and underlying programmatic and curational logics—as well as the business models that sustain them and have fuelled their rise to such soaring heights. It also reflects on the relationship between the platforms and the political climate in which they arose and exist, including the ideological emphasis on free speech in the context of American national and political values, and the far more pragmatic, and covert, requirements of American (and other) national security, intelligence and policing agencies to access user data for their purposes.

A key argument in this chapter is how these social, technological and political forces have aligned to promote data-driven capitalism (also known as surveillance capitalism [Zuboff, 2019]) at the expense of individual privacy. While this question has been significantly addressed from the Global North perspective, the impact this very concept has on the Global South is still playing out. This section ends with a discussion of how the tension between freedom and privacy exists as a key driver in ongoing policy debates, and how related concerns about content moderation and the efforts to monitor and limit the spread of problematic content are likewise key concerns for the social media companies.

The users of social media have changed and adapted as the technologies, infrastructures and cultures of practice have evolved throughout the history of social media, which is the core focus for Chap. 4. From earlier online community formations that sought to connect and improve users' lives, through to the more divisive and damaging practices across the contemporary platforms—including harassment, bullying, doxing and extremist vitriol and online abuse—users have assembled with like-minded individuals. This is the basis for individuals to perform their online identities and connect with networked individuals and online communities. With these practices and interpersonal relationships, social media users continue to evolve from the earlier back-stage formations (Goffman) to highly polished versions of their Insta-moods. Building on these individual identities and collective practices, the emerged space of emotions has emerged through liquid love practices (Hobbs).

This chapter builds on the established platform practices of this book to highlight how individuals and groups of users effectively operate on social media. This chapter highlights the implications of user relationships from dating, to influencing, to political and lobbying practices across the suite of social media platforms. From influential Instagram campaigns to political Twitter, vlogging and YouTube, and livestreaming on Momo, users continue to develop new ways of attracting audiences and engaging them for a variety of purposes. It lays the foundation for the future chapters that uses rich ethnographic data to describe how users play the visibility game (Cotter) and engage in cultural intermediation practices to highlight value within cultural production (Hutchinson) on social media platforms.

Social media platforms have provided new employment opportunities for creative content producers all over the world. In Chap. 5, we highlight that they connect content-hungry users with savvy producers to provide highly engaged experiences for these stakeholder groups. But the process of creating content is relentless: producers must produce regularly, align with algorithmic determined interest areas, have no set start and finish times, have no union representation and are required to align with the terms and services of these platforms to continue to operate. At the same time, the platforms have the power to de-monetise these often highly popular producers for their past actions if they deem them to not align with the overall trajectory of the platform provider. To combat this, online content producers have developed procedures and mechanisms to operate effectively in these entirely precarious environments. Collaborations, meet and greets, and new live online experiences such as AMA (ask me anything) and livestreaming have enabled many online content producers to create new and innovative ways to keep a check on how they preserve their labour efforts in an 'always-on' environment. Intermediaries such as digital agencies and multichannel networks have also found a specific niche to connect online content producers with large audiences through platform affordances. Chapter 5 highlights the practices and surrounding industries of social media content producers by exploring the precarious labour models, the role of agencies and the new content production models that are created by online content producers. It also explores how other operators outside of the famous and influencer space conduct business on social media.

Building on from the previous chapter, Chap. 6 examines how surveillance capitalism has impacted on how news companies operate, and on how other techno-social aspects of news and information gathering, reporting and distribution are transformed through social media. The role social media plays in the generation, distribution and consumption of news has emerged as a major concern due to the perceived impact of news coverage and consumption on public debate on key social issues (such as marriage equality), environmental issues (such as climate change), public health issues (like vaccinations and the COVID-19 pandemic) and political events (like the Brexit vote in the UK and national elections in the US, the Philippines, Malaysia, Kenya, France and many others. Media technologies have historically had a role in how societies collectively discuss and debate important issues and have been pivotal tools for those seeking to influence opinions and thus shape societies through its impact on news, journalism and public opinion. Social media has joined pre-existing sources of news and information, transforming the news environment in several profound ways. The way journalists work to gather information, interview subjects and report the news is different, for example social media posts have largely replaced the 'vox pops' or sound bites of yesteryear. News has been severely affected by social media and search companies (especially Facebook and Google) entering and then dominating the advertising market, making it difficult for commercial news organisations to survive on advertising revenue and leading some of them to erect paywalls and subscription-only news services.

Also, social media (and search) are a major source of news for many audiences and in many different ways. This impacts the way news generated by journalists circulates, gets attention, and has impact. It also creates new opportunities as social media users can access news and information from non-traditional sources. Citizen journalism and online opinion by, for example, prominent personalities on YouTube, offers alternatives to mainstream news media. Chapter 6 addresses these issues in the context of the dire differences in understanding of public affairs between social media users and journalists. It also discusses research into the role that social media users play in the distribution of news via posting and sharing, and how this varies according to the reputation of the source, the type of content, the 'first-mover' advantage, the type and level of connection between the audience and the story, and other matters. The freedom and opportunity social media provide to non-traditional news sources contribute to a media ecosystem where accidental misinformation and deliberate disinformation (what we might problematically refer to as 'fake news') are able to easily and cheaply developed, distributed and promoted. Social media networks provide a dynamic system where 'fake news' can thrive and have significant detrimental impacts on public debate, on trust in news and in governments, scientists and other experts. This chapter concludes with a discussion of the connections and crossovers between news, fake news, and—in an introduction to the subsequent chapter—influence campaigns.

The relationships between social media and online political influence campaigns have generated great interest and considerable anxiety. Chapter 7 takes topics raised in the previous two chapters—social marketing techniques (Chap. 5) and the impact of social media on the 'public sphere' (Chap. 6) and develops them to highlight more specifically how 'influence' campaigns operate, who conducts influence campaigns, and with what effects on politics, social campaigns, and international relations. The chapter considers how marketing techniques are applied to political and social change campaigns. It includes attempts at persuasion, and manipulation, through the digital advertising technologies that are available from both legitimate and shady sources (the mainstream and black markets in adtech). It includes case studies of political influence campaigns that have been run within borders, and those conducted by foreign powers. Of the latter, we include examples of 'foreign influence' campaigns and responses to them by governments, and defence and intelligence agencies, who regard (and respond to) these campaigns as a form of 'grey-zone warfare', as the 'weaponisation of information'. Social media company actions to detect and remove 'coordinated inauthentic behaviour' are also included. This chapter also outlines and critiques the attitudes and approaches to the regulation of political speech by the social media companies, including a case study of the 2016 and 2020 US Presidential elections and the actions by Twitter, Facebook and others to limit or impact political speech. Social media users' attitudes towards the potential or actual influence that social media has on election campaigns and political content, and their variation according to political partisanship, are also discussed.

Chapter 7 goes further to describe the fears that social media has a negative impact on democracy and the public sphere are well-founded, but there is another, equally important story to tell about the role of social media for social justice and pro-democracy movements. Because social media is more individualised and more participatory than traditional media, it offers opportunities for users to express their own opinion, expression, or ideas and to link individual self-expression with civic and political participation to support democracy. Social media has facilitated political participation in reform movements globally: the Arab Spring, the Indignados Movement in Spain, the Occupy Movement in North America, the Umbrella Movement in Hong Kong, the Tunisian Revolution and the Save KPK 2015 in Indonesia. The participants in both movements utilised social media to communicate, raise awareness, recruit participants, coordinate information, and mobilise people. While social media in political revolutions and campaign was beneficial, enabling the group to develop a large-scale of networks and to pressure the government to do actions. However, there are challenges of using social media for digital activism as it led to the movement only having a short lifespan with the volunteerism, loose connections and lack of leadership.

Chapter 8 uses some key themes from the previous section on political communication and extends into the international arena, focussing on the use of social media as a means of engaging in conflict, and as a vehicle for fostering amity between nations. The section on conflict outlines the recent history of known interference campaigns by foreign nations, including case studies in the US, UK, Hollands, Ukraine, Estonia, Taiwan, and how these are like and different from earlier examples of information warfare, propaganda, and psychological warfare. It discusses the tactics and strategies employed by those who use this type of malicious interference, and how they seek to remain in the 'grey zone' or 'littoral zone' below the level of outright conflict. These types of communication campaigns rely on the same technologies and many of the same tactics, of typically marketing and advertising campaigns, making them particularly insidious and difficult counter. This section therefore considers also how the commercial and social aspects of social media that are fundamental to their existence, and their success, are key attributes in information warfare. These include elements such as the size, scale and speed of networked information systems, and the design of social media platforms that promote emotional appeal to increase screen time and engagement. A key point in this section is that information warfare seeks to exacerbate pre-existing tensions and fissures within societies, rather than create them.

Responses to information warfare include technological, regulatory, and social have focussed on traditional national security and defence tropes, including deterrence, detection, denial, disruption and destruction. We catalogue some of these approaches, based on government and research institute reports, and critique them. We consider how alternative approaches, such as media literacy and building trust and social cohesion, may need to play a larger role. The second section of Chap. 8 looks at how social media has impacted on normal, diplomatic relations between nations, using case studies and highlighting best and worst practice. We outline how the Ministries of Foreign Affairs had been slow to adopt digital diplomacy, then over-enthusiastic about its potential. The research we introduce outlines how social media's usefulness varies greatly from nation to nation but can be generally considered to be more useful in countries with smaller, younger and poorer populations.

Social media platforms and social websites/bulletin boards are sites, including spaces like 4chan and 8chan, where illegal, immoral and anti-social behaviour can proliferate and be celebrated. This dark side of social media is the focus of Chap. 9, and it examines some of the bad online behaviours such as everyday harassment and bullying; doxing (identifying private and anonymous individuals); using hate speech and promoting hate crimes and otherwise celebrate, perpetrate and spread hate and violence. Other criminal behaviour that has successfully moved online and onto social media platforms includes drug and human trafficking, including sexual trafficking on children. At the same time, the dark side of social media has emerged as a response to the increase in surveillance capitalism highlighted in the earlier chapters. This chapter examines the socio-technological aspects of social media that facilitate these types of behaviour such as the (semi-)anonymity of the Internet and the ability to hide in the dark web, and the sheer volume of users and online activity. It considers how regulation regimes that protect social media companies from responsibility for the content posted on their platforms have contributed to this sense of lawlessness, and why the social media companies have fiercely resisted content regulation by governments. It looks at the online cultures associated with shitposting and trolling, their histories and impacts on contemporary society, and their uses of specific discursive and visual communicative practices. It also looks at the role of governments, in terms of their attempts to monitor and govern these seemingly out of control spaces.

Chapter 9 uses cases studies to examine this apparent dark web emergence from both sides of the debate. This includes gamergate, QAnon, the Christchurch Massacre, the persecution of the Rohingya people in Myanmar and the attacks on journalists and political activists in the Philippines to outline the role that social media has played in hate and violence. Alternatively, it uses the lens of the dark web to understand how activist groups such as Anonymous operate, alternate search engines have emerged outside of Google's strangle hold, and initiatives such as SecureDrop have emerged for whistleblowers and journalists to meet and share information.

Finally, Chap. 10 discusses how social media facilitates activism, connective action and social change. Social media can contribute to citizen mobilisation and participation. Activism and campaigning become easier and cheaper, expanding activists' capacity to communicate, coordinate, and mobilise information and society. Characteristics of this new type of connective action include personal expression and voluntary coordination without organisational infrastructure or leadership. The logic of collective action emphasises the important of goal orientation, the high costs of group formation, and groups' executive power relation to individuals (Papacharissi & Trevey, 2018). This chapter introduces research from diverse communities in the Global South, noting the diversity of political and cultural contexts which impact on social media activism and seeking to some extent to address the relative paucity of research into and discussion of social media campaigns outside of North America and Europe. The research in some areas of the Global South, for example, indicates, inter alia, how people who believe that social media activities can affect changes at the community level, they are more likely to feel capable of effecting change at national and international levels: in other words, social media can be empowering. Examples of promoting, establishing and supporting campaigns from local to national include the ForBALI movement (the Balinese People's Forum to Reject Reclamation in Bali Island); those from national to global include The Earth Hour campaign; and from local to global to local (glocalisation) include the Black Lives Matter movement. However, in other contexts, in a form of 'astroturfing', the strategies and tactics social media activism can be co-opted by malign and misleading actors. This chapter also points to prospects for an improved digital future for generations to come. It considers how social media users are, for good or ill, more digitally immersed and grow up with more access to information and connections. It considers, in principle and practice, digital media literacy as a strategy for addressing the concerns and promoting the productive and critically reflexive uses of social media.

The chapter, and the book, concludes with several prominent remaining questions, concerns and possibilities for the next stage of social media's history: how can individuals, communities and polities shape social media and its impacts on society for our mutual and collective benefit?

## REFERENCES

Aichner, T., Grünfelder, M., Maurer, O., & Jegeni, D. (2021). Twenty-Five Years of Social Media: A Review of Social Media Applications and Definitions from 1994 to 2019. *Cyberpsychology, Behavior, and Social Networking, 24*(4), 215–222.

Barth, F., & Bergen, U. i. (1969). *Ethnic Groups and Boundaries: The Social Organization of Culture Difference*. Little, Brown.

boyd, d. (2014). *It's Complicated: The Social Lives of Networked Teens*. Yale University Press. https://doi.org/10.12987/9780300166439-002

boyd, D. M., & Ellison, N. B. (2007). Social Network Sites: Definition, History, and Scholarship. *Journal of Computer-Mediated Communication, 13*(1), 210–230.

Cohen, A. P. (1985). *The Symbolic Construction of Community*. Tavistock Publications.

du Gay, P., Hall, S., Janes, L., Madsen, A. K., Mackay, H., & Negus, K. (2013). *Doing Cultural Studies: The Story of the Sony Walkman*. SAGE Publications.

Goggin, G. (2021). *Apps: From Mobile Phones to Digital Lives*. Wiley.

Habermas, J. (1991). *The Structural Transformation of the Public Sphere: An Inquiry into a Category of Bourgeois Society*. MIT Press.

Hebdige, D. (1979). *Subculture, The Meaning of Style* (1st ed.). Routledge.

Hogan, B., & Quan-Haase, A. (2010). Persistence and Change in Social Media. *Bulletin of Science, Technology & Society, 30*(5), 309–315.

Jensen, K. B. (2015). What's Social about Social Media? *Social Media + Society, 1*(1). https://doi.org/10.1177/2056305115578874

Jensen, K. B., & Helles, R. (2011). The Internet as a Cultural Forum: Implications for Research. *New Media & Society, 13*(4), 517–533.

Kay, A., & Goldberg, A. (1999). Personal Dynamic Media. In P. A. Mayer (Ed.), *Computer Media and Communication: A Reader* (pp. 111–119). Oxford University Press. (Original work published 1977).

Lasswell, H. D. (1948). The Structure and Function of Communication in Society. In L. Bryson (Ed.), *The Communication of Ideas* (pp. 37–51). Harper and Row.

Lüders, M. (2008). Conceptualizing Personal Media. *New Media & Society, 10*(5), 683–702.

Majias, U. A., & Couldry, N. (2019). Datafication. *Internet Policy Review, 8*(4), 1–11.

Mauran, C. (2022). *How to Survive the 'Vibe Shift' It's Coming. Are You Prepared?*. Mashable. Retrieved January, 10, 2024, from https://mashable.com/article/vibe-shift-survival-guide

McQuail, D. (2010). *McQuail's Mass Communication Theory* (6th ed.). SAGE Publications Ltd.

Newman, N., Fletcher, R., Eddy, K., Robertson, C. T., & Nielsen, R. k. (2023). Reuters Institute Digital News Report 2023. Retrieved from Oxford, https://reutersinstitute. politics.ox.ac.uk/sites/default/files/2023-06/Digital_News_Report_2023.pdf

Papacharissi, Z. (2015). *Affective Publics: Sentiment, Technology, and Politics*. Oxford University Press.

Papacharissi, Z., & Trevey, M. T. (2018). Affective Publics and Windows of Opportunity: Social Media and the Potential for Social Change. In Z. Papacharissi & M. T. Trevey (Eds.), *The Routledge Companion to Media and Activism* (pp. 1–10). Routledge.

Rafaeli, S., & LaRose, R. J. (1993). Electronic Bulletin Boards and "Public Goods" Explanations of Collaborative Mass Media. *Communication Research, 20*(2), 277–297.

Shirky, C. (2009). *Here Comes Everybody: How Change Happens When People Come Together*. Penguin UK.

Staab, P., & Thiel, T. (2022). Social Media and the Digital Structural Transformation of the Public Sphere. *Theory, Culture & Society, 39*(4), 129–143. https://doi.org/10.1177/02632764221103527

Standage, T. (2013). *Writing on the Wall: Social Media—The First 2,000 Years*. Bloomsbury Publishing USA.

Tierney, T. (2013). *The Public Space of Social Media: Connected Cultures of the Network Society*. Routledge.

Wellman, B., & Gulia, M. (1999). Virtual Communities as Communities. *Communities in Cyberspace*, 167–194.

Wellman, B., Salaff, J., Dimitrova, D., Garton, L., Gulia, M., & Haythornthwaite, C. (1996). Computer Networks as Social Networks: Collaborative Work, Telework, and Virtual Community. *Annual Review of Sociology, 22*, 213–238.

Wellman, B., Hogan, B., Berg, K., Boase, J., Carrasco, J.-A., Côté, R., … Tran, P. (2005). Connected Lives: The Project. In P. Purcell (Ed.), *Networked Neighbourhoods*. Springer.

Zuboff, S. (2019). *The Age of Surveillance Capitalism*. Profile Books.

## CHAPTER 2

# Studying Social Media

## Introduction: What Can and Can't We Study: Users, Content, Technologies, Industries

In 2015, the Australian Broadcasting Corporation was given permission to release the metadata of one of their journalists, Brett Ockenden, as an experiment to understand what the implications of metadata are. This was a response to the shift in local laws requiring Internet service providers to retain data on each of their customers for up to two years. In the lead up to this regulation, there was much debate on what metadata is, how it can be manipulated and how it could be used against the Australian citizens. The ABC experiment showed some alarming results of what can be concluded from seemingly harmless information—or social media data. By observing Ockenden's data, much of which was produced when his phone connected to communication towers, the public could work out where he works and lives, how he commutes, when he moved house, where his parents live, what flights he takes and when he leaves the country, and some basic information about who he called. The significant take away from the experiment suggests that most people are unclear about the trade-offs we agree to when using social media. As users, we need to be aware of what is happening in the background, for example who is watching and what are they doing with our data, and to also ensure we are engaging in appropriate tools that protect our online activities.

This chapter is designed to deepen our understanding of the tension between social media and its use: do social media platforms provide us with greater access at the cost of surrendering our privacy? Is being connected to our family and friends worth having our data taken and used in ways that we probably didn't expect to happen? What are the consequences of having access to wrong or misleading news and information? And as social media researchers, how do we access these data for good, and what is our responsibility when we have that information? Broadly speaking, the general push was that social media were

J. Hutchinson et al., *Social Media in Society*, https://doi.org/10.1007/978-3-031-66360-4_2

being created for the benefit of the public: a kind of public service. Social media are also being created as a response to a market, however, which has an increasingly incessant desire to take our everyday movements and place them on mobile platforms. This has become increasingly the focus of all criticisms of social media in recent years, given not only the opaqueness of the platform industries, but also the role these platforms have played in significant moments of individuals and societies.

According to Jeremy Hunsinger (2014), this arrangement between platforms and users is problematic from three perspectives. First, governments shift laws that transform once friendly driven Internet practices into market centred practices. This may mean users can be sued by corporations who own the IP of content that was originally created by them because they have agreed to specific terms and services that sign over the copyright of their material to the platform. Secondly, the way corporations acquire a user's consent to perform activities that we are likely to not even know about, nor understand, is entirely questionable. To present a social media user with a 'choice' to accept an agreement more than 200 pages of legally written terms of services, or end user agreement as they are also known as, as they sign up to a service provider, is entirely unreasonable. Thirdly, social media users are for the most part unaware of the infrastructures that facilitate social media use, for example the copper wires or servers that store information, and changes to these infrastructures can be manipulated to serve the purpose of some and not others. While a social media user might access their Instagram account on a smart phone in Germany, the activities they perform are associated with physical infrastructures that are in several regions, each with different legal and operational requirements.

What is most concerning about these issues is that changes to how users are using and being made to perform in particular ways to do so, occur very slowly and those changes are often unnoticed. In the case of interface changes, users will typically react negatively, but this reaction usually concludes with those changes quickly becoming standardised practices. A standard example of this is whenever Facebook changes their interface. There is usually general disdain demonstrated from users against such changes to their social media platform experience, but this negative attention is usually short lived as users become accustomed to the interface and continue to use the system as usual. However, the changes underneath *are* of consequence, and require further investigation, beyond expecting users to simply accept the shifts that are placed upon them for their everyday communication experiences. We are also nudged by the larger infrastructure organisations that decide and manage the protocols on which our social media platforms operate, often with the goal of increasing watch time, for example, which will attract more advertising revenue. While many of these social media platforms are designed and operated to operate within a free and open Internet, they are managing multiple regions, cultures and uses, each of which have unique and specific perspectives on how social media infrastructures should work.

The protocols that social media platforms operate on and within have been established through telecommunications protocols and standards, but maintaining their relevance is always challenging as new cultural uses and technologies emerge. Goggin (2018) highlights the gap between a so-called *Universal Service* and disability rights to critique the shortfall between the end experience of some social media users and the lagging of government policies. In short, this approach highlights the tensions between the infrastructures of social media as a specific subset of communication infrastructures, the governing policies and the experience, which is often suboptimal, for end users. To remind us, WSIS, the UN World Summit on the Information Society, reaffirms that all information society users are entitled to freedom of speech and expression. One of their key principles is "Everyone, everywhere should have the opportunity to participate and no one should be excluded from the benefits the Information Society offers" (United Nations, 2023).

If, for example, we were to look at how Facebook uses algorithms to control which updates users are exposed to, this is a helpful example of how the WSIS concept of everyone having access to information can be construed and manipulated by vested interests. While some social media platform users engage in their everyday practices, some may be aware of the data that is being generated while a large majority of users are not. The fact that users have given consent to third party platforms to have access to that information should not be an issue, however what the platform providers are doing with that data is deeply concerning (Flew, 2022). Are we, for example, okay with personal data being sold on to advertising agents so that platform providers can earn additional income (Crocco et al., 2020)? Or for researchers to gather information about our political opinions (Bruns, 2013)? And are we okay with developers and designers deciding which functionality we have access to before we know which tasks we want our technology to undertake for us? These are some of the issues we must think about and keep questioning as social media continues to evolve and become increasingly central to our everyday lives.

There are similarities between those who use social media and those who research it, so understanding what functions and data we each have access to is important for all users surrounding platform studies. Significantly, it is important to understand not only the changes to these aspects of social media over time, but also how they lay the foundation for contemporary and future communication technologies that build on social media principles. Much of these data associated with the questions above are available but only to the platform providers themselves. This is expected given this is also the commercial intellectual property of these businesses and they are therefore designed and produced by developers of systems that we either cannot see or do not have access to. This chapter will use this as a starting point to highlight the tensions that exist between complete transparency of social media platforms and the economic and political models that determine how they operate, and the implications of such arrangements. There have been moments in the last decade that have enabled researchers to access these data and infrastructures which drove critical enquiries of the uses of these spaces—we will unpack this in detail in the coming chapters. Unfortunately, these primarily public good research tools were also exploited by commercial enterprise (see specifically Cambridge Analytica) which not only challenged users to understand who has access to their data, but also prompted governments to request changes to how data is brokered by social media platforms—privacy and trust has become a key concern of regulators and civic rights groups. The next section helps us understand what data we have available to us as an entree for what we can then do with it, which begins to unpack the changes and challenges of studying social media data. Perhaps more importantly, understanding how and what we can and cannot research within social media can be applied to the broader experiences of everyday social media users and ensuring they have positive interactions when engaging these technologies.

## How Do We Study What We Cannot See?

As previously outlined, the infrastructures and data that operate on top of them are often not accessible, if tangible at all. The process of communicating across social media is something that, instead, is often aggregated and reported to users in very particular ways designed by the platforms themselves. A helpful example is the yearly *Spotify* 'Unwrapped' report to users. This is a rather entertaining method of informing a user of what they listened to, what was the new music they found, who else was listening to their favourite artists, favourite genres, and many other specific insights from how a specific user has engaged with the platform over the past twelve months. These reports are possible through the collection of personal data and the aggregation of what we can describe as data analytics.

What are data analytics and how do they function within the context of social media? Data analytics can be understood from a few perspectives. From a social science perspective, it 'is the application of advanced analytics techniques on big data' (Elgendy & Elragal, 2014, p. 214). Computer science uses data analytics as 'methods of data preprocessing and data analysis: data and relations, data preprocessing, visualisation, correlation, regression, forecasting, classification, and clustering' (Runkler, 2020, p. 1). From a qualitative research perspective, we would argue they are a collection of data that tell us something about social media conversations, that can be aggregated and used in a variety of applications, including research, but not limited to academic purposes alone. Some examples of data analytics include the number of Facebook likes on a post, or how many X followers an account has, or how many times a video has been played on YouTube. Each data point is not only helpful for the user of the platform, but they tell a particular aspect of the story that describes social media use. For example, the likes on a post is one metric that might determine popularity, but looking at other aspects such as when the content was published, how other users commented, where was it shared, how did others engage with it, and many other ways begins to tell a broader picture of how data analytics are helpful to understand social media more broadly. In essence, data analytics are a way to quantify content, conversations and human interaction across social media.

Social media analytics built on datafication are now at the core of contemporary society. Datafication 'is a contemporary phenomenon which refers to the quantification of human life through digital information' (Mejias & Couldry, 2019, n.p.) and is 'the collection, databasing, quantification and analysis of information, and the uses of these data as resources for knowledge production, service optimization, and economic value-generation' (Flensburg & Lomborg, 2023, p. 1451). Through the datafication process, data analytics because of social media use, has enabled new and fascinating ways of understanding what happens on social media. Social media analytics are used in advanced computer learning, health and medicine, marketing and PR, information systems, events, mobilities, crisis communication, goods and services production and transportation among many other aspects of our contemporary information societies. Commercially, social media producers are likely to use analytics to gain insights into their customers. This is often referred to as social listening. Social media data are collected, monitored, analysed, summarised and graphically visualised to generate insights into the behaviour of users. Understanding user behaviour is not only about collecting data on activity such as how many times content is viewed, however. It also includes what can be deduced from these figures about user opinions, views, emotions, evaluations and attitudes—in short, why users might behave as they do.

Understanding how humans operate and function within larger groups through their media activities is of great interest in the academic world where a dedicated field of research has emerged around political, civil unrest, psychological, sociological and cultural studies of social media analytics, using scientific methods to analyse large social data sets—computational social science. While we unpack computational social science in greater detail below, it is worth highlighting that social media data provides a rich and dynamic representation of human activities, communication patterns, emotions and reflections, and ways in which we engage with the world and others around us. The automated systems that decipher these conversations are complex, and most times have been designed by those who work within platform providers yet are also a source of analytical enquiry for academia, too. These are the processes that assist users, content creators, platform providers and those who regulate these systems a variety of large-scale insights on social media.

If we look at a Facebook Ads Manager page insights for example, which is the entry point to obtain analytics from users who 'like' your Facebook page, we are presented with several tabs. Within those tabs are numerous numbers, graphs, suggestions, and of course calls to 'boost' your audience based on these numbers. This is the exact space that a social media manager will likely use when setting up an advertising campaign for their brand or service, so it is again a way of aggregating all the datafied, big data insights from user activity. Before a social media manager uses data analytics to monitor and develop a social media campaign for a project, it is important that they define what they want their social media activity to achieve. Some questions that might guide these considerations may include:

- What is the purpose of the social media campaign? Is it to build an audience, develop brand awareness, or to drive traffic to a website?
- Are they undertaking social conversation to generate a social media buzz beyond taking out traditional, paid advertising?
- Are they attempting to gain endorsement from strong social media influencers for the 'brand'? Note that the brand in this context can include a cause, event or even a person.
- Geographically, where is brand awareness needed to grow?
- What types of conversation will they engage in?

They will likely establish a clear set of key performance indicators, or KPIs, that will allow them to gauge success. Establishing the KPIs before enables them to clearly focus on improving certain strategic areas, rather than trying to grow everything. What are success measures in these areas? Is it increased followers or subscribers? Content being shared more frequently? Or increased activity around a call-to-action? Social media analytics can help address these questions and many more, but it is crucial to understand the measurements prior to designing the foundational questions outlined above—and especially before investing in them. Most social platforms use the same or similar sorts of measurements so, given that Facebook has a comprehensive set of data metrics, let's look at their Insights page in detail.

*Likes* – *the total number of people who like your page. Could also be called fans, followers, friends etc. Likes are also often separated into 'organic' and 'paid' measures to offer an insight into where business money is being spent. This differentiation might address whether your social media spend for last month resulted in new likes for your account?*

*Reach* – *This number indicates where your content has ended up. For example, how many news feeds did your Facebook page update end up in? Again, this separates paid and organic measures to indicate if your money has been targeted well and your message has been sent to the most appropriate consumers.*

*Page views* – *how many people looked at your page.*

*Posts* – *this is a crucial measurement as it indicates which posts attracted the most traffic. Did people engage with the posts, for example click the 'like' button or comment on the content? Did they share it with their network? If they did share it, what was the impact on the post's reach?*

*People* – *this is the final insight of general significance as this gives you a very clear and highly useful understanding of the socio-demographic of your audience members. Are they female? What age group? What languages do they speak? Where are they located? What sort of device do they use to access your content?*

With each of these metrics, a content creator, and thereby a broader group of stakeholders looking to understand how people operate on social media, can begin to understand how targeting audiences through the interpretation of metrics is crucial. This is the way in which visibility of content becomes crucial, which, as we will explore later, is significant not only for content creators, but also for politicians, marketers, journalists and a range of other social media users who 'game the system' to increase their visibility (Cotter, 2018). For example, if a content creator posted a comment about a sunflower with a slogan saying "Resilience", they may notice their metrics move slightly to reflect how people saw and engaged with this content. It may attract a particular demographic who are likely to engage and will probably share the content a handful of times. However, if at the same time next week, they post a photo of a sunset with the slogan, "#vanlyfe" they may find there is an enormous spike in the interactions and shares of the content. It may be that the content is better for their audience, or it may be that the content creator has identified a different demographic who are interacting with them and have shared it vigorously with their friends. In either case, it is through identifying and understanding how the metrics have shifted that enables the creator to adjust and learn who they are talking with, while working within the parameters of the platform. Alternatively, content could be posted for a local market at lunchtime, when the audience are likely to be on a break, or at 9 pm when many are looking at Facebook before they doze off to sleep at night. Time is also a key indicator of identifying and manipulating one's exposure through content creation by finding the ideal time to post your content.

These examples indicate that social media is a trial-and-error type of approach, where each time a campaign is designed, the social media manager in this case will learn an incredible amount about the people they are talking to and feed that information into the next action—a new piece of content or another campaign entirely. Beyond a few basic ground rules on what, when and how information should be posted, social media analytics are helpful to monitor what is successful amongst audiences and how to create content that is highly applicable to them. While this is located within the social media content creation space, the same principles apply to the research space which has been puzzled by researching only what is visible. Social media metrics, and data analytics, enable researchers to access insights about societies more broadly and we look further into this approach in the next section.

## Developing Meaning from Data

We referred to analysing and interpreting social media analytics as social listening in the last section. Social media producers observe their audience through analytics, deducing who they are, where they come from, what their interests are and how they communicate. This is the way in which meaning is extracted from the datafication process—that is the translation of data into concepts, meaning and understanding. Social listening is the way in which the broader directions of individuals within publics, groups and societies is understood and where necessary, acted upon. While this has helped in many instances such as political activism (Hutchinson, 2019), crisis communication (Bruns et al., 2012), and journalism (Hermida, 2012), there are still many moments where social media has hindered the way in which society functions. The anti-vaccination campaign that was prevalent prior and through the COVID-19 pandemic is an excellent example of this (Smith & Graham, 2017), or in the recent Australian context, how the Voice to Parliament referendum was manipulated through misinformation on social media (Graham, 2023). Why then do social media disasters occur if we have access to such incredible data?

There is a deeper level of understanding of users that can be accessed beyond what are typical rudimentary audience representations. The social media metrics are useful, but do not tell us things like attitudes, political preference, intelligence and societal standing among many others. Analytics are part of the picture, but they need to be combined with other nuanced approaches such as social listening to effectively communicate with an audience, or to correctly inform an audience with information. With a broad understanding of the type of social media analytics available to us, for example Likes, Reach, People, or Views, we move towards how these insights are integrated to create social media campaigns within empirical examples as a way of demonstrating how meaning is embodied in social media data.

We have previously suggested that certain messages may work more efficiently with different types of audiences at particular times in the day. But there are many other ways we can use this data to tell us how to manage a social campaign. Let's look at an example of some empirical, de-identified social media research. This research has appeared previously in Media International Australia (Hutchinson, 2015), but for the purposes of this book we will focus on the extraction meaning in social media beyond the process of social TV.

The graphic (Fig. 2.1), while admittedly interesting to gaze upon, is pretty much useless if you do not understand how to read it—let alone produce it. This graphic represents empirical research conducted with the Australian Broadcasting Corporation (ABC) to understand who was conversing and what those participants were talking about for a scripted television comedy programme, #7DaysLater. This programme was produced by the ABC in corporation with Ludo productions and engaged social media as one of its core elements for not only distribution, but for seeking the creative process of producing the programme.

The idea of #7DaysLater was to co-create the next episode of the programme with direct audience involvement across social media platforms within seven days. The producers would seek input from Facebook, Twitter, Instagram, the now defunct Google Groups and email from the audience members. They would then use these ideas, concepts, creative pieces and other artefacts to co-create the next episode of the programme within the next seven days. It was a great programme that was well received at the time and won the producers an

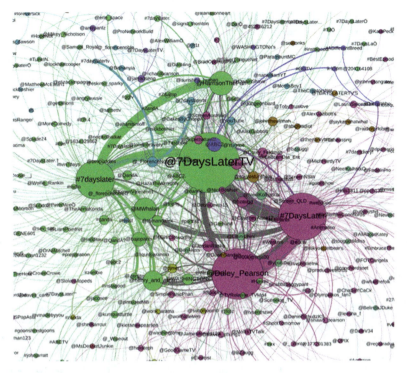

**Fig. 2.1**   The social network analysis of the Twitter audience for #7DaysLater

Emmy. As part of the process, the research team harvested the Twitter conversation for six weeks of production and followed the @7DaysLater Twitter handle to understand who was talking with whom and what they were talking about. The following analysis appeared in the 2015 article, which describes the research in detail (Hutchinson, 2015). As a broad overview of the results:

> *An example of the connectedness of the network influencers is @Daley_Pearson, the #7DaysLater director. Not surprisingly, his node is centrally located and has a large, connected community, with the hashtag #7DaysLater strongly connected to his conversation. Daley's connections indicate he frequently talked to his network about #7DaysLater, which was very significant in the conversation. Comparatively, the @ tokyostuntbear node, as one of the commissioned directors, indicates that they are centrally located to the #7DaysLater conversation, but their network is not as extensive as Pearson's, nor does it have as much impact. The quantitative analysis established the top ten users and topics, shown in Table 2.1.*

If we eliminate the ABC staff Twitter handles (@7DaysLaterTV, @Daley_Pearson, @bajopants, @ABC2, @JordanRasko and @tomandalex), along with celebrities and external production professionals (@henry_and_aaron, and

**Table 2.1** The top ten users and topics within the #7DaysLater network

| Users | Topics |
|---|---|
| @7DaysLaterTV | #7DaysLater |
| @Daley_Pearson | #qanda |
| @HarrisonTheFan | #ZandA |
| @MWhalan | #spooky |
| @henry_and_aaron | #Animation |
| @bajopants | #FlightoftheConchords |
| @ABC2 | #Western |
| @WASHINGTONx | #Hawaii |
| @JordanRasko | #ggtv |
| @tomandalex | #zombie |

Washingtonx), @ HarrisonTheFan and @MWhalan are the top two network influencers. To enable a sizeable sample of contributors to investigate, @zenjito, @jarradseng and @Mikey_Nicholson were also included. From the highest engaged topics, it is also clear that Episode 3, Zombies Flight for Equality (#ZandA) and Episode 5, A Bullet with Braille on It, were the most engaged-with episodes of the season—a fact confirmed during the interview with supervising producer Richard Huddleston. This quantitative analysis provides the basis for the qualitative research: interviews with the #7DaysLater team and the most influential Twitter contributors.

Along with some additional fine-grained, qualitative approaches such as interviews and focus groups, it was possible to make sense of the broader Twitter conversation. In terms of the graphic, it is important to help one understand the broader trends alongside the usual sorts of vanity metrics outlined above. In Fig. 2.1 above, there are colour, size and space differences. The graphic was produced using the open source program Gephi, which is a social network analysis tool. Using a combination of different algorithms from within the program can reveal certain things about the conversation across the network, including the users, the communities and the topics. In the graph above, the things to note to help explain the detail after the algorithmic processing include: the more important users and topics are located towards the centre of the graph; the larger nodes are the more connected users or topics within the network; and the different colours represent different online communities.

Knowing how to read this network graph at a basic level immediately indicates there are very influential users located near the centre of the graph. This was due to their relationship with the production crew, or because they were highly active in contributing, or perhaps had relative and creative ideas. For a full analysis, the article highlighted above describes all the outcomes in detail. However, from a social media producer perspective, or even a social media researcher perspective, these highly connected and influential users are the people who are most useful to communicate with. For example, to use a brand's Twitter account just to randomly comment has very little impact on a social conversation. It will have very minimal reach and is not likely to attract much interaction in the way of responses, shares and contributions. However, if the same message is targeted at one of the highly influential users who is likely to engage with the conversation regardless, then the potential for your effort to reach a much wider audience is exponentially improved. The communication instigator is now talking to the networks of the network participants, which may be millions of users.

In this regard, it is important to remember a few things when extracting meaning out of social media data. A crucial aspect to remember is that social media data needs time—it is not ideal to take a snapshot of social media metrics to understand the broader picture. There are many factors that need to be considered when analysing the data, and again this is not only from the perspective of a qualitative researcher, but also for content creators, students, social media producers and all other roles that evolve around social media activities. It is, however, especially helpful to think like a social media content creator/producer to approach social media analytics for better insights. The following questions will help in designing projects and analyses for social media data:

- An informed sense of how to start social media campaigns will inform how to research them: Who are the participants talking with? What do they say? When do they say it?
- Monitor the conversation by engaging with the social media metrics: Which posts attract the most interaction? At what times? What type of content is more appealing to the audience? These are points of interest for the broader group of social media users.
- Analyse and visualise the networks: identify who the network influencers are in the network and strategically target conversation with those people or identify the conversations that emerge around those users.
- Reinforce organic conversational techniques using social media, with paid advertising to maximise audiences, exposure and engagement levels.

## USING DATA ANALYTICS FOR SOCIAL MEDIA CAMPAIGNS

Just as a researcher might approach social media campaigns, so too do social media strategists where the sense-making techniques used are similar. To unpack these analytical similarities in detail, it is helpful to think through how social media analysts, community managers and marketers can undertake their social media research. These two approaches are similar while potentially having different motivations for undertaking the analysis of social media data. The iterative approach to identifying data, analysing it, extracting insights, then revisiting the empirical space is essentially the same for a variety of perspectives with research data. To understand the cyclical approach, it is helpful to examine how social media producers operate.

A social media campaign may have great success with content creation that is received well by its users, and therefore has, by their measures, successful audience reach, engagement and participation. This could include videos that went viral, content that is picked up by traditional media, or any of the social media influencer examples that sees YouTube, Instagram or TikTok creators promoting their life of fun, health or happiness surrounded by an array of life-style products. These examples typically correlate with high levels of traffic, engagement and audience contribution during the larger media campaigns in which they sit. But how do these campaigns maintain relevance and continue to increase their audience size and participation? Often, their success is achieved through iterative social media design.

Social media producers engage in what's called an iterative design cycle, where Tsai et al. (1997, p. 297) liken this approach to what they call spiral lifecycle in the software development environment. They say a spiral lifecycle is cyclical where 'analysis and design follow an incremental and iterative process. Each phase can provide information which involves the modification of results at other phases, including some previously completed phases'. This idea is borrowed from the literature on design research (Chakrabarti, 2010) and the methodology within social media design directly uses four specific phases:

1. Research
2. Requirements
3. Design
4. Evaluate

The *research* phase investigates questions such as the best platforms to use, the key message, who the audience is, and how to talk with them. The r*equirements* stage reveals the form of content that is likely to be needed: a behind the scenes video, a chat with the CEO, a product highlight, or a discussion about the next social good campaign, for example. The *design* phase is production where the copy, video, image, updates etc. are produced, implemented and published across the variety of social media platforms. And finally, the *evaluate* stage is where social media analytics are gathered and assessed to understand the effectiveness of the cycle.

In the evaluation stage, the social media producer carefully examines the activities on all the social media platforms to assess when high engagement moments occurred, what was of interest to the users, and the sorts of user activities that emerged around the content. Based on our own empirical research with a variety of creative agencies located in several cities around the world, the types of data they will look for include:

- What was the best time to publish posts to attract engagement?
- What was the most successful form of content that was produced?
- What sort of content attracted the most engagement?
- How did users respond?

- Did they want to share the content?
- Was the response positive or negative?

When the answers to these questions have been extracted and understood, another design cycle is initiated, this time with a more nuanced understanding of the potential outcomes of the communication strategy. An iterative design cycle can vary in time depending on the focus of the campaign, but from our research it is typically around the three-month timeframe. This timeframe is normally reflected in the three-month content calendar that is constructed to align with the broader design cycle. It is common practice among social media producers to establish the key communication platform of the campaign, design conversational social media posts that represent that pillar, and then schedule the updates to occur in three months. It is the role of the social media producer to then monitor how these are received and adjust the campaign accordingly.

In this iterative research design context, social media analytics are crucial to bolster the social listening of the producer by providing quantifiable insights—much the same as how we might research social media broadly. For example, while a starting point might suggest the social conversation is happening on Monday at 2 pm, the data indicates the conversation spike is at 1:45 in the afternoon. It is the social media researcher's role to monitor the time bracket here, use the analytics to provide evidence, then adjust the publishing plan to align with both the data insights and the designer's lived experience of the social world. This approach, of course, echoes the approach of the social scientist or qualitative researcher.

An example of how this operates in the empirical world can be seen in the food and beverage industry. A greengrocer may want to boost their business customer base and decides to engage in a social media campaign across several platforms. The content they post initially focuses on their weekly specials, which attracts a small amount of attention. Their social media producer/researcher notices that the key audience views their page around 10:30 am, is aged between 21 and 38 and tends to save their updates and share them with their network. The research might suggest, based on this demographic and user behaviour data, this group of users are likely to be stay-at-home/work-from-home parents who are likely looking for inspiration for their young family's evening meal. The published content is then adjusted to include recipes, updates on the local suppliers and background knowledge on how to prepare and cook particular ingredients, for example. The social media producer would then roll out a slew of this kind of content and examine how it is received and glean those insights to inform how the next round of content will be produced. It is the informed decisions on how to create content that is important to focus on here, along with the iterative approach to understanding how content is received and engaged with by the audiences, who are generating the accompanying social media data.

So, if this is the process that follows, we can observe a few insights on how social media audiences engage with content, the sorts of data that those interactions generate, and then how analysts such as social media producers use those data to make informed decisions about future content creation. This social media story is only possible when the social media researcher, (a) understands how to read the vast amount of social media analytics and (b), can translate those findings into content production that reflects these insights. When an iterative cycle is engaged by the social media producer, this type of social media management is possible. The overall concept is to understand your audience, communicate with them, grow its size and then continually improve the use of social media both through social listening and by interpreting social media analytics.

Metrics and social listening are only two ways in which a social media researcher can gather data. There are several other ways in which researchers can collect, clean, analyse and interpret the data to explain why certain things happen, the sorts of users that are involved in the process, and the kinds of implications these communication habits contribute. The following sections explore the idea of application program interfaces (APIs) in detail, followed by a more detailed examination of digital methods that have been designed especially for social media researchers. After working through these sections, the reader will be fully equipped on how to do social media research—it is at that point that we then ask the question, is that ethical? These concepts lay the foundation for understanding the remainder of this book and its research into the many and varied locations that social media is implemented.

## APIs and the Backdoor of Data

Application program interfaces, more commonly known as APIs, have emerged as the tool of choice for many social media researchers. In contrast to the UI (user interface) the API serves as the back door to accessing platforms and is how scholars can obtain metadata from posts such as likes, comments and shares, as well as batch download large datasets (Lomborg & Bechmann, 2014). An API's intended purpose is to be the backchannel by which websites and apps communicate with one another. If you have ever used a Facebook log-in to access Spotify, that happens through an API. When you access Google Maps from your car's entertainment console, it also happens through an API. In short, if the user interface UI is how people interact with a website or app, the API is how websites and apps communicate with each other across platforms and the 'Internet of Things' (IoT).

From a distance, accessing an API may look like a complicated process, but typically any person with basic programming knowledge can use one, provided the platform company has granted them access. These serve not only as an alternative way to access a website or app, but they also provide access to certain features that aren't normally available via the UI. Social media researchers use these APIs to do high-volume data collection, often in the form of batch collecting posts and their metadata. The data can be output into formats that are ready for large-scale quantitative analysis. Manually doing this without an API is possible too, but it would probably take a large team and months of work to conduct. Below we can see an example of data collected from YouTube using its API (see Table 2.2). The contents include the title of the video, how many views it has received, and then its likes and dislikes. It also contains a unique ID consisting of letters, numbers and characters. The full version would include another 50 columns of metadata and over 1000 posts.

Using content and metadata obtained from APIs researchers have been able to perform a range of different analyses, including:

- Sentiment analysis of Twitter posts at scale using natural language processing (Trupthi et al., 2017)
- Comparative analysis of user engagement with election campaigning on Twitter (Bruns et al., 2021)
- Network analysis to identify the use of bots and inauthentic activity in environmental campaigning (Hobbs et al., 2020)
- Analysis of user interest in international diplomatic missions on Facebook (Spry, 2018).

These mixed method approaches have meant that media and communication scholars frequently collaborate with computer science researchers and data analysts, as processing the data requires skills not traditionally deployed by media and communication scholars. Indeed, we now see some media and communication researchers upskilling and developing this programming and data science knowledge as part of their researcher's toolkit. APIs have also opened a doorway to a scale of research that wasn't previously possible. Content analysis conducted before APIs would normally have sample sizes of only a few

**Table 2.2**  Results of a data query taken from the YouTube API[a]

| id | snippet.title | statistics. viewCount | statistics. likeCount | statistics. dislikeCount |
|---|---|---|---|---|
| 9p2wMpVVtXg | Justin Bieber - Intentions ft. Quavo | 9,067,739 | 920,915 | 20,228 |
| KM3j_TXeqfc | The Pussycat Dolls - React | 773,185 | 101,600 | 2470 |
| c-yRN55iaQY | Lil Nas X - Rodeo (ft. Nas) [Official Video] | 5,532,710 | 449,564 | 19,112 |
| 1FJRvKQmOwg | Tobi & Manny - Destined For Greatness | 1,794,863 | 376,543 | 2372 |
| LOVxwVvUe_c | Nicki Minaj - Yikes (Official Audio) | 783,447 | 126,320 | 4376 |
| K09_5IsgGe8 | Joji - Run (Official Video) | 3,390,394 | 411,413 | 3584 |
| 4rNo-UuGDfA | Meek Mill - Believe (feat. Justin Timberlake) | | 876,192 | 73,520 | 1478 |

[a] Found on https://www.kaggle.com/datasets/eliasdabbas/youtube-data-api-datasets/

hundred or more, whereas social media scholars might mine datasets with posts numbering in the tens or hundreds of thousands (and beyond).

To access an API, researchers require a couple of resources. Primarily it requires API access which can vary from platform to platform. As of 2023, YouTube and Facebook both offer researcher-level access to their APIs, but they must be applied for. This high-level access allows for high-volume queries (data requests) to their sites. Researcher access will grant the researcher a digital token which is a string of characters that is used like a limited-time key for accessing the API. Then, assuming the researcher has sufficient programming knowledge, a query is developed using Python code and the data is outputted using the desired format of the researcher. This typically comes in the form of a .csv or .json file. Not all APIs require researcher access, and not all require programming knowledge either. Facebook and Instagram data can be collected using a service called CrowdTangle which is more user-friendly than Python. YouTube and Reddit APIs can also be accessed by the general public, but the volume of queries that can be made is significantly less than those with researcher-level access.

## The Development of Digital Methods for Research

The environment for media and communication research was shifting during the early 2000s, especially with the emergence of social media platforms and their APIs that enable access to the data. This moment promised a new way of examining the digital worlds we have previously looked at through traditional qualitative approaches, with particularly amazing developments in the ethnography space (Tacchi et al., 2003; Hearn et al., 2008). This work would become foundational for the slew of research in the mid-2010s as digital ethnography became the standard for research within social media environments (Pink et al., 2015).

However, at the same time the combining of computational science methods *with* traditional and emerging media and communication methods was gaining momentum. It is at this point that researchers begin to see how quantitative and qualitative approaches towards digital media research are important as we can find new stories within the environments we had been researching for the last decade or so.

The combining of quantitative with qualitative methods was enabling researchers to understand so much more about the digital media environment that so many users occupied. It was quickly established however, that good digital methods as it was becoming known as, relied on complementary and useful qualitative research approaches—neither was better than the other, but rather the combination of both was incredibly powerful for knowledge generation. Pure computational methods missed nuances of digital cultures in favour of satisfying predetermined problems, while pure ethnography missed the opportunity of research at scale and access to the sways of data that was available through social media platforms. Collectively, both approaches were able to start to understand how research could look at the close read, while also being able to accurately read the broader picture. It was the starting point for digital methods.

In describing digital methods in his 2013 book, *Digital Methods,* Richard Rogers asks the question in the opening pages of researching Twitter, 'How may the digital objects be combined and recombined in ways that are useful not so much for searching Twitter but rather for social and cultural research questions?' (p. 1). While he is talking about data points such as tweets, retweets, likes, shares etc., he is also prompting us to think about the process of finding new research questions through new access to data. So far, we have looked at how social media producers access these data and employ them to direct social media campaigns, yet here Rogers pushes this further to say, well what if our research questions aren't that interesting? How might we use new techniques to create new research questions and approaches? What might we find in doing so?

Digital methods shifted how we approach and understand our digital media environments, yet at that stage it was a foreign language for many humanities and social science scholars. The missing link was the computational science that worked with researchers to develop tools that were more user-friendly without having to undertake a computer science degree to undertake new research projects. This was the focus of many researchers coming to this space, with the University of Amsterdam and later the Queensland University of Technology bringing these two fields together. The University of Amsterdam was especially important in the earlier stages as they would host an annual digital methods workshop for postgraduates and emerging scholars to work with and develop new tools for this research approach. The result was the Digital Methods Initiative (DMI) that posted a collection of digital media tools for researchers to extract digital objects from digital media environments and uncover new questions and new knowledge (Fig. 2.2).

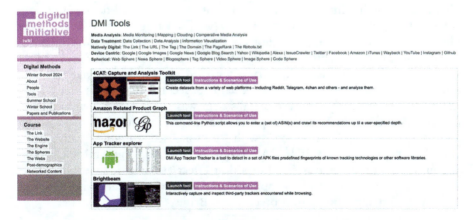

**Fig. 2.2**  The Digital Methods Initiative and the tools list for researchers

For many of the social media tools, they were built on APIs as backdoors to data as we previously discussed. One tool in particular became very powerful for Twitter researchers, TCAT—the Twitter Capture and Analysis Tool. Once this was set up on a server, the researcher could enter the hashtags, users or terms that they were interested in following and they were then able to capture the conversation, but also begin the large-scale analysis of those conversations. This was the missing link for many researchers who were then able to apply their existing expertise to new environments to understand new knowledge. One example of this research bridge is Alana Mann's (2021) work on food activism, *Beyond the Hashtag: Social Media Ethnography in Food Activism*. As a non-computer scientist but a trained communication scholar, Mann was able to apply these emerging practices to her own work and deeply read how activists were using Twitter as an activism site for food politics.

However, APIs became the devil's advocate for media researchers in the late 2010s as we soon realised that commercially oriented platforms were rarely able to support the efforts of scholars. Once active research projects that relied on API access could sadly be defunct in the following day if the API changed. This was not only impacting current research projects, but also the enormous amounts of public funding that went into the development of the tools that enabled researchers to access these data. The following section outlines this scenario in detail as one of the most problematic times of social media research.

## THE API APOCALYPSE AND ITS IMPACT ON UNDERSTANDING SOCIAL MEDIA

Access to platform APIs has increasingly become a sore issue for the technology companies that own and control them. Their popularity among social media researchers and third-party app developers has not diminished this tension. This situation is partly due to public and regulatory scrutiny over the mishandling of user data. The Cambridge Analytica scandal in 2018 is a notable example, highlighting the vulnerability of user's personal data. Cambridge Analytica, a political consultancy firm, exploited Facebook's API to harvest identifiable information from millions of users through an app featuring a personality quiz named "This Is Your Digital Life". This app not only accessed the users' information but also their friends list, made possible by the API's lax limits on accessing user data. The breach exposed the data of as many as 87 million users, primarily in the US. This data was used for microtargeting—a controversial political campaigning method involving data mining to profile and target groups of users with personalised political advertising (Papakyriakopoulos et al., 2018). Although current research on microtargeting is limited and only demonstrates a modest effect (Kruikemeier et al., 2016), the practice has strong ethical implications and has prompted firms to revisit their APIs and apply limits to protect users (Bruns, 2019).

Historically, social media companies were proactive in granting researchers, journalists and civil liberty groups access to their APIs. However, as a response to exploited user data and issues of liability, this backdoor is now closing for many. Bruns (2019) outlines the changing landscape for data access on platforms like Facebook and Twitter/X. Popular tools such as Netvizz, TwapperKeeper and Texifter have progressively shut down due to API restrictions. In recent years, these restrictions have intensified. In 2023, both Twitter/X and Reddit imposed significant limitations on their APIs, making them nearly inaccessible for researchers (Calma, 2023; Park, 2023). While the companies cite the cost of access as a reason for these limitations (Park, 2023), the use of this data for training large language models (LLMs) has also been a concern (Issac, 2023).

These methods have been beneficial for researchers, affording media and communication scholars access to datasets of unprecedented size, but some scholars have noted that these methods come with their own ethical questions. Puschmann (2019) describes this period as the "Wild West" of social media research. They suggest that the extant methods of API access, scraping and platform partnerships are no longer viable and flawed from the outset—noting that none of these methods were developed with researchers in mind which leads to issues of validity and reproducibility.

As API access becomes more restricted, alternative methods like data donation are emerging. With this method, researchers use a browser plug-in to collect data on user content consumption. Data donation offers bespoke research designs focusing on specific data points like time spent on platforms and content consumption behaviour, which differs qualitatively from the likes, comments, and shares collected via API. This demand-side data capture method allows researchers to connect browsing habits with social factors not readily available on platforms, such as age, gender and political affiliation. Some consider this approach more ethical, as it involves data from willing participants who can better consent to its use and understand how their information is utilised (Boeschoten et al., 2022). As APIs become more limited, the use case for data donation becomes more compelling—not only is the data more ethically acceptable, but the quality of the data is also richer and opens possibilities to a wider range of research designs.

## THE ETHICS OF SOCIAL MEDIA RESEARCH

*Just because we can, doesn't mean we should.*

So far, this chapter has worked through the possibilities of accessing social media data to understand an audience better and to tailor content for them. Ethical considerations are a key point of consideration when accessing this kind of content and in this section, we will explore the many aspects of ethics. Ethics in this sense is somewhat related to those that are present within University research processes, which in the Australian context is defined by the Code of

Responsible Conduct of Research (2018), the National Statement on Ethical Conduct in Human Research (2023), and a range of other national policies that guide how researchers conduct themselves. Most countries will have a version of this guiding national document on ethical research which is ultimately a way of ensuring the risk never outweighs the benefit of this kind of work.

In social media spaces, it is a little different, albeit built on similar principles. While industry has emerging regulations to follow, which is dependent on the region the user is in (more on this in Chap. 3), often there are a host of industry 'best practices' that guide how users conduct themselves while using social media. There is also community management which is a tool to help how users conduct themselves. However, when it comes to researching social media, there are often a different set of rules to work by, based on, again, risk versus benefit. In its first iteration of social media research, there was a rhetoric of 'it's public data so I can basically do what I want with this', which, granted, most researchers had the interests of the users front and centre. However, it became obvious very quickly that reassessing how we approach social media research was a different process, with a different approach towards harvesting, cleaning and talking about those same data.

Often when users sign up to a social media platform, they are agreeing to terms and conditions of that platform provider. However, many of those platforms also operate with an application program interface or API which enables third party operators to perform additional tasks with the platform, for example include a Facebook like button on a blog post for example. What users are not signing up for are intermediaries mining their data and performing tasks that might align them with certain conversations, or locations or political activities. This is an ethical concern, and one that universities are addressing in how their researchers undertake this work and ensure those 'scooped up' in the process are respected.

Professor Tama Leaver from Curtin University notes that, "every month, thousands of foetal images are shared and publicly tagged as ultrasounds... For many young people, this type of sharing will be their first mention on social media" (2015, p. 1). In these instances, the social media users are not aware of their online personas being constructed for them—arguably another ethical social media situation. This is precisely an example of why the Association of Internet Researchers (AoIR) produced the AoIR Ethics 3.0 document to highlight some of the implications of social media research and how researchers need to think and how they can operate in these environments to ensure participants are respected. In many cases, it is impossible to seek consent from every social media user in research projects, yet it is incredibly important to, on the same account, understand how users talk about political elections, or how important it might be to be exposed to trans information groups, or indeed how users find out about local sporting events in their neighbourhoods. Because of the risk versus benefits ideology, a vast range of techniques are now employed to protect users, while also advancing our understanding of these sorts of environments.

## *AoIR Ethics 3.0*

The premise for this collection of guiding ethical principles is built on almost twenty years of research into the field of Internet research and more recently the push to understand social media spaces. The report itself says:

> *IRE 3.0 is then illustrated by way of two elements—namely, (greater) attention to stages of research (a continuation of distinctions developed in 1.0 and 2.0) and what has become a standard problem of informed consent in particularly (but not exclusively) Big Data research approaches. We then list and briefly discuss the primary additional ethical challenges in IRE 3.0 as identified by the AoIR Ethics Working Group (EWG). We offer a general structure for ethical analysis, designed to help identify the ethically relevant issues and questions, along with additional suggestions for how to begin to analyse and address these challenges in more detail.*

For more specific detail, a full copy of the document can be sought here: [https://aoir.org/reports/ethics3.pdf].

Beyond the risk versus benefit approach of all ethical research, one of the defining issues with social media research is, building on the two previous sections, the capacity to scrape large amounts of communication data. While this has been useful for some of the more cutting-edge research projects that have driven social and political change, there are several unseen risks that emerged as this research was increasingly used. One of the key issues was that users who sign up for social media platforms, didn't necessarily agree to having their data collected and analysed by social media researchers. The lack of informed consent is paramount, as researchers often analyse users' publicly available data without their explicit consent, potentially infringing on privacy rights. While someone may have been having a 'public' conversation with their network, they did not necessarily know or agree with someone else collecting that conversation and referring to them as an outcome.

Secondly, the responsible handling of sensitive information, such as personal details or user-generated content, is essential to prevent harm or misuse. In the earlier phases of APIs, the amount of detail that was contained within the scrapes was likely 'throw away' material, but it often also included sensitive material. Further, these sensitive data were not obvious until they had been collected and analysed, making them obvious in some instances to the researcher first without the participant being aware of this. A famous example of this was the Target case in which a young girl was identified as pregnant by the sorts of information she was leaving behind as she purchased and explored items online and in the physical shop. The data points alone are likely not that exciting, but when they are connected into a larger picture, they can be incredibly revealing of personal and private information.

Thirdly, maintaining the anonymity and confidentiality of participants is crucial to safeguard their identities and data. When social media research had been undertaken in the past, the username, location and potentially other sensitive information was also included in these data. In the very first wave of social media research, usernames were often included in the results of the research, and it was not until Internet researchers questioned the process that it was thought to be important to anonymise the data—or at least describe an aggregate version of the data. Anonymisation and aggregation became standard practice in social media research, and always done by ethical researchers, but the personal information remains in the scrape of the dataset and required an additional step of de identifying the information.

Additionally, the potential for bias and discrimination in data collection and analysis must be rigorously mitigated to ensure equitable research practices. Moreover, transparency in research methods and intentions is vital to maintain trust between researchers and the public. Lastly, social media platforms' terms of service and ethical guidelines should be respected, and any ethical dilemmas related to data ownership and user rights should be carefully navigated. Addressing these ethical concerns is imperative to ensure that social media research is conducted responsibly and ethically, benefiting both researchers and the broader online community.

Unfortunately, not all researchers abide by the sorts of standards that are present in the AoIR Ethics documents, and as we have seen through various examples in the last decade (see for example the Cambridge Analytica scandal), additional steps had to be taken to protect user information. This forced platforms to rethink how they allowed access to the user data and what others could be doing with that data—this included social media researchers. This process slowly restricted the access to the APIs, and in many cases resulted in the APIs disappearing completely.

With a solid understanding of the sorts of data that are available to users and researchers, it is possible to understand the dynamics of social media more broadly. The remainder of this book looks at specific case studies and phenomena surrounding social media, which has been drawn out from accessing and examining social media data. Chapter 3 takes the approach of understanding the social media industry as one that provides the tools and platforms that users engage with for their social media lives.

## References

Australian Code for Responsible Conduct of Research 2018 National Health and Medical Research Council R41. Retrieved from www.nhmrc.gov.au/guidelines/publications/r41978-1-86496-013-6

Boeschoten, L., Ausloos, J., Möller, J. E., Araujo, T., & Oberski, D. L. (2022). A Framework for Privacy Preserving Digital Trace Data Collection Through Data Donation. *Computational Communication Research, 4*(2), 388–423.

Bruns, A. (2013). Faster than the Speed of Print: Reconciling 'Big Data' Social Media Analysis and Academic Scholarship. *First Monday, 18*(10), 1–5.

Bruns, A. (2019). After the 'APIcalypse': Social Media Platforms and their Fight Against Critical Scholarly Research. *Information, Communication & Society, 22*(11), 1544–1566.

Bruns, A., Burgess, J., Crawford, K., & Shaw, F. (2012). #qldfloods and @QPSMedia: Crisis Communication on Twitter in the 2011 South East Queensland Floods (Media Ecologies Project, Issue).

Bruns, A., Angus, D., & Graham, T. (2021). Twitter Campaigning Strategies in Australian Federal Elections 2013–2019. *Social Media + Society, 7*(4), 20563051211063462. https://doi.org/10.1177/20563051211063462

Calma, J. (2023). *Twitter Just Closed the Book on Academic Research.* Retrieved from https://www.theverge.com/2023/5/31/23739084/twitter-elon-musk-api-policy-chilling-academic-research

Chakrabarti, A. (2010). A Course for Teaching Design Research Methodology. *Artificial Intelligence for Engineering Design, Analysis and Manufacturing, 24,* 317–334.

Cotter, K. (2018). Playing the Visibility Game: How Digital Influencers and Algorithms Negotiate Influence on Instagram. *New Media & Society, 21*(4), 895–913.

Crocco, M. S., Segall, A., Halvorsen, A.-L., Stamm, A., & Jacobsen, R. (2020). "It's Not Like They're Selling Your Data to Dangerous People": Internet Privacy, Teens, and (Non-)controversial Public Issues. *The Journal of Social Studies Research, 44*(1), 21–33.

Elgendy, N., & Elragal, A. (2014). Big Data Analytics: A Literature Review Paper. In P. Perner (Ed.), *Advances in Data Mining. Applications and Theoretical Aspects.*

Flensburg, S., & Lomborg, S. (2023). Datafication Research: Mapping the Field for a Future Agenda. *New Media & Society, 25*(6), 1451–1469.

Flew, T. (2022). *The Challenge of Trust in Digital Societies: Digital Platforms and New Public Spheres.* Retrieved from https://ssrn.com/abstract=4151098 or https://doi.org/10.2139/ssrn.4151098

Goggin, G. (2018). [From Universal Service to Communication Rights: Connecting Everyone in the Internet & Mobile Age].

Graham, T. (2023, September 8). *Understanding Misinformation and Media Manipulation on Twitter During the Voice to Parliament Referendum.* https://doi.org/10.31219/osf.io/qu2fb

Hearn, G. N., Tacchi, J. A., Foth, M., & Lennie, J. (2008). Action Research and New Media Overview. In R. E. Rice (Ed.), *Action Research and New Media: Concepts Methods and Cases* (pp. 9–21). Hampton Press.

Hermida, A. (2012). Social Journalism: Exploring How Social Media is Shaping Journalism. In E. Siapera & A. Veglis (Eds.), *The Handbook of Global Online Journalism* (pp. 309–328). Wiley-Blackwell.

Hobbs, M., Della Bosca, H., Schlosberg, D., & Sun, C. (2020). Turf Wars: Using Social Media Network Analysis to Examine the Suspected Astroturfing Campaign for the Adani Carmichael Coal Mine on Twitter. *Journal of Public Affairs, 20*(2), e2057.

Hunsinger, J. (2014). Interface and Infrastructure in Social Media. In J. Hunsinger & T. Senft (Eds.), *The Social Media Handbook* (pp. 5–17). Routledge.

Hutchinson, J. (2015). Public Service Media and Social TV: Bridging or Expanding Gaps in Participation? *Media International Australia, 154,* 89–100.

Hutchinson, J. (2019). Microplatformization for Digital Activism on Social Media. *Information Communication & Society, 24*(1), 35_51.

Issac, M. (2023). *Reddit Wants to Get Paid for Helping to Teach Big A.I. Systems.* Retrieved from https://www.nytimes.com/2023/04/18/technology/reddit-ai-openai-google.html

Kruikemeier, S., Sezgin, M., & Boerman, S. C. (2016). Political Microtargeting: Relationship Between Personalized Advertising on Facebook and Voters' Responses. *Cyberpsychology, Behavior, and Social Networking, 19*(6), 367–372.

Lomborg, S., & Bechmann, A. (2014). Using APIs for Data Collection on Social Media. *The Information Society, 30*(4), 256–265.

Mann, A. (2021). *Beyond the Hashtag: Social Media Ethnography in Food Activism (Version 1).* University of Tasmania. Retrieved from https://hdl.handle.net/102.100.100/533163

Mejias, U. A., & Couldry, N. (2019). Datafication. *Internet Policy Review, 8*(4). https://doi.org/10.14763/2019.4.1428

Papakyriakopoulos, O., Hegelich, S., Shahrezaye, M., & Serrano, J. C. M. (2018). Social Media and Microtargeting: Political Data Processing and the Consequences for Germany. *Big Data & Society, 5*(2), 205395171881184.

Park, J. (2023, June 14). *The Reddit Blackout of 2023: A Deep Dive into the Conflict and Its Implications.* Retrieved from https://hackernoon.com/the-reddit-blackout-of-2023-a-deep-dive-into-the-conflict-and-its-implications

Pink, S., Horst, H., Postill, J., Hjorth, L., Lewis, T., & Tacchi, J. (2015). *Digital Ethnography: Principles and Practice.* Sage.

Puschmann, C. (2019). An End to the Wild West of Social Media Research: A Response to Axel Bruns. *Information, Communication & Society, 22*(11), 1582–1589.

Runkler, T. A. (2020). Introduction. In *Data Analytics: Models and Algorithms for Intelligent Data Analysis* (pp. 1–4). Springer Fachmedien Wiesbaden.

Smith, N., & Graham, T. (2017). Mapping the Anti-vaccination Movement on Facebook. *Information Communication & Society,* 1–19.

Spry, D. (2018). Facebook Diplomacy: A Data-driven, User-focused Approach to Facebook Use by Diplomatic Missions. *Media International Australia, 168*(1), 62–80. https://doi.org/10.1177/1329878x18783029

Tacchi, J., Slater, D., & Hearn, G. (2003). *Ethnographic Action Research—A User's Handbook Developed to Innovate and Research ICT Applications for Poverty Eradication* (1st ed.). United Nations Educational, Scientific and Cultural Organisation UNESCO.

Trupthi, M., Pabboju, S., & Narasimha, G. (2017). *Sentiment Analysis on Twitter using Streaming API.* Paper Presented at the 2017 IEEE 7th International Advance Computing Conference (IACC).

Tsai, B. Y., Stobart, S., Parrington, N., et al. (1997). Iterative Design and Testing within the Software Development Life Cycle. *Software Quality Journal, 6,* 295–310.

United Nations. (2023). *World Summit on the Information Society (WSIS).* Retrieved from https://sustainabledevelopment.un.org/index.php?page=view&type=30022&nr=102&menu=3170

## CHAPTER 3

# Social Media Platforms: Technologies, Companies, Industries

## INTRODUCTION

In the twenty-first century, launching a social media platform stands out as one of the more lucrative ventures for technology companies. Listings of the last decade's most profitable and valuable global companies show a field dominated by four main sectors: resources, manufacturing, banking and information and communication technologies (Statista, 2023b). Nearly all new entrants are 'Big Tech' firms and the owners of social media platforms, the likes of which include Alphabet, Meta and Tencent. Whether a tech giant, manufacturing titan, or resource magnate, many of the world's most profitable companies share common business strategies; they either have exclusive access to a resource, own large parts of a supply chain, or both.

In manufacturing, conglomerates like Johnson & Johnson and Volkswagen have become powerful entities by acquiring their former competitors and substantial parts of their supply chains—a process that happens through years of mergers, acquisitions and vertical integration. Similarly, resource giants like ExxonMobil or Saudi Aramco hold exclusive access to some of the most valuable global commodities like petroleum oil. Social media parent companies like Meta and Alphabet follow a similar strategy. They seek to establish a strong foothold in online advertising and aim to own various elements of their supply chain infrastructure (Giblin & Doctorow, 2022). In turn, this enables these technology firms to extract value at scale from a user base numbering in the billions. How they achieve this requires us to examine further the foundations of their enterprises—an interplay of technology, corporate culture, and business models.

What also makes these developments noteworthy, is the sheer speed in which social media platforms, Silicon Valley start-ups and Big Tech have achieved their success. What began as a few small businesses in a family garage or college fraternity are now some of the most profitable companies in the

J. Hutchinson et al., *Social Media in Society*,
https://doi.org/10.1007/978-3-031-66360-4_3

world. This achievement can be attributed in part to technological development discussed later in this chapter such as Web 2.0 and smartphones, but also to the business cultures that these companies emerge from, and the power of venture capital (Hoffman & Yeh, 2018). The mindset and resourcing that accompany social media and tech companies are qualitatively different from those of other sectors.

We must also consider that users are an integral component of this success and that products usually become popular because customers like or need them. Social media platforms afford users the ability to create their own media content and display it on a network that can number in the billions. This is a significant paradigm shift away from the broadcast era that was the twentieth century. As such, social media platforms have been the birthplace for much of contemporary culture, from memes to user-generated news, from the career revival of forgotten stars to a whole new generation of micro-celebrities and influencers.

This chapter considers how social media companies like Facebook, YouTube, Instagram and TikTok operate from an industry perspective. From the technologies the platforms are built upon, the corporate players who control them, and the new economics of attention and user producers. This chapter will also discuss the joint trajectory of smartphones, Web 2.0 and machine learning algorithms. We will define Big Tech, Silicon Valley and social media platforms, and identify the important overlap between these business spheres. We will look behind the digital curtain to examine how platforms, power and personalities have coalesced in the twenty-first century to create what are now some of the most successful companies in the world.

### CASE STUDIES: ARAL'S *LEVERS OF POWER* AND THE EARLY LIFE OF A SOCIAL MEDIA PLATFORM

What are the features that shape a social media platform and what is it that makes them so valuable? Is it the user base, the content or the technology that supports it all? It is most likely a combination of all three, but the significance of each might vary depending on the perspective of whom you ask. When it comes to media it can be said that if you aren't paying for a service, then you are the product. This expression is epitomical of dual markets such as social media, and traditional broadcast mediums such as television and radio. Users come to the platforms for content and the network, and mostly get that service free of charge. Conversely, businesses come to the platform for the attention of users and to sell them products, which is a privilege they pay for. Social platforms mediate these interactions and facilitate the networking of users, content creators, and advertising. It is from these stakeholders and technology that the commodities of attention and data emerge, but it also creates a co-dependency between interest groups by which power struggles can also form.

In their book The Hype Machine, Sinan Aral refers to four "levers of power" that shape social media companies including their profitability, structure and the content that we see, these are norms, code, money and laws (Aral, 2021, pp. 61–63). Norms are the behaviours of individuals on platforms such as what is acceptable, their purpose for using the platform, the rituals, and the languages employed. Money represents the financial and economic incentives that influence the business models pursued by platforms. Code represents the programming and the physical infrastructure that support the network. Laws are the governance of these platforms and represent the diverse legislative frameworks that these global firms and user bases have to navigate. We can better understand the relationships of these levers by examining how these platforms start and where these factors of influence come into play.

Hypothetically, the early life of a social media platform may resemble the following. First, a tech start-up develops a social networking site with an easy-to-use UI and a unique aspect of the product offering that helps attract users out of interest. For Facebook this unique offering was originally the relationship status of users, for Instagram it was filters (Leaver et al., 2020) and for Twitter it was microblogging (Burgess & Baym, 2022). A few celebrities now join in—because that is where the fans are—and you are on track for an exciting online community. Indeed, it is the critical mass of users that afford social media platforms their power. A desire to be part of a community or in-group affords social media companies a power and influence often referred to as network power (Castells, 2011). At this point, the platform would be primarily influenced by code and norms, and if you only saw users as consumers, you might not need to do much else. A few tweaks to facilitate quality content, prevent harmful behaviour and make it easy for people to find each other, and you should have a flourishing ecosystem. Technical aspects such as server speed, stability and ease of use are important, but maintaining a critical mass of users on the platform is paramount.

At the same time, we begin to observe Aral's second lever of power, the influence of money. Running a platform often requires enormous capital investment and revenue to meet its fixed costs. This includes research and development, servers, content moderation and other business overheads. For some platforms, monetisation comes later while for others it is clearly integrated into their business plans from day one. How a platform company generates its revenue will likely affect every aspect of product development. For traditional media services like print, radio and television there are three ways of generating revenue: user subscriptions, advertising or government funding (McQuail & Deuze, 2020). For social media, there is little precedent for user subscriptions and government funding comes with many constraints. If users pay to use a platform, it raises the financial barrier of entry which makes it harder to bring people onto the platform. We also know that user density is essential to a thriving community. LinkedIn might be the first true success story for a subscription model. Their annual revenue from subscriptions, by some estimates, is thought to exceed that of advertising (Statista, 2022). X has also experimented with a subscriber model since being purchased by tech billionaire Elon Musk, but the success of the model is still unclear (Chen & Mac, 2023). Comparatively, advertising is a tried and tested revenue model with some wealthy clients who are looking for a large and global audience. This business model often used in media industries, wherein firms serve both audiences and advertisers through two closely connected markets, is commonly referred to as a dual-product market (Albarran, 2013). With traditional media markets, broadcasters and papers have provided audiences with content in exchange for their attention (a.k.a. the battle for eyeballs), and then that attention is sold to advertisers in exchange for money. With social media companies though, they also collect user data on a scale that isn't seen from traditional media firms (Zuboff, 2015, 2019).

At this point in the early life of a platform, maintaining a balance between user satisfaction and advertiser interests, while generating revenue, is a crucial aspect of business operations. Theoretically, a thriving community and compelling content attract substantial advertiser investment, creating a sustainable ecosystem. Nonetheless, this dynamic is further complicated by the inclusion of a third pivotal stakeholder: investors.

While tech start-ups often tout humble beginnings, like working out of their parents' basements, a college dorm or garage, the road to ubiquity is often paved by investor finance. As a platform grows the need to increase scale of operations can, and often does, require huge capital investment (Hoffman & Yeh, 2018). Funding their premises, purchasing platform infrastructure and hiring programmers, lawyers, accountants and marketing and sales personnel requires considerable access to capital. Going to a bank for a loan is possible in theory, but you would need a steady flow of income from day one to service that loan. Instead, many social media companies have relied on investor finance to grow. Investor finance is the provision of capital by investors to companies, projects, or individuals. Initial seed funding from investors may come with a few milestones but is mostly contingent on the promise of future returns on investment through interest, dividends or capital gains—ubiquity now, profit later. Investors also obtain, through their purchase of the company, some sway in the board of directors and therefore the operations of the company.

This dynamic, between three key stakeholders—users, advertisers and investors—each with their own levers of power, is at the core of the social media economy (Aral, 2021). If the users are unhappy, they can abandon the platform. If the advertisers are unhappy, they will stop buying ad space. Then finally, if the shareholders are unhappy, they can terminate the board or executive and put new management in place. In 2023 we saw some of these dynamics at play with the user revolt at Reddit or the mass exodus of advertisers on Twitter (now X).

For Reddit, a June 2023 announcement of a restrictive pricing structure for third-party app developers resulted in a widespread blackout of their community forums known as subreddits. The new cost structure meant that many users were no longer going to have access to popular third-party apps for viewing the platform as they were dependent on unrestricted API access to function. In response to these changes, Reddit's volunteer community moderators closed over 6000 of their forums—a protest that lasted months (Park, 2023). It had been speculated that Reddit's decision to throttle API access was motivated by a long-awaited initial public offering (IPO) which is a process by which a private company offers shares to the public for the first time, thereby becoming a publicly traded and owned entity. These IPOs are often an important part of a platform's business journey, which often requires getting a firm's financial matters to make the purchasing of shares as enticing as possible. In this instance, the pursuit of profitability came at the cost of user satisfaction. Many of Reddit's most popular communities went dark, which resulted in another power struggle whereby some of the volunteer moderators were replaced with mods from other subreddits.

X has faced its own swathe of power struggles since its purchase by the controversial CEO and entrepreneur Elon Musk in late 2022. Musk, the self-declared "free speech absolutist", insisted on a sweeping array of changes to the platform. This included the restoration of thousands of previously banned accounts, such as those of Kanye West and Donald J Trump, as well as far-right trolls and QAnon conspiracy theorists with extremist views. Famously, they also insisted on making verified accounts to pay a monthly subscription fee of 8 dollars (Chen & Mac, 2023). Musk himself also had his account granted special privileges so that his posts were prioritised by the platform's algorithm so they would frequently appear in people's feeds and at the top of conversations (Schiffer & Newton, 2023). In this time, both users and advertisers have left the platform in droves with reports suggesting that advertising revenue has decreased by as much as 59% (Mac & Hsu, 2023), while monthly users are down 15% (Spangler, 2023).

These two examples demonstrate the challenges that platforms face while trying to keep their various stakeholders satisfied. In both, we can see the enormous sway that investors and shareholders can have in creating top-down change, but social media platforms are also built on communities and users will always have their say. Alongside users, advertisers and shareholders, there is also a final stakeholder who is also able to exercise their influence over these levers of power, and that is government.

The political economy of social media is both wide-reaching and complex. Media is said to have two values, one is economic and the other political (Just, 2009). The economic function is to generate income, create value through goods and services, drive innovation and employ workers. The political value is to inform the public, generate dialogue and in the instance of news, be a 'fourth estate' that seeks to provide truth and insight to matters of public interest. For lawmakers, this presents a challenge as the pursuit of these two values is prone to regulatory conflict.

In the early stages of development for the Internet and social networking sites, these companies were mostly able to avoid political scrutiny and cumbersome regulation. Lawmakers were worried that intervention too early in the life of these firms might inhibit innovation and therefore their profitability

(Flew, 2021). This pursuit and promise of economic value have been a shield for many of these companies and as such has allowed firms like Meta and Google to scale up rapidly and become some of the most powerful and profitable companies in the world. As time has gone on though, the anticompetitive practices of these firms alongside the range of political and social issues that have arisen from their behaviour has led to intensified political scrutiny and intervention. Media and communications scholar, Terry Flew (2021), argues that we are now moving into a regulatory era of online platforms. They suggest that the shift from a free Internet to a platformed Internet has led to concerns regarding the social and economic implications of Big Tech and Silicon Valley companies. The anti-competitive practices of these companies, the exploitation of user data and concerns for political polarisation have led to increased scrutiny and regulatory intervention for social media companies.

It is at this point we arrive at the current moment for most social media companies and the path forward isn't entirely clear. Each of these phases of the early life of social media companies demonstrate Sinan Aral's 'levers of power' for social networking sites (Aral, 2021, p. 92). The programmers deliver the code, while users establish the norms of the platform. Early investors and advertisers offer money and then government introduces laws and regulation. It would seem that the fight for control of these levers between users, owners and regulators will likely determine that future.

## TECHNOLOGIES

In many ways, the power of platforms is based on their ubiquity, scale and desirability. These outcomes are facilitated in part by a suite of technologies working in conjunction together to make a platform that is greater than the sum of its constituent pieces. In this section, we consider three broad categories of technological development that have played a critical role in influencing the social media paradigm: smartphones, Web 2.0 and machine learning.

### Smartphones

In the discussion of social media platforms and their rapid growth in popularity, it is difficult to overlook the development and popularisation of smartphones. The path to ubiquity for smartphones has also coincided with a path to ubiquity for social media. Through mobile apps, social platforms have been able to move away from periodic interaction with users to ubiquitous and 'always-on' modes of engagement (Marwick, 2015). The Apple iPhone was introduced in 2007, and while it wasn't the first smartphone, the launch of the product would prove to be a landmark moment for the tech industry. The use of ease and the introduction of a touch screen that encompassed most of the face of the device meant that the development of apps could be more versatile and dynamic, especially in the design of their user interface. These devices were also much easier to type on and included high-quality cameras on their rear.

This further reduced the barrier for entry for user-generated content which was already a popular feature of the Web 2.0 era. Indeed, social media platforms such as Instagram, TikTok, Snapchat and BeReal are for the most part dependent on users owning smart devices with cameras. X was also a response to the move to mobile devices, as its short character limit was a necessity due to the limited character length available on short messaging services (Burgess & Baym, 2022, p. 5). This led to the rapid introduction of apps as points of access for many existing websites including social networking and user-generated platforms. One cannot overstate the importance of the development of widespread, high-speed wireless Internet infrastructure as part of this equation too. As the smartphone industry has grown, so too has the social media industry. As such, it is no surprise that social media apps are among the most popular apps available (Goggin, 2021, p. 8) (see Fig. 3.1).

For social media companies, the app-ification of their platforms also meant greater access to user data. Now companies like Facebook, Instagram, YouTube and X could get access to user location and behavioural data in real time which is then commodified (Zuboff, 2015) and used to suggest content, connections and advertising (Aral, 2021). Should there be any uncertainty regarding the important role smartphones play in the economics of social media platforms, one can refer to the instance of Apple's 2021 iOS update. The update meant that if an app wanted to monitor user activity on other apps, such as Facebook monitoring your web browsing in Chrome or Safari, they would need to obtain explicit permission from the user. When one considers that in countries such as the United States, Canada, Australia and the United Kingdom that iPhones represent anywhere between 50% and 60% of the mobile phone market, this is a significant threat to the surveillance economy of social networking apps. Following that announcement, the parent company of Facebook, Instagram,

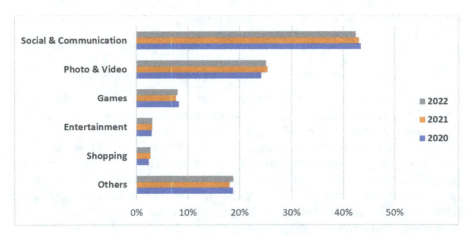

**Fig. 3.1**  Distribution of global time spent on mobile in 2020 to 2022, by category (derived from Statista, 2023a)

and WhatsApp, Meta Platforms, experienced a near immediate 26% decline in its share price (Olson, 2022). Without smartphones, there is no doubt the contemporary landscape for social media industries would look vastly different.

## Web 2.0

Anderson (2016, p. 1) states that Web 2.0 is "a group of services that have become deeply associated with the term: blogs, wikis, podcasts, Really Simple Syndication (RSS) feeds etc., which facilitate a more socially connected Web" and that "pulls in economics, technology and new ideas about the connected society". Sometimes referred to as the social web or the dynamic web, Web 2.0 refers to a technological shift for the browser-based Internet, starting in the late 1990s and early 2000s. During this period, an upgrade in programming and infrastructure meant that websites went from static to dynamic pages. During this same period, the added ability for users to upload content and more readily interact with pages meant that users started having more direct input into the content of these sites. Examples of the innovations in user interfaces and hosting during this time include the introduction of comments and rating in online stores, video hosting services such as YouTube, the ability to upload photos for websites such as Flickr and Tumblr (Hinton & Hjorth, 2019). Prior to this period, the content present on webpages was almost wholly dictated by the owner of those pages. The front pages for websites would often be bloated and slow to load. Content was also the same for every user. The shift to Web 2.0 meant that a service could start offering a more tailored experience, with the use of tracking features, such as cookies, allowing websites to follow users and then offer content that might be more suited to them. While early use of the term social media predates this period by 5 years, many scholars identify this advancement as one of the eminent technological contributions which lead to the development of social media platforms. Part of which, this change indicated a semantic shift from one-to-many to many-to-many as a communication protocol (O'Reilly, 2005).

## Recommender Systems, Algorithms and Machine Learning

The other integral technology behind social media companies is the use of algorithms, recommender systems and machine learning processes. With a large content inventory containing millions of images, videos and text-based posts, navigating that library can be quite difficult. Platforms such as Instagram or TikTok might receive millions of pieces of content per minute into their inventory, most of which won't be relevant to any one user at that point in time. A system is required to ensure that the content users view meets their interests or needs. So how do you design a system that helps filter out content and ensure that users see only what is relevant and engaging?

On Reddit, this system is rather simple. Content is up-voted by other users, or down-voted, and this determines its placement on the front page. Content is also categorised by subtopics (subreddits), and users can opt in and out of the subreddits that interest them. Combining these two features, the content from your subreddits is pooled together and then sorted based on user ratings to determine what users see on their accounts. Their algorithm then deprioritises content which has been on the platform longer, with upvotes acting as a counterbalance to downvotes plus the time the content has spent on the platform. On platforms such as Facebook and X, the content uses more sophisticated algorithms to sort content and ensure that users see what is of interest to them. These are algorithmic controls referred to as recommender systems.

Recommender systems are one of the overlapping technologies between social media and other tech firms such as Amazon, Netflix or Spotify (Milano et al., 2020). These algorithms can interpret user data and content metadata in such a way that they can make predictions for the kind of content a given user might find interesting. The news or For You feeds on these platforms might draw upon existing consumption habits or data regarding your friendship circle to curate their content. Emerging research has shown that some users, in developing knowledge regarding how these systems work, have been proactive in influencing their algorithms to help ensure the content curation meets their needs (Stepnik, 2023, 2022).

## COMPANIES

Understanding the business models and philosophy behind social media companies also requires us to consider the broader technological and business traditions that many social media platforms emerge from; these are Big Tech and Silicon Valley. What is referred to as 'social media', at an industry level, might be better understood as the nexus between Big Tech, Silicon Valley and social platforms.

While Big Tech, Silicon Valley and social platforms aren't synonymous, there is considerable overlap between these industry paradigms. From Big Tech's propensity to gatekeep resources and buy its competitors, to Silicon Valley's libertarian values and desire to "move fast and break things", these combined with social networking sites' business models of surveillance capitalism and attention economics to arrive at an industry that transformed the media and telecommunications landscape in just a few short decades (Fig. 3.2).

### *Big Tech*

Big Tech refers to a particular class of technology conglomerates, with large market capitalisations, global reach, significant vertical integration and an expansive product ecosystem. The largest and most famous of these are Alphabet, Apple, Microsoft, Meta Platforms and Amazon, or AAMPA for short. We would also consider the Chinese tech conglomerates Alibaba, ByteDance and Tencent in this category. These companies have a lot in common with many of the non-tech super corporations of today. Vertical

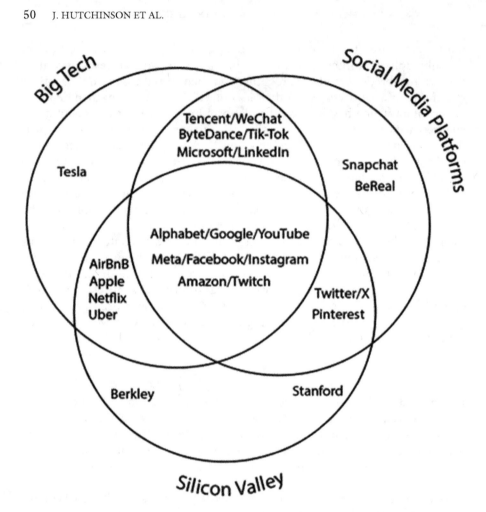

**Fig. 3.2** A Venn diagram showing the overlap of Big Tech, Social Media Platforms and Silicon Valley

integration—the ownership of multiple aspects of the supply chain—allows companies a greater opportunity to exercise control over how their products are created and the costs involved. For instance, if you own your own server farm and hosting service, you are no longer required to negotiate with other firms on costs and service provision. Furthermore, the infrastructure can be used to provide services to other companies. In the instance of Amazon, Google and Microsoft, each offers cloud computing services to other businesses as well as a range of enterprise solutions that draw upon the infrastructure they already required for their core services. Through vertical integration and acquisitions these conglomerates can further diversify their product offerings but also create resilience to market-specific changes.

In the English-speaking world, Meta Platforms Inc is undoubtedly the centrepiece of this social media industry. Their 'Family of Apps'—Facebook, Instagram and WhatsApp—are some of the most popular platforms in the world. While Google, Microsoft and Amazon each own platforms (YouTube, LinkedIn and Twitch), Meta is the only firm that one could confidently say is primarily focused on social networking sites as its core business. Their emerging products such as the Metaverse and Threads (the new X competitor) are also social platforms. The company also owns the popular business communication tool Workplace and VR headset company Oculus. Meta's push into the 'Metaverse' and submarine cable investment can also be seen as examples of this vertical expansion, alongside their earlier acquisitions of Instagram, WhatsApp and Oculus. Should their core product in Facebook begin to decline, the parent company is still able to sustain itself through these other offerings.

### Silicon Valley

Silicon Valley might be best understood through an ethnographic or geographic lens. The Valley is a region of northern California spanning from San Francisco to San Jose that is host to over 30 of the most well-known tech companies in the United States including Alphabet, Meta, Apple and Amazon. Indeed, the only company from the 'Big 5' of tech not based in Silicon Valley is Microsoft. As the previous figure shows, there is considerable overlap between Big Tech and Silicon Valley, but making a distinction between these industry paradigms allows us to better understand the ambitions and influences of social media companies. While the Valley is a geographically bound region, it is also a culture that comes with its own brand of ideology or 'mindset'. For much of the twentieth century, Silicon Valley was host to several transformational tech innovations. This included the development of radio stations, semiconductors and the Internet. This was in part facilitated by the location of the US Navy's research and development base as well as two major universities, Stanford and Berkeley UoC. The mindset of Silicon Valley, of libertarianism (Flew, 2021), entrepreneurialism, disruption and the cultivation of 'the founder' mythos (Cohen, 2018) are characteristics not necessarily shared by all Big Tech companies, but are a common feature of firms based in the region. Furthermore, there are a number of Silicon Valley companies that might not be designated as social networking companies either, such as Uber or Netflix, but do use similar models of data surveillance and disruption or have used venture capital as a means to quickly achieve scale.

Marwick (2017, p. 315) contends that many of the recent Silicon Valley start-ups draw upon social media concepts and logics including "user generated content, peer production, marketplaces, collaboratively generated information, (and) datafication". As such it is unsurprising to see the two paradigms conflated. Silicon Valley companies often seek to disrupt existing markets by bringing innovative information and communication technology solutions to what were previously stagnant or concentrated industries. For instance, Uber has been a disruptor for taxis and food delivery, Spotify has been a disruptor for music, Netflix was a disruptor for film and television, while Facebook has been a disruptor for many industries but perhaps none more so than the news media (see more in Chap. 6). This is facilitated by the sheer mass of programmers, tech experts, investors and entrepreneurs living in the area. This culture has also led to the introduction of 'incubators', exclusive office spaces that are owned and hosted by entrepreneurs which are offered to start-ups for free in exchange for shares in their companies should they prove successful.

Craig and Cunningham (2019) reflect upon this culture and its differing logic and strategies in their book *Social Media Entertainment: The new intersection of Hollywood and Silicon Valley,* noting that while Hollywood and the media giants of the 1990s have been a slow but sure section of the media industry, the social media entertainment companies of northern California have had considerable turnover for firms. They also note that traditional media has a stronger focus on the ownership of content as an intellectual property, which is not something shared by the tech industry, and has tended to be less possessive of content, instead focusing on the technology and the service.

### Social Media Platforms

From an industrial perspective, social media platforms maintain several similar features, be it Facebook, Instagram, LinkedIn, Pinterest, Snapchat, TikTok, X, Weibo and YouTube. Each platform allows users to generate, share and interact with content, establish a profile and communicate with people through instant messaging or other dialogue features. They all do this at scale, with user bases in the high millions or billions. Platforms use advertising as their primary form of revenue generation. They each collect data on users too, to enhance their services and target users with advertising based upon demographics and inference (Zuboff, 2015, 2019). At the same time, there are differences between them in terms of their primary use-case which in turn shapes the style of networks and content they produce.

Social media platforms are a product of the Web 2.0 era—a period of development for the worldwide web that meant users were able to produce, upload and share content online without owning their own server space or requiring any programming knowledge. The tracking features (i.e. cookies) commonly found on websites also were popularised during this period. These features form much of the backbone of social networking sites. Another core component for most social networking sites is the app-ification of their platforms and expansion into smartphones and other devices. This technology not only affords these companies greater access to user data but is also essential to them becoming ubiquitous and omnipresent in the lives of their users. Without smartphones, these platforms would be limited to desktop computers and laptops.

Designating a platform as 'social media' creates several conceptual challenges (see Chap. 1). Both YouTube and WhatsApp have been referred to as social media from time to time, but the two services could not be more different. One is a content sharing website more akin to a broadcast medium while the other is an instant messaging app which depends on dialogue to be effective. This difference emphasises how broad the social media paradigm is. At the same time, there are common technological threads that connect the diverse range of platforms available, including the medium (primarily smartphones) and the industry behind them. Within the social media paradigm, we might understand there to be three main categories of platform: social networking sites, content sharing platforms and instant messaging services.

Social networking sites (SNSs) are platforms that allow users to create profiles, connect with other profiles and build a network which to share information and content (boyd & Ellison, 2007). While most social platforms have network features, Facebook and LinkedIn might be said to have the strongest network focus, whereby the design of the platform is centred around enabling communities specific to the user that might mirror and extend their offline relationships. Content sharing platforms by comparison have a stronger focus on content and content creators. YouTube and TikTok are perhaps the most popular of this category, with Reddit and X also being industry stalwarts. These platforms are more likely to generate celebrity content and interaction and also have a stronger emphasis on entertainment (Craig & Cunningham, 2019). While there is some argument as to whether instant messaging services count as social media platforms, there is no doubt they are an important part of the paradigm and the infrastructure. Most social networking sites have some sort of messaging service attached to it. WeChat, WhatsApp and Facebook Messenger are among the most commonly used depending on your region. X, TikTok and Instagram all feature their own direct message function too. Interestingly, YouTube removed its direct messaging feature in September 2019, with some speculation it wasn't popular enough to warrant its continuation (Moon, 2019).

### The Myth of the Founder

Behind every Big Tech company, it would seem, there is the myth of a 'founder'. Well-known examples like Bill Gates, Steve Jobs, Jeff Bezos, Larry Page & Sergey Brin, and Mark Zuckerberg have become subjects for biographers and historians alike. There also appears to be a repeated pattern among tech companies of fostering enigmatic CEOs and mythologising their founders as rebels and geniuses. In their book *The Know-It-Alls*, Noam Cohen (2018) describes a number of features, typical of a Silicon Valley CEO. First is the proclaimed pursuit of serving mankind and trying to make a better world. The second is the promotion and mythologising of themselves as tech geniuses. Third is the promotion of libertarian viewpoints veiled behind political agnosticism. The fourth and last is the reduction of matters of social or cultural significance into mere engineering problems.

The awe and attention that comes from being a tech founder is a valuable asset in its own right. Companies can often cash in on the cultural cachet of their founders as a public relations tool and to corral investors. It was reported that in early 2023 that during a Tesla shareholder meeting, X owner and CEO, Elon Musk bragged about his social media account's follower count and went so far as to suggest it was a valuable asset to their company and that "Twitter is actually an incredibly powerful tool for driving demand for Tesla" (Serrano, 2023). Only a few weeks later, developers at Twitter changed the platform's recommender settings to prioritise tweets from Musk (Schiffer & Newton, 2023).

The enchanting spell of the tech founder myth has also been used to disguise fraudulent and abusive behaviour in the tech sector too. Famous examples of Elizabeth Holmes and Sam Bankman-Fried (SBF for short), show how presenting oneself as a philanthropic tech genius can be used to attract billions of dollars in investor capital and shield oneself from proper scrutiny. Elizabeth Holmes, a Stanford drop-out, was convicted of fraud in 2022 after raising over $700 million US dollars in venture capital and then lying about the product capabilities of medical-tech company Theranos—the company of which she was both the founder and CEO. Holmes styled herself in the fashion of Steve Jobs and Mark Zuckerberg was seen rubbing shoulders with Bill Clinton and Joe Biden. Like many founders and CEOs, she and her company made grandiose claims about changing the world.

### Attitudes to and Actions Towards Regulation

In recent years there has been a push towards increased regulation for social media companies. In the early days of these platforms, policymakers took a hands-off approach towards regulation as to avoid stifling innovation and growth. Now it would seem the pendulum has swung in the opposite direction (Flew, 2021). Among the main concerns for policy makers have been user privacy, copyright, national security, youth safety, misinformation, protecting the news industry and anti-competitive behaviour. The libertarian mindset commonly seen among Silicon Valley types (Flew & Martin, 2022) is often opposed to regulation. A common rhetorical position presented by these firms is that they are technology companies, not media companies or content producers (Napoli, 2019).

## INDUSTRIES

In analysing the business models of social networking companies, we see some common features with the media and telecommunication companies of the past, but also some unique features, specific to Big Tech and Silicon Valley. The business models of most social media companies are focused primarily on using attention and user data as their commodities. It is through these two resources that they can generate revenue, by inserting ads into the user experience and using data both to target users and to refine their platforms to promote further consumption.

### 'Surveillance Capitalism', Attention Economy and Smartphones

In this chapter's introduction, we referred to big oil companies like Saudi Aramco and ExxonMobil having exclusive access to valuable commodities. While oil tycoons have a stranglehold on one of earth's most precious resources, platform companies like Meta and Alphabet have been able to create their own exclusive resource in the form of user data. Shoshana Zuboff (2015, p. 75) argues that big data "is above all the foundational component in a deeply intentional and highly consequential new logic of accumulation that I [sic] call surveillance capitalism. This new form of information capitalism aims to predict and modify human behaviour as a means to produce revenue and market control".

It is the large-scale capture and commodification of user data, alongside the network power that comes from capturing the attention of millions of users, that social networking sites use to achieve business success. Social media companies and ad brokers can gather big data sets about users and consumers through the collection and trading of input data, behavioural data and inference. This data analysis is then used for the purpose of targeted advertising and the further refinement of platforms. Facebook, YouTube, X, Instagram and TikTok all use some form of targeted advertising. The ambition of which is to improve the relevance and suitability of advertising on these platforms. That said, the reliability of user data and inference to target consumer data has come also into question. In their book *Sub-prime Attention Crisis*, Tim Hwang suggests that the accuracy and predictive powers of ad brokers online with studies is overstated (Hwang, 2020). He cites research which found variability in accuracy for targeted ads was on average worse than random selection (Neumann et al., 2019).

Harnessing the attention economy is one of the features of new media that is comparable to the business models of traditional media. The more screen time or viewership a platform has, the more valuable ad space becomes. One of the distinguishing features of social media within the attention economy is the ubiquity of smartphones. While traditional media has been spatially limited in the way that it can be broadcast with audiences, smartphones have a life that extends beyond the breakfast table or the living room. These devices are with people regardless of whether they are on the bus, in a park, at the office or in a restroom. Therein the opportunity to engage the attention of audiences is much greater than before.

### Economies of Scale

Two key features of any media or telecommunications market are high fixed-costs and low marginal-cost (Noam, 2006). What this means is that for the business to perform its most basic functions such as providing a platform, printing a newspaper or providing wireless Internet, it requires a significant upfront expenditure on behalf of the business. Consider the resources necessary for developing, hosting and managing a social networking site like Facebook or X. It often requires thousands of employees and an enormous amount of technical infrastructure. This is the fixed cost. If you have one customer or one billion, there is a certain amount of capital that is required to provide the minimum service and for many entrepreneurs and would-be businesspersons, that cost is prohibitively high. That said, if you can afford the initial investment, the costs associated with serving additional customers is considerably less. The marginal cost is the cost of serving any additional customer. As social media companies serve larger and larger consumer bases, that marginal cost is reduced even further. These high fixed-costs and low marginal-costs encourage economies of scale, whereby firms attempt to serve as many consumers as possible. This has helped to make some of the most profitable companies in the world, but it also creates issues within markets that are not easily resolved.

In the earlier days of the Internet, the cost of entry for a social media company was much lower than it would be today. As such, early entrants were able to slowly build up their companies and establish new markets. In the era of tech giants and the platformed Internet (Flew, 2021), a small handful of platforms command much of the western public's attention. For a new entrant to achieve the same level of scale and network power, the slower, more steady method of scaling up over time isn't as viable. Instead, new firms rely on one of Silicon Valley's most hazardous strategies, blitzscaling, to achieve the same success. LinkedIn founder Reid Hoffman and Chris Yeh describe this business-building strategy whereby entrepreneurs deliberately burn through their investor capital in a haphazard manner to scale up their business as quickly as possible (Hoffman & Yeh, 2018). The assumption is that, as a media and communication company, if you have a large enough user base you will be certain to find a way to be profitable.

### *Produsage*

Part of the edge that social media companies have over traditional media companies and streaming services is the joined production and usage of content by users. Television, radio, streaming and print companies depend upon teams of professionals and production resources to create content, either through commissioned work or paying to use content libraries. Social networks are instead able to extract enormous value from their users by affording them the platform and tools to create content of their own. The Web 2.0 era, of which many social networks emerge, affords users much a greater opportunity to produce and publish their content online. This represented a significant change in how audiences interact with the media economy. Media scholar, Axel Bruns refers to the process of 'user-led' production or 'produsage'. They contend that "the role of 'consumer' and even that of 'end user' have long disappeared, and the distinctions between producers and users of content have faded into comparative insignificance" (Bruns, 2008, p. 2). While some scholars, like Henry Jenkins, have had much praise for participatory culture and its potential benefits to society, others, such as Fuchs, have identified the problematic nature of the relationship between producer-users and the owners of platforms who profit from it (Fuchs, 2017). Fuchs suggests that the exchange of value between users and platforms is one of exploitation and that taking pleasure in engaging with the platforms does not erase that platform owners are profiting from the labour of users. It is in these changing dynamics that we see a shift under social media in how we understand creative labour, the consumer and producers. This raises new questions regarding the ownership of content and the rights and responsibilities for both users and platforms. If the user is simultaneously the producer, consumer and the product, internal and governmental policy frameworks need to reflect these dynamics.

## CONCLUSION

In this chapter we have considered how—via the intersection of technology, users and business cultures—social media firms have come to be some of the most profitable and valuable companies in the world. Using a combination of old business models, such as advertising and subscriptions, and new models such as data brokerage and in-app sales, these firms have been able to generate income from a global user base numbering in the billions. At the same time, they still use common business strategies deployed by behemoths in manufacturing and resource sectors, these being conglomeration and exclusive access to valued commodities in the form of user data and attention.

We also explored the business traditions of these firms, examining the influence of Big Tech and Silicon Valley on the social media sphere. Social media technologies have been enabled largely by the developments of Web 2.0 and smartphones. The app-ification of social networking and content-sharing sites has led to a level of ubiquity never seen by traditional media companies. The 'move fast and break things' attitude of Silicon Valley has promoted a culture of disruption and innovation while libertarian viewpoints have made them reluctant to partner with governments in regulation efforts.

The interplay of what Sinan Aral refers to as the 'levers of power' for social media companies, of norms, code, money and laws, help to articulate the dynamics of the power and struggles at play in the social media world. Businesses, users, investors and government have each, at times, had competing interests in the future success of these platforms, and balancing those interests has proven to be both challenging and sometimes costly. To make an industry out of platforms means the further encroachment of economic interests into once aspects of the social world once thought to be free from commercialisation. A new era of cultural commodification that is ubiquitous, global and 'always on'.

## REFERENCES

Albarran, A. B. (2013). *The Social Media Industries*. Routledge.

Anderson, P. (2016). *Web 2.0 and Beyond: Principles and Technologies*. Chapman & Hall.

Aral, S. (2021). *The Hype Machine: How Social Media Disrupts Our Elections, Our Economy, and Our Health—And How we Must Adapt*. Currency.

boyd, d., & Ellison, N. B. (2007). Social Network Sites: Definition, History, and Scholarship. *Journal of Computer-Mediated Communication, 13*(1), 210–230.

Bruns, A. (2008). *Blogs, Wikipedia, Second Life, and Beyond: From Production to Produsage* (Vol. 45). Peter Lang.

Burgess, J., & Baym, N. K. (2022). *Twitter: A Biography*. NYU Press.

Castells, M. (2011). Network Theory | A Network Theory of Power. *International Journal of Communication, 5*, 15.

Chen, B., & Mac, R. (2023, 31 March 2023). *Twitter's Blue Check Apocalypse Is Upon Us. Here's What to Know*. Tech Fix. Retrieved from https://www.nytimes.com/2023/03/31/technology/personaltech/twitter-blue-check-musk.html

Cohen, N. (2018). *The Know-It-Alls: The Rise of Silicon Valley as a Political Powerhouse and Social Wrecking Ball*. Simon and Schuster.

Craig, D., & Cunningham, S. (2019). *Social Media Entertainment: The New Intersection of Hollywood and Silicon Valley*. NYU Press.

Flew, T. (2021). *Regulating Platforms*. Wiley.

Flew, T., & Martin, F. R. (2022). *Digital Platform Regulation: Global Perspectives on Internet Governance*. Springer Nature.

Fuchs, C. (2017). The Power and Political Economy of Social Media. In *Social Media: A Critical Introduction* (2nd ed., pp. 121–152). Sage Publications Ltd.

Giblin, R., & Doctorow, C. (2022). *Chokepoint Capitalism: How Big Tech and Big Content Captured Creative Labor Markets and How We'll Win Them Back*. Beacon Press.

Goggin, G. (2021). *Apps: From Mobile Phones to Digital Lives*. Wiley.

Hinton, S., & Hjorth, L. (2019). Understanding social media. In *Understanding Social Media* (pp. 1–232).

Hoffman, R., & Yeh, C. (2018). *Blitzscaling: The Lightning-Fast Path to Building Massively Valuable Companies*. Currency.

Hwang, T. (2020). *Subprime Attention Crisis: Advertising and the Time Bomb at the Heart of the Internet*. FSG Originals.

Just, N. (2009). Measuring Media Concentration and Diversity: New Approaches and Instruments in Europe and the US. *Media, Culture & Society, 31*(1), 97–117.

Leaver, T., Highfield, T., & Abidin, C. (2020). *Instagram: Visual Social Media Cultures*. Wiley.

Mac, R., & Hsu, T. (2023, 2023 June 5). *Twitter's U.S. Ad Sales Plunge 59% as Woes Continue*. Retrieved from https://www.nytimes.com/2023/06/05/technology/twitter-ad-sales-musk.html

Marwick, A. E. (2015). Instafame: Luxury Selfies in the Attention Economy. *Public Culture, 27*(1 (75)), 137–160.

Marwick, A. (2017). Silicon Valley and the Social Media Industry. In *The SAGE Handbook of Social Media* (pp. 314–329).

McQuail, D., & Deuze, M. (2020). In D. McQuail & M. Deuze (Eds.), *McQuail's Media & Mass Communication Theory* (7th ed.). Sage Publications.

Milano, S., Taddeo, M., & Floridi, L. (2020). Recommender Systems and their Ethical Challenges. *AI & SOCIETY, 35*, 957–967.

Moon, M. (2019, August 20). *YouTube is Removing its Direct Messaging Feature in September*. Retrieved from https://www.engadget.com/2019-08-20-youtube-killing-direct-messaging.html

Napoli, P. (2019). *Social Media and the Public Interest: Media Regulation in the Disinformation Age*. Columbia University Press.

Neumann, N., Tucker, C. E., & Whitfield, T. (2019). Frontiers: How Effective is Third-Party Consumer Profiling? Evidence from Field Studies. *Marketing Science, 38*(6), 918–926.

Noam, E. M. (2006). Deregulation and Market Concentration: An Analysis of Post-1996 Consolidations. *Federal Communications Law Journal, 58*, 539.

O'Reilly, T. (2005). Web 2.0: Compact definition.

Olson, C. (2022, February 5). *Meta Rivalry with Apple Inflamed as Facebook Parent Company Share Price Plummets*. Retrieved from https://www.theguardian.com/technology/2022/feb/04/meta-rivalry-apple-inflamed-facebook-parent-company-share-price-plummets

Park, J. (2023, June 14). *The Reddit Blackout of 2023: A Deep Dive into the Conflict and Its Implications*. Retrieved from https://hackernoon.com/the-reddit-blackout-of-2023-a-deep-dive-into-the-conflict-and-its-implications

Schiffer, Z., & Newton, C. (2023, February 15). *Yes, Elon Musk Created a Special System for Showing You all his Tweets First*. Retrieved from https://www.theverge.com/2023/2/14/23600358/elon-musk-tweets-algorithm-changes-twitter

Serrano, J. (2023). *Elon Tries to Convince Tesla Investors That Twitter Isn't a Problem, Really*. Retrieved from https://gizmodo.com/tesla-twitter-elon-musk-earnings-1850033951

Spangler, T. (2023, October 27). *One Year After Elon Musk Bought Twitter, X Monthly Users Are Down 15% and Ad Revenue Has Slumped 54%*. Retrieved from https://variety.com/2023/digital/news/musk-twitter-x-acquisition-one-year-user-revenue-decline-1235770297/

Statista. (2022). *Revenues Generated by LinkedIn from 2019 to 2021, by Segment*. Retrieved from https://www.statista.com/statistics/226863/linkedins-quarterly-revenue-by-segment/

Statista. (2023a). *Distribution of Global Time Spent on Mobile in 2020 to 2022, by Category*. Retrieved from https://www.statista.com/statistics/435324/share-app-time-category/

Statista. (2023b). *Leading Companies in the World in 2022\*, by Pre-tax Income*. Retrieved from https://www.statista.com/statistics/269857/most-profitable-companies-worldwide/

Stepnik, A. (2022). Active Curation for Cultural Commentary: Young Adults, Algorithms, And News Content On Social Media. In *AoIR Selected Papers of Internet Research*.

Stepnik, A. (2023). Active Curation: Algorithmic Awareness for Cultural Commentary on Social Media Platforms.

Zuboff, S. (2015). Big Other: Surveillance Capitalism and the Prospects of an Information Civilization. *Journal of Information Technology, 30*(1), 75–89.

Zuboff, S. (2019). In S. Zuboff (Ed.), *The Age of Surveillance Capitalism: The Fight for the Future at the New Frontier of Power*. Profile Books.

## CHAPTER 4

# Social Media and the Social Self: Individuals and Relationships

## INTRODUCTION: SOCIALLY MEDIATED LIVES

Social media users have changed and adapted as the technologies, infrastructures and cultures of practice shift within platformed media. From earlier online community formations that sought to connect and improve users' lives, through to the more divisive and damaging practices across contemporary social media platforms—including harassment, bullying, doxing and extremist vitriol and online abuse—users have typically assembled with other like-minded individuals. This connection through connectivity is the basis for individuals to construct and perform their online identities with what others have identified as networked individuals (Papacharissi, 2012) and online communities (Baym, 2000). With these practices and interpersonal relationships, social media users continue to evolve from the earlier back-stage formations (Goffman, 1956) to the more obvious and highly polished versions of contemporary influencers. Building on these individual identities and collective practices, the evolving space of digital emotion has also emerged, especially through what Hobbs (2015) describes as liquid love practices.

This chapter builds on the established social media platform practices of this book to highlight how individuals and groups of users effectively operate on social media. This chapter highlights the implications of user relationships from dating, to influencing, to political and lobbying practices across the suite of social media platforms. From influential Instagram campaigns to political X, vlogging and YouTube, and livestreaming on Twitch and other platforms, users continue to develop new ways of attracting audiences and engaging them for a variety of purposes. This chapter lays the foundation for the future chapters that uses rich ethnographic data to describe how users play the visibility game (Cotter, 2018) and engage in cultural intermediation practices to highlight value within cultural production (Hutchinson, 2017) on social media platforms.

J. Hutchinson et al., *Social Media in Society*, https://doi.org/10.1007/978-3-031-66360-4_4

## Social Media and the Self

How is it that we represent ourselves online? For example, if I am on my Facebook page which is predominantly made up of friends and family, I might behave differently than how I will on my LinkedIn profile which is used for my professional life, which is also different to how I present myself on TikTok, Grindr, YouTube and many other unique and specific platforms. Each of these platforms attract significantly different practices which guide users on how to create and publish content while simultaneously using and consuming other media. Yet, the uses of social media are a socially constructed process that evolves with the users of these communication technologies over time. Facebook, as one long-term example of an evolving communication technology, is now a place of commerce and connectivity and is moving towards becoming its own self-functioning environment through Meta (see Chap. 3). Facebook has significantly shifted from its first conception of rating other American college students. This evolution extends across all social media platforms as users engage with the technology and shape and transform its use as the social and cultural application emerges over time.

In the first instance of our self-identity construction in social media spaces, it is useful to think about who we are and how we represent ourselves on each specific social media platform. Are we using our professional persona? Am I representing myself as a weekend hobby person? What is different about myself on my dating app profile? Perhaps I'm a professional sporting personality setting up a behind-the-scenes TikTok account? In each of these examples, there are certain personality characteristics present with more emphasis on those than others—this in itself has been a significant shift from when social media first became a tool to the very much controlled individual spaces of contemporary social media. Images, videos, actions and textual representation also differ in how we assemble and construct our cultural and social symbols, which are not only how we present ourselves, but how others understand us. Lizardo (2016, p. 199) notes that such cultural symbols are 'motivated mappings between external form and cognitive meaning, used for both the private evocation of and the public externalization of those meanings'. It is useful to think of identity as a form of language construction that is sent and received across social media.

We might also think of our online selves as a disembodied communication process, where Durham Peters (2012, p. 228) outlines the process of communication beyond speech itself. They note:

*'To talk on a telephone is to identify an acoustic effigy of the person with an embodied presence. In "communication" the bodies of the communicants no longer hold the incontrovertible tokens of individuality or personality. Our faces, actions, voices, thoughts, and transactions have all migrated into media that can disseminate the indicia of our personhood without our permission. Communication has become disembodied'.*

This is also true of social media in that we are disembodied from this communication practice and rely on the construction of symbols and texts to represent who we are in the online space. This disembodiment on social media can be demonstrated through a few different and distinct ways. First, the way we talk and the language we use. We are likely to use a more formal style of language and talk in a matter-of-fact tone in professional spaces. Whereas we might use a more relaxed language in personal networks and rely on styles such as satire or sarcasm to convey messages. Linking practices (online content sharing) such as providing the URL address of a particular webpage to our social networks and other resources from the Internet is also a powerful way of demonstrating one's online personality. In a professional sense, we might post links that refer to current affairs or perhaps a political event. In personal spaces, we might post a link to a humorous story or perhaps even an activist site that we understand our friends would be interested in. One other textual representation for our online selves could be the sorts of images we post. Again, using the professional/personal dichotomy, our professional self might post a graph or statistic of information, whereas our personal space might include photos of our friends and family, or recent holidays for example.

Yet it is also in how we compare ourselves to other users on social media that can also determine the construction of our identities, and sometimes not in a positive sense. Taylor-Jackson and Moustafa (2021) highlight the relationship between social media and depression, self-esteem, anxiety, and loneliness. Through a series of surveys of western states in the US, they consider the two predominant ways of explaining the relationship between social media use and the impacts on mental health. First, they describe identity development and impression management which is the practice to exhibit and withhold information to influence perceptions and manage impressions held by others. This technique enables users to portray an ideal version of themselves that may be unachievable in real life and relies on social identity theory and group categorisation. Second, social comparison theory which suggests individuals define their abilities and evaluate their sense of self-worth through comparison with others. Jiang and Ngien (2020) through their study of 388 Singaporean participants note that while social media can increase anxiety, it is not platform specific but does connect with the issues associated with social comparison online. While highlighting significant negative impacts of identity construction for social media, these two studies alone indicate the importance of understanding how users and their identities are located within the networks we construct, both for positive and negative outcomes.

This may prompt us to ask, what happens when social media personas collide? The consequences of identity collision are often not obvious and can lead to significant repercussions. Networks can collide which can bring disparate and unique personas of the same person together in formations that were not determined by the owner of those personas. Social media is often criticised for presence bleed, which Gregg (2011) defines as the way our personal and professional selves intersect with one another in social media spaces. For a broad

Fig. 4.1   The contentious Scott MacIntyre tweet on ANZAC day

range of social media users, presence bleed will not cause an issue, but for some users it can be catastrophic. One way of examining social media identity construction and presence bleed is to look at an empirical example which erupted in Australia during 2015, when the Special Broadcasting Service (SBS) journalist, Scott MacIntyre, was fired for his social media use during his day off (Fig. 4.1).

April 25 is known as ANZAC Day, which is a day of remembrance for the Australian and New Zealand soldiers who have served during the wars these countries have participated within. While it is a day of remembrance for many Australians and New Zealanders, it can be a day of political tension between anti-war folk and the families of those who served. However, in 2015, the now sacked SBS sports journalist Scott McIntyre was the example of presence bleed when he tweeted from his personal X account: 'Wonder if the poorly-read, largely white, nationalist drinkers and gamblers pause today to consider the horror that all mankind suffered'. These comments attracted condemnation from the then Prime Minister, Malcolm Turnbull, asking for consequences to his 'offensive' comments, which resulted in the journalist being stood down from his role as a journalist for the SBS. Regardless of whether users agreed with his comments or not, in this then X space he was representing his employer, the SBS (who were also at threat of having their funding cut by the Australian Government at that time) and as such his thoughts reflected his employer. His employment manager, Michael Ebeid AM, responded that the SBS did not agree with his views, and stood him down from his professional duties almost immediately. This was a landmark social media case in Australia that prompted employers and employees to review their practices across social media because of presence bleed, with many, if not all, places of employment designing and implementing a set of social media standards for all staff.

Social media identity is not only limited to professional versus private domains, but rather across the entire spectrum of who we are online. Judith Butler (2014) is one of the leading scholars on gender and identity and can be drawn on here to think through some of the implications of representation in the online environment. She notes that we embrace an identity through our sexuality because we own a certain gender and we understand that gender, for example what it is meant to be, how it operates, how we position that gender across the spectrum of gender identification. If this is the case, we use aspects of our identity to convey certain messages, through the disembodiment of communication beyond human speech. We construct our identity through an assemblage of symbols, including our language, tone, images, avatars, taglines, and shared content. Just as Butler notes we do this through our sexuality, we also operate in a similar mode across social media. We are a collection, or assemblage, of technological artefacts, social media experience and sociality (Taylor, 2009) through the communication texts and symbols which are demonstrated through what we say, what we post, and what we share.

### The Performative Pursuit of Perfectionism

At the time of writing, the #thatgirl hashtag has accumulated over 4 billion views on TikTok and around 600,000 posts on Instagram. Designed as an inspirational space for young women, the #thatgirl hashtag is typically a collection of health-related diet ideas such as green smoothies and juices, wellbeing tips that range from how to feel good in the morning to relationship advice, fashion and makeovers suggestions, and other inspirational content. The #thatgirl content is undertaken in a playful way to engage and entertain users looking for a piece of escapism in their social media day. Content creators typically make social media content that represents healthy and happy young women living a positive life, happily sharing, or promoting, their lives with others following the conversation.

**Fig. 4.2**   The typical #thatgirl styled social media content

However, as the *Wall Street Journal* reported from the leaked internal study by Facebook into Instagram (Wells et al., 2021), one in three young women feel increasing pressure to conform to the content they see on their social media spaces. Sadly, many survey respondents noted they had a 'desire to kill themselves' due to high levels of body dissatisfaction compared with the young women they see in their social media feeds. The #thatgirl hashtag denotes the previously discussed disembodiment phenomenon across social media communication spaces: that is, while a topic or conversation emerges across social media spaces to inspire and strengthen young women, it has instead become toxic and a source of much sorrow, anxiety and depression across the same demographic it sought to address. Through the collection of its pieces that make up the entire hashtag feed across multiple social media spaces, #thatgirl has evolved to a space of ridicule, satire and anger of what young women are pushing back against: the perfect young women's life (see for example Vice's Shamani Joshi who documented her attempt at 'I tried to be TikTok's 'That Girl' for a week' https://www.vice.com/en/article/5db8ek/tiktok-youtube-viral-trend-that-girl-internet-genz-challenge) (Fig. 4.2).

Here, the misalignment between one's self identity and their representation of it comes under fire as exemplary of social media more broadly. Beyond the misogynistic practices that women have to endure daily on platformed media, the over-saturation of influencers has distorted how users perceive their own social media spaces. The #thatgirl conversation is an example of how something that is designed to be a positive conversation space is met with high levels of suspicion from readers who are wary of the commercial products just under the surface. Is this health information being presented so I can buy a health tea, or new facial routine? Health is incredibly commercialised through social media, and the ways in which users have aligned their online identities with this scene has been of interest to many social media researchers [cite, cite, cite]. The process itself brings the concept of authenticity into sharp view for the broad array of users.

## SOCIAL MEDIA AND SELF-PRESENTATION: MEDIATED AUTHENTICITY

Building on the idea of authenticity among social media users, Luoma-aho et al. (2019) have provided unique insights that extend beyond simply endorsing products that influencers might assume their audiences like, but to also prime them. In a study they undertook with a US-based travel vlog, they found that users would perceive authenticity differently if they were primed in either a negative or positive approach. For example, if users were told the social media post was done for money, they would react negatively to the content, and vice-versa. They also found that the user approach towards authentic content was neither positive nor negative if the content creator called upon the audience to participate with the content. This controlled environment experiment is a strong example of what is called mediated authenticity (Enli, 2014, p. 5)—'the idea that our understanding of society is based on mediated representations of reality'. To bring authenticity on social media alongside mediated authenticity, is to also begin to unpack the sorts of ideas and concepts that design and guide how mediation is undertaken and why it occurs.

Mediated authenticity extends beyond perception and into notions of power and networks. Social media and self-representation are the concept of the individual and communication power. Foucault (1977, p. 331) notes that identity within the media is a particular power: "This form of power that applies itself to immediate everyday life categorises the individual, marks him by his own individuality, attaches him to his own identity, imposes a law of truth on him that he must recognise and others have to recognize in him" (p. 331). If we broaden this concept across the contemporary gender conversation and apply it to social media, why is it that only some users can start movements, trends or memes that become popular and highly engaged with across social media spaces? Why do certain campaigns gain traction on social media when posted by certain users, while other campaigns by other users are somewhat dead in the water? The difference between popularity and engagement can be attributed to the concept of individuality as a form of power, where some users are more influential than others because of the authority they command when using social media platforms. They subject themselves in ways that reject the common flow of communication. Within an environment that has an enormous amount of communication potential, and one that speaks to highly niche audiences as social media does, power across platforms is gained through what Wellman (2001) notes as networked individualism.

Personal community networks give rise to the individual as the primary unit of connectivity, which provides the basis for the social structure called networked individualism. In thinking about how online communities form and the lead users that appear from within, we can focus on the mediated authenticity of personal autonomy and agility to strengthen the value of member connections due to additional knowledge resources—popular people have a perceived presence to know more things and demonstrate higher levels of unique knowledge. Therefore, their high levels of expertise and experience is another formation of identity symbols that an individual will use as a means of constructing their online representation in a social media environment. The knowledge that one individual brings to a collection of individuals is directly related to how they construct a power relationship, and are often referred to as lead users, or social media influencers. It is the lead users that can construct significant power relations and mobilise specific social media movements.

Fuchs (2014) provides us with a great empirical example of communication power through identity: one of mass self-communication and a desire and will to keep the Internet free and open. The group Anonymous is one of those examples of a civil liberty group, often referred to as 'hackers', that will pursue civic freedom through digital technologies above all. Often, Internet freedom civil liberty groups such as Anonymous, are vocal and can mobilise large amounts of individuals around the globe through their connected networked individualism. By collectively engaging in the 'anonymous' identity which is portrayed through the Guy Fawkes mask, Anonymous members are engaging in mass self-communication to collectively push an ideal amongst a broader group of individuals with a common purpose of keeping the Internet free and open. Ironically, Anonymous are one of the more successful social media groups who demonstrate strong identity and online representation through their faceless-ness operation.

To sum up the key points of a social media user's online identity and how they present themselves, there are four key areas that highlight how users represent themselves in an authentic social media environment. First is the language they choose to use. This determines in which circles they are communicating and how they align with particular pre-existing discourses. Users also have the ability to switch **language**, for example how a user might interact with a dating app is likely to be very different to how they use a LinkedIn profile. Second is the **imagery** users choose to attach to their social media selves. Given the rise of visual communication in the networked communication environment, the use of imagery, for example how we construct avatars and profile images, or the way users construct their palettes of imagery in Instagram, for example, demonstrates identity and an insight into one's self in a social media environment. A profile picture on X might be a professional profile shot, while an Instagram profile might be more playful, for example a selfie atop Santorini on a holiday adventure. Third, the **links** shared by users demonstrate considerable identity indicators: users may want to share information to demonstrate they are across the most recent events in social experiences, or that they are up to date with the latest information in relation to that crypto currency movement or stock market shift. Finally, the specific and niche **knowledge** that users bring to online identity is crucial for constructing an authoritative voice on the conversations they engage with. This is especially important when mobilising groups or what we might consider to be online communities. A high level of knowledge in a particular area of expertise is likely to attract like-minded individuals and, by engaging in networked individualism, social media users can start campaigns and build momentum behind specific issues of interest—be that good or bad.

## SOCIAL MEDIA AND INNER LIVES: MEANING MAKING ONLINE

*'"Meaning" highlights the generative process by which users negotiate the communicative potentials and constraints of a text or a medium vis-a-vis the individuals' pre-existing mental models, expectations, and intentions in context.* (Lomborg, 2015, n.p.)

Media and meaning has a long history across media and communication studies (McQuail, 2010; McLuhan, 1964) and other closely related disciplines such as cultural studies (Hall, 1999) and science and technology studies to name a few. While the evolution of social media and the meaning through media that it has generated has not fundamentally shifted, the way in which we make sense of the world around us and the pace at which this process is undertaken has dramatically impacted our lives. Further, how we look at our societies and those who exist within them has seen a shift in the recent years, particularly with the rise of misinformation within tense political situations and key medical moments. So how is meaning created and shared amongst social media users and what are its impacts?

Media has arguably been noted as communicatively grounded (Carey, 1989), situated (Goffman, 1956), and negotiated and shared (Miller, 1984). Media users bring their own context and understandings to media, locate that meaning in their own worlds and engage with it to ensure it makes sense from their perspective: meaning making is cumulative and generative amongst its audiences. Langlois (2014, p. 7) makes a useful observation that these actions within digital media are not simply producers and consumers of content, but rather a mix of many stakeholders who complicate the meaning process. 'These sites, I would add, are composed of users, audiences and producers, institutions, policies, rules, routines, professional hierarchies and ethics, aesthetics and technologies all in the service of enabling the production, storage, and distribution of meanings'. It becomes clear in this space, that meaning is not simply generative and cumulative as once thought, but indeed loaded with several perspectives all attempting to nudge meaning along.

If we reflect on the previous sections in this chapter, it becomes clear that social media messages can become distorted through individuals who have strong understandings of how platforms and users operate on them, the sorts of languages and norms that are used, and how they construct their identities to position themselves as significant network influencers. In these circumstances, these users have demonstrated high levels of knowledge to ensure their authority and thereby authenticity is pushed forward, in that case strengthening the meaning they are distributing in their media. This authority in meaning, of course, works in both positive and negative arrangements.

## TRIBES AND MEMES: COMMUNICATING COMMUNITY

There is much discussion about online communities as a collection of users presenting their online identities, where often terms that describe online community are conflated. These ways in which we understand online community as a descriptor provide an understanding for how we look at groups of individuals collectively operating online together for a shared purpose. This approach is even more obvious with social media, where the inherent transaction is to be social with one another within these spaces. But how do these spaces differentiate between networks, groups, communities, cliques, squads or hangouts for those inside and those outside looking in? This section unpacks the tribes of social media by examining what the characteristics are for these social arrangements and the sorts of identifiers that connect them to particular groupings. Imagine the following two scenarios. These two examples are often collapsed into the same online community category. In fact they are quite different both through their characteristics, and in how they operate.

Scenario 1:

*Gabriella loves gaming. She spends a great deal of her time conquering lands, leading armies, creating new weapons and building up treasures in her favourite, networked massive open online game, or MOOG. On a recent gaming quest, she had to determine how to march her armies faster but didn't have the approximate six hours in real time to strategise how her troops could arrive at the next kingdom. So, she called on her team alliance to help her out with some expertise. Luckily, Gabriella has previously helped others in a variety of scenarios and there is a high level of reciprocity, or give and take, within her online community of fellow gamers. They help her quickly with the resources to make the march faster.*

Scenario 2:

*Manuel has a mid-level management position. He relies on his strong network of industry contacts to keep him up to date with the latest ideas and information about trade relationships within the steel industry. He has been on LinkedIn for several years and is continually adding and refining his list of industry contacts relevant to his professional role. In this capacity, Manuel is using LinkedIn as a social network site to find people of a similar calibre to glean information and look for opportunities. His online network is strong, with similar interests, but is not so inclined to reciprocate beneficial activities.*

To identify what is online community and what is not in the above examples presents an opportunity to identify and define the term more broadly. Historically, online communities began as early versions of ad hoc online communication then evolved to become sophisticated networks modelled on offline communities. The existence of makeshift computer mediated communication (CMC) technology, for example the early Internet chat rooms developed by like-minded individuals, made it possible for the first online communities to emerge. In the early 1990s, Howard Rheingold (1994) observed and recorded the interaction and organisation of 'virtual' communities, based on his experience as a member of the Internet chat space, the Whole

Earth 'Lectronic Link or WELL as it is fondly remembered. Central to Rheingold's definition of online community is the sense of belonging with other participants who share a similar interest, or a "personal relationship in cyberspace".

Other scholars, such as Barry Wellman (1998), identify online communities as computer-supported social networks as a mechanism between "people as well as machines" to "link globally with kindred souls for companionship, information, and social support from their homes". Wellman attempted to understand what online communities would look like and how they would operate given their limited social presence and geographical proximity. This was the precursor for understanding the larger societal impact of online communities, or virtual communities, through increased connectivity afforded by information and communication technologies. As communities extend beyond their localised versions where individuals are born into their networks, people begin to choose who is in their networks. Here we see the emergence of what Wellman, Bernie Hogan and others (2005) note as "personal community networks: fragmented multiple social networks connected only by the person (or the household) at the centre". Simply put, this describes a mode of network connection between smaller clusters of individuals, rather than the larger cluster. This viewpoint provides, as they describe, "diversity, choice, and manoeuvrability at the probable cost of cohesion and long-term trust". Personal community networks give rise to the individual as the primary unit of connectivity, which provides the basis for the social structure described by Wellman as networked individualism. The loss of cohesion and trust within the community setting is counterbalanced by increased personal autonomy and agility, strengthening the value of member connections due to additional knowledge resources.

There are, however, arguments to support the collective benefits of individuals connecting en masse across ICT networks. When defining online communities, Bonniface, Green and McMahon (2006) incorporate Papadakis' offline community features of commonality, reciprocity, identity and collective action. They suggest the online community evolves into more than a collective connection of individual interests or circumstances. In terms of an online community, there are connective and personal traits that suggest users are coming together to benefit each other as they strive to achieve a similar goal. This is somewhat different to a network.

Building on the social relations of online communities, we might think about networks as actors connected through nodes and lines, typically represented as network graphs. However, the concept of the 'network' emerged through the explicit work of Kirt Lewin and Jacob Moreno who applied 'space' to those social relations. Through sociometry, described as the social fabric or social web that can explain the interaction, motivations and actions of individuals, we can begin to understand group dynamics (Treadwell, 2016). Agency is how an individual interacts with the social structure of the network, where Bruno Latour (2005) provides us with three ways to think about this. "The first one is to attribute to them naturality and to link them with nature. The second one is to grant them sociality and to tie them with the social fabric. The third one is to consider them as a semiotic construction and to relate agency with the building of meaning." In other words, individuals operate within networks organically, socially, or as meaning makers.

If we return to Scenario 2 above, Manuel and his use of LinkedIn, he is using the concept of the network somewhere in between the formation of the social fabric and the relationship between agency and the building of meaning. By constructing a social fabric, that is a network of similar minded individuals, he is opening the possibility of access to knowledge. It is the agency of those users that determine how that knowledge is transferred, accepted and ultimately shared with others within the network.

Online community is the heart of communication and the social fabric of social media platforms. Defining our relationships in a way that describes shared commonalities and goals, reciprocity, respect and civility amongst its users, is the basis of an online community. However online communities do not represent every gathering of individuals on the Internet, particularly those using social media. Networks exist and they too have social fabric at their core. This is essentially how users find each other and connect—through commonalities. But unlike the reciprocity and civility that is common amongst online communities, networks are designed and operate around the concept of user agency. How we construct our networks entirely depends on the authority of those with knowledge and demonstrated agency within those groups. Beyond the superficial difference of navigating forums versus profile pages, the interactions are somewhat different between the network and the community. Network favours agency, while community favours reciprocity.

## SOCIAL MEDIA AND PROBLEMATIC PSYCHOLOGIES: NARCISSISM, ADDICTION

'Two things that I cannot change: I'm a Millennial, and I am an addict. A social media addict' wrote Brit A on January 24, 2018, on her Medium page. Unpacking newly found knowledge about their place in an online space, they unpack how it is situated within undergraduate studies, and how computer-mediated communication theory helps them to understand how to operate in this space. For Brit A, they pointed out two key aspects of their social media life: they found support from their network of friends and followers, yet they struggled with having a life outside of social media.

The social media addiction rhetoric has gathered traction over the past decade as people tend to increasingly spend more time on their smartphones and engage with people in the online world. Yet, it has also become obvious, particularly to media studies scholars, that often the notion of media addiction is associated with moral panics and too often with the health of our children—every moment spent on a screen is time taken away from the romanticism of climbing a tree or kicking a football around. But as the field of media studies, its technologies and histories has consistently shown us, this is rarely the case as media technologies always find routine and space in our existing lives.

Yet narcissism is a recurring argument that exists within the aftermath of social media. In fact, work such as Casale and Banchi's (2020) continue to perpetuate the idea that there is a connection between narcissism and social media by introducing the term problematic social media use (PSMU) by highlighting that social media is somehow promoting the narcissistic aspects of social media through 'grandiose narcissism'. While these scholars do highlight the connection between social media and some significant mental disorders such as anxiety, depressive symptoms, body image dissatisfaction and disordered eating, this is a difficult argument to mount considering the other positive aspects of social media.

A better way to understand the moral panic reaction to social media and narcissism is through the research by Tiidenberg and Gómez Cruz (2015, p. 77), who systematically describe the selfie phenomenon as a practice of freedom. They note, 'For our participants, self-shooting is an engaged, self-affirmative and awareness raising pursuit, where their body, through critically self-aware self-care, emerges as agentic, sexual and distinctly female'. By engaging in empirical research with users who share their images across the then sex-friendly Tumblr platform, these scholars challenge existing normative ways of understanding social media practices, especially not safe for work (NSFW) selfies, as more meaningful ways that users are actually engaging in their thoughtful and inspiring ways. This places the legitimacy of examining social media and selfies as narcissistic practices into question and develops a more nuanced understanding of how to read contemporary social media practices.

Katrin Tiidenberg is a wonderful media studies scholar that explains this arena of social media users, particularly through the concept of selfies. By avoiding moral panic approaches, and by introducing concepts such as the term by Lucy Suchman, configuration, it is possible to unpack the why and how people undertake the sorts of social media practices they do. In doing so, we can avoid the objectification of things like selfies by giving it one hard definition—'A selfies is…'. Instead, the term selfie as a social media practice means many different things to many different people—a memory, a significant moment, a medical snapshot, or perhaps a cultural insight. Through Suchman's configuration lens, we can unpack how cultural objects like selfies are a result of a changing world—'In this light, selfies are a new configuration, a moment of coming together, within a process of ongoing technological and cultural shifts in networked, photographic self-representation' (Tiidenberg, 2018, p. 18). Here, it is clear that selfies have become an important part of cultural representation and documentation beyond any aspect of problematic social media use.

However, it is remiss to suggest that social media is all rainbows and unicorns. Andreassen et al. (2017) undertook a study aimed at the associations between addictive use of social media, narcissism, and self-esteem. A cross-sectional sample of 23,532 Norwegians (Median age = 35.8 years; range =

16–88 years) completed an open web-based survey that included questions related to Bergen Social Media Addiction Scale (BSMAS), the Narcissistic Personality Inventory-16, and the Rosenberg Self Esteem Scale. The results demonstrated that demographics within lower age, being a woman, not being in a relationship, being a student, lower education, lower income, lower self-esteem and narcissism were associated with higher scores on the BSMAS. The study suggests that basic demographic variables (primarily age and sex), narcissism and self-esteem are all associated with addictive use of social media. Addictive social media use was related to lower age, being a woman, not being in a relationship, lower education, being a student, lower income, having narcissistic traits and negative self-esteem.

While both sides of the argument continue to make headlines, for example The Times front cover that screamed the "Me Me Me Generation: Millennials are lazy, entitled narcissists who still live with their parents" above a photo of a young women talking a selfie on her smartphone, it is important to place this debate in context. There is no denying that social media contributes to some of our society's most significant mental health issues, but at the same time they enable a great deal of innovative and important social practice. To reduce the social media practice to addictive and/or narcissistic alone is simplistic and ignorant of the broader field. A better way to approach social media users and their practices is to understand the environment in which these practices emerge—that is they are a result of a combination of cultural and technological assemblages that present a continual change in the way meaning is produced around us.

## Social Media and Relationships

If all media are social, why then are social media associated with human relationships? It may be because they are ever-present in our everyday lives, carried around in our bags and pockets to be easily ignited at our choosing. Or it might be because access has never been easier with technologies becoming smaller and cheaper. Or perhaps it could be because practices of content creation are now almost part of our everyday lives, signifying a semantic shift in how we communicate with each other and audiences of varying sizes. But it's not always about communicating for communication's sake: at the heart of social media is the capacity to build strong and powerful relationships. These relationships are built in several ways including through memes and other communication devices.

One way of thinking about the building of relationships is through memes and the 'tribes' that emerge within this powerful communication process. Winocur (2019) presents the results of an online ethnography which evidences, on the one hand, how such parodic resources are expressed when creating tribal identities and strategies of social inclusion and exclusion. On the other hand, the author presents the epistemological and methodological suitability of not separating the creation and the consumption of content from the production of sense, undertaken in the study of adolescent practices on social media. Their selected case study was the Facebook page Uruguayan Memes for Young Citizens (UMFYC), which has 2328 followers. Uruguayan Memes for Young Citizens was created to publish satires based on regional/Uruguayan events. The researcher discovered that, in the same way as it happens in other urban tribes, in the meme tribe there are "role plays" which exclude those who do not know or do not share identity codes. The adolescents in this research chose memes to represent the identity of the tribe because they constitute parody resources with possibilities of open and encoded communication at the same time. Danks (the identity assumed by the members of the tribe who founded the meme page) resorted to a kind of satirical humour and dialectal codes which combine the use of colloquial English with Spanish and the jargon from anime and video games. Although there is no explicit intention of excluding people from the page, such codes act, as a matter of fact, as a semantic barrier to leave others aside.

Similarly, Dafaure (2022) discusses how the alt-right has brought back traditional tenets of the reactionary, xenophobic and often racist far-right and made these tenets appear as novel, provocative, and updated to the twenty-first-century U.S. society and digital environment through memes. Dafaure argues that alt-righters relied heavily on the creation, and sometimes reappropriation, of enemy images, with the ultimate goals of provoking outrage, instilling fear and/or hatred towards specific groups, reinforcing a sense of belonging within their own community, or more broadly manipulating collective perceptions and representations notably through examples of far-right domestic terrorism in the US, and their place in an age of post-truth, fake news, and alternative facts. Focuses on "otherness" of Hispanics and Muslims ("rapefugees") which easily appeals to rampant islamophobia. The second enemy image created by the alt-right consists in its ideological opponents. The third enemy image is a common thread (or threat) in far-right ideologies, cultural Marxism. Ultimately, the use of big banner issues is used to create communality between lead and fringe groups (through meme culture).

Beyond the darker side of social media relationship building are the more productive groups and progressive thinking. After Tumblr's Terms of Services changed during 2019, which saw the platform post a blog noting that NSFW content would not be allowed any longer, which was defined as explicit sexual content and nudity 'with some exceptions'. From the Tumblr perspective, this was to reduce the amount of pornography on the platform, but at the same time it had a very negative impact on groups who used the space for other sexually oriented reasons beyond pornography alone. Of those most impacted was the LGBTIQ communities who used Tumblr as a safe space to meet, connect, support and engage with each other. To many, this was the death of the platform where its user base pushed back but to no avail, causing a major exodus from the site.

Not long after, *OnlyFans* emerged as a platform where users could pay content creators for their work. The sort of content that was most popular on this space aligned with sex workers who were able to safely undertake their profession while being able to earn an income. OnlyFans is financially supported by three major American banks—Bank of New York Mellon, Metro Bank and JPMorgan Chase—who urged the platform to announce a ban on sexually explicit content. After significant backlash from its users, they redacted the announcement stating on X that:

> *"We have secured assurances necessary to support our diverse creator community and have suspended the planned October 1 policy change," and "OnlyFans stands for inclusion and we will continue to provide a home for all creators."*

The Tumblr and OnlyFans experiences are moments that highlight how sexual expression is significant in not only communication and exchange of ideas, but also a strong process for building relationships across social media. Kath Albury (2018) writes extensively about sexuality on social media and has highlighted the importance of platforms within this conversation. Through exploring sexual expression, Albury notes that sexuality, intimacy and social media practices might be constrained or enabled by technical elements such as design features and platform affordances. While these evolving practices of sexual expression have promoted freedom of expression for sexual minorities, they have also raised legitimate concerns regarding the costs of increased visibility for a range of groups, including young people, LGBTQ people, and members of BDSM and kink subcultures.

Nonetheless, social media plays a significant role in building both intimate and non-intimate relationships. Through the often hurtful and extreme views of the alt-right and their use of memes such as *Pepe the Frog*, through to queer culture and its incorporation of signifying symbols, social media is an important communication tool for gathering individuals together and building relationships. Within this same conversation are the affordances of the platforms themselves, which was further discussed in Chap. 3, and how key policy decisions that are made in these spaces can severely impact the lives of those individuals developing relationships across social media.

## SOCIALLY MEDIATED MASS-SELF COMMUNICATION: ALWAYS, EVERYWHERE, EVERYONE

The always on idea of social media emerges from the foundational concepts of how and why we communicate using these technologies. Social media platforms can be defined as "sites and services…that allow participants to create and share their content" such as photos, videos, audio, and text (boyd, 2014, p. 6). Since their rise in the early 2000s, social media platforms have become a ubiquitous presence in our lives, connecting billions of people around the world and even "[structuring] the flow of information in society" (Aral, 2020, p. 58). One of the most popular social media platforms is X, which allows users to communicate through short messages/updates known as 'tweets'. Like all social media platforms, X creates a 'networked public', because its users imagine themselves as part of an online community (boyd, 2014, p. 8–9). The properties of this networked public, known as X's 'affordances' and 'constraints', shape how the platform can be used (Ronzhyn et al., 2023).

X has a variety of affordances, including 'persistence', 'visibility', 'spreadability', and 'searchability'. According to boyd (2014), these are the four affordances that "shape many of the mediated environments…created by social media" (p. 11). Firstly, persistence refers to how tweets remain visible and accessible on the platform indefinitely. This persistence allows users to revisit and ongoingly engage with old tweets/conversations. Another affordance of X is visibility. Whilst a user's tweet is shown to anyone who follows them, it also has the potential to appear on each user's 'For You' timeline. This personalised timeline is curated by a recommender system that analyses a user's connections, interests, and engagement metrics in three stages—candidate sourcing, ranking, and heuristics and filters (Twitter, 2023). By appearing on 'For You' timelines, tweets have the potential to go viral and have an amplified reach.

Furthermore, X affords high spreadability due to its unique 'retweet' feature in which users can instantly reply to another person's tweet and then reshare it with their followers. Not only does this enable the rapid dissemination of information, but it encourages users to interact with one another by "[providing] a structure for conversation and comment" (Geboers & Van De Wiele, 2020, pg. 751). Finally, X affords high searchability because it allows users to search for specific keywords, topics, and hashtags. These searches can then be filtered via location, recency, and popularity, thus making it extremely quick and easy for users to find a wide range of topics and engage in ongoing tweets/conversations (Geboers & Van De Wiele, 2020). Overall, these four main affordances make X a handy platform for sharing information, with the potential to facilitate robust, mass communication.

When considering X's overall net value to users, it is necessary to understand that the platform's affordances and constraints are closely related and do not have strictly positive or negative effects on user behaviour (Ronzhyn et al., 2023). For example, X's 280-character limit can be seen as an affordance because it fosters clear and concise communication, contributing to the platform's high engagement levels and spreadability (Guo & Saxton, 2014). However, this character limit could also be viewed as a constraint that does not allow for the expression of complex ideas, thus leading to sensationalism, decontextualisation and miscommunication.

Another example is how X's affordances of spreadability, visibility and searchability can make it a powerful tool for activism and social movements whilst conversely creating dangerous 'echo chambers'. For instance, during the Black Lives Matter Movement, X "played a crucial role" by "[drawing] attention to the movement's core ideas and…[mobilising] supporters for protests" (Klein et al., 2022, p. 1). However, Bouvier and Rosenbaum (2020) note that "while technologies have afforded activists with the ability to reach wider audiences across physical and social boundaries, they have also limited who might hear about certain events through the algorithms put in place" (p. 121). This highlights the fact that X and its algorithms can form "echo chambers" in which users are only exposed to content that supports their existing beliefs (Aral, 2020). This severely constrains users' abilities to access diverse perspectives, potentially resulting in the polarisation of public discourse. Additionally, the spreadability and real-time nature of X can enhance the dissemination of false news and misinformation because tweets can rapidly go viral before being fact-checked.

Overall, affordances and constraints can be considered "complementary" and "equally necessary for activity to take place" on social media (Ronzhyn et al., 2023, p. 14). The platform, X, has many affordances, including persistence, visibility, spreadability, and searchability, all of which are closely intertwined with the platform's constraints, such as the character limit, echo chambers, and fake news. Despite these constraints and challenges, X is of net value to users, because it is an immensely powerful tool for communication, activism, and social change. According to Nagy & Neff (2015) affordances provide a "middle ground between technological determinism and social construction", therefore, believing that X has no net value to users would completely disregard the ways in which "people shape their media environments, perceive them, and have agency within them" (p. 1–2).

Content that is uploaded to social media stays visible until the person on the other end reads the message or the content gets deleted. This is called persistence, and this allows for asynchronous communication (boyd, 2014), meaning that one user could send a message to another user, however the user may not open this message for weeks on end and it will still sit there. Instagram in this instance, has affordances with its features. Most of the features on the application are not on a timed basis, meaning they are asynchronous. However, images sent in private messages, the user sending the message can choose to have them on a timed basis or allow the image to be looked at for extended periods of time. Users can also comment publicly for all to see on others' posts, allowing for people to read the user's comment, then re-read it again. A constraint of the persistence aspect is that messages and comments can be deleted, thus meaning users can manipulate chats and comments, however this must occur to allow user privacy.

## REFERENCES

Albury, K. (2018). Young People, Digital Media Research and Counterpublic Sexual Health. *Sexualities, 21*(8), 1331–1336.

Andreassen, C. S., Pallesen, S., & Griffiths, M. D. (2017). The Relationship Between Addictive Use of Social Media, Narcissism, and Self-esteem: Findings from a Large National Survey. *Addictive Behaviors, 64*, 287–293. https://doi.org/10.1016/j.addbeh.2016.03.006

Aral, S. (2020). *The Hype Machine*. Harper Collins.

Baym, N. K. (2000). *Tune In Log On: Soaps Fandom and Online Community*. Sage Publications Inc..

Bonniface, L., Green, L., & Swanson, M. (2006). Communication on a Health-Related Website Offering Therapeutic Support—Phase 1 of the HeartNET Website. *Australian Journal of Communication, 33*(2), 89–107.

Bouvier, G., & Rosenbaum, J. E. (2020). *Twitter, the Public Sphere, and the Chaos of Online Deliberation.* Palgrave Springer.

boyd, d. (2014). *It's Complicated.* Yale University Press.

Butler, J. (2014). *Bodies that Matter: On the Discursive Limits of Sex.* Routledge.

Carey, J. W. (1989). *Communication as Culture: Essays on Media and Society.* Routledge.

Casale, S., & Banchi, V. (2020). Narcissism and Problematic Social Media Use: A Systematic Literature Review. *Addictive Behaviors Reports, 11*(2020), 100252. https://doi.org/10.1016/j.abrep.2020.100252

Cotter, K. (2018). Playing the Visibility Game: How Digital Influencers and Algorithms Negotiate Influence on Instagram. *New Media & Society, 21*(4), 895–913.

Dafaure, M. (2022). Memes, Trolls and the Manosphere: Mapping the Manifold Expressions of Antifeminism and Misogyny Online. *European Journal of English Studies, 26*(2), 236–254.

Enli, G. (2014). *Mediated Authenticity: How the Media Constructs Reality.* Peter Lang.

Foucault, M. (1977). *Discipline and Punish.* Vintage Books.

Fuchs, C. (2014). *Social Media: A Critical Introduction.* Sage.

Geboers, M. A., & Van De Wiele, C. T. (2020). Machine Vision and Social Media Images: Why Hashtags Matter. *Social Media + Society, 6*(2).

Goffman, E. (1956). *The Presentation of Self in Everyday Life.* University of Edinburgh.

Gregg, M. (2011). *Work's Intimacy.* Wiley.

Guo, C., & Saxton, G. D. (2014). Tweeting Social Change: How Social Media are Changing Nonprofit Advocacy (November 12, 2012). *Nonprofit and Voluntary Sector Quarterly, 43*(1), 57–79. Available at SSRN: https://ssrn.com/abstract=2247136

Hall, S. (1999). Encoding, Decoding. In S. During (Ed.), *The Cultural Studies Reader* (pp. 91–103). Routledge.

Hobbs, M. (2015). Designing Desire. In T. Chalkley, M. Hobbs, A. Brown, T. Cinque, B. Warren, & M. Finn (Eds.), *Communication, Digital Media and Everyday Life* (2nd ed.). Oxford University Press.

Hutchinson, J. (2017). *Cultural Intermediation and Audience Participation in Media Organisations.* Palgrave Macmillan.

Jiang, S., & Ngien, A. (2020). The Effects of Instagram Use, Social Comparison, and Self Esteem on Social Anxiety: A Survey Study in Singapore. *Social Media + Society.* https://doi.org/10.1177/2056305120912488

Klein, P., Fairweather, A. K., & Lawn, S. (2022, September 29). Structural Stigma and Its Impact on Healthcare for Borderline Personality Disorder: A Scoping Review. *International Journal of Mental Health Systems, 16*(1), 48.

Langlois, G. (2014). *Meaning in the Age of Social Media.* Palgrave Macmillan.

Latour, B. (2005). *Reassembling the Social: An Introduction to Actor-Network-Theory.* OUP Oxford. Retrieved from http://books.google.com.au/books?id=DlgNiBaYo-YC

Lizardo, O. (2016). Cultural Symbols and Cultural Power. *Qualitative Sociology, 39*(2016), 199–204.

Lomborg, S. (2015). "Meaning" in Social Media. *Social Media + Society.* Online First. https://doi.org/10.1177/2056305115578673

Luoma-aho, V., Pirttimäki, T., Maity, D., Munnukka, J., & Reinikainen, H. (2019). Primed Authenticity: How Priming Impacts Authenticity Perception of Social Media Influencers. *International Journal of Strategic Communication, 13*(4), 352–365. https://doi.org/10.1080/1553118X.2019.1617716

McLuhan, M. (1964). *Understanding Media: The Extensions of Man.* Routledge. Retrieved from http://books.google.com.au/books?id=R2bqSaC5TlkC

McQuail, D. (2010). *McQuail's Mass Communication Theory* (6th ed.). Sage Publications Ltd.

Miller, J. G. (1984). Culture and the Development of Everyday Social Explanation. *Journal of Personality and Social Psychology, 46*(5), 961–978.

Nagy, P., & Neff, G. (2015). Imagined Affordance: Reconstructing a Keyword for Communication Theory. *Social Media + Society, 1*(2).

Papacharissi, Z. (2012). Without You, I'm Nothing: Performances of the Self on Twitter. *International Journal of Communication, 6*(2012), 1989–2006.

Peters, J. D. (2012). *Speaking Into the Air: A History of the Idea of Communication.* University of Chicago Press.

Rheingold, H. (1994). *The Virtual Community—Homesteading on the Electronic Frontier* (1st ed.). HarperCollins Publishers.

Ronzhyn, A., Cardenal, A. S., & Batlle Rubio, A. (2023). Defining Affordances in Social Media Research: A Literature Review. *New Media & Society, 25*(11).

Taylor, T. L. (2009). The Assemblage of Play. *Games and Culture, 4*(4), 331–339.

Taylor-Jackson, J., & Moustafa, A. A. (2021). The Relationships Between Social Media Use and Factors Relating to Depression. *The Nature of Depression,* 171–182. https://doi.org/10.1016/B978-0-12-817676-4.00010-9

Tiidenberg, K. (2018). *Selfies: Why We Love (and Hate) Them.* Emerald Publishing Limited.

Tiidenberg, K., & Cruz, E. G. (2015). Selfies, Image and the Re-making of the Body. *Body & Society, 21*(4), 77–102.

Treadwell, T. (2016). J. L. Moreno: The Origins of the Group Encounter Movement and the Forerunner of Web-Based Social Network Media Revolution. *The Journal of Psychodrama, Sociometry, and Group Psychotherapy, 64*(1), 51–62. https://doi.org/10.12926/0731-1273-64.1.51

Twitter. (2023). *Violent Threats Policy.* Retrieved from https://help.twitter.com/en/rules-and-policies/violent-threats-glorification

Wellman, B. (1998). *Loose Connections: Joining Together in America's Fragmented Communities.* Harvard University Press.

Wellman, B. (2001). Physical Place and Cyber-Place: Changing Portals and the Rise of Networked Individualism. *International Journal for Urban and Regional Research, 25*(2), 227–252.

Wellman, B., Hogan, B., Berg, K., Boase, J., Carrasco, J.-A., Côté, R., Kayahara, J., Kennedy, T. L. M., & Tran, P. (2005). Connected Lives: The Project. In P. Purcell (Ed.), *Networked Neighbourhoods.* Springer.

Wells, G., Horwitz, J., & Seetharaman, D. (2021, September). Facebook Knows Instagram Is Toxic for Teen Girls, Company Documents Show. *Wall Street Journal,* (14). Retrieved from https://www.wsj.com/articles/facebook-knows-instagram-is-toxic-for-teen-girls-company-documents-show-11631620739

Winocur, R. (2019). The Tribe of Memes. A Virtual Territory of Inclusion-Exclusion Among Adolescents. *Comunicación y Sociedad (Guadalajara, Mexico),* 1–22. https://doi.org/10.32870/cys.v2019i0.7327

## CHAPTER 5

# Social Media as a Creative Industry: Labour, Workplaces, Markets

Social media platforms have provided new employment opportunities for creative content producers all over the world. They connect content-hungry users with savvy producers to provide highly engaged experiences for these stakeholder groups. But the process of creating content is relentless: producers must produce regularly, align with algorithmic determined interest areas, have no set start and finish times, have no union representation and are required to align with the terms and services of these platforms to continue to operate. At the same time, the platforms have the power to demonetise these often highly popular producers for their past actions if they deem them to not align with the overall trajectory of the platform provider.

To combat this, online content producers have developed procedures and mechanisms to operate effectively in these entirely precarious environments. Collaborations, meet and greets, and live online experiences such as AMA (ask me anything) and livestreaming have enabled many online content producers to create new and innovative ways to keep a check on how they preserve their labour efforts in an 'always-on' environment. Intermediaries such as digital agencies and multichannel networks have also found a specific niche to connect online content producers with large audiences through platform affordances. This chapter highlights the practices and surrounding industries of social media content producers by exploring the precarious labour models, the role of agencies, and the new content production models that are created by online content producers. It also explores how other operators outside of the famous and influencer space conduct business on social media.

J. Hutchinson et al., *Social Media in Society*, https://doi.org/10.1007/978-3-031-66360-4_5

## INTRODUCTION: FROM CREATIVE INDUSTRIES
## TO BEDROOM SUPERSTARS

This section provides an in-depth exploration of the creative industries, a dynamic and rapidly evolving sector that encompasses a wide range of activities, from film and music production to advertising and design. Understanding the economic and political environment in which social media operates is critical and paves the way for how we understand the sorts of business models that have emerged because of platformed media. It delves into the historical evolution of the creative industries, their economic significance and the various subsectors within this expansive domain. Additionally, it highlights the challenges and opportunities facing creative professionals in the digital age and examines the role of policy and innovation in shaping the future of this sector. It then casts this late 2000s policy concept against the contemporary space which sees users become superstars beyond the traditional creative industries—a point social and platformed media plays a significant role within.

The creative industries gained increasing prominence on the global economic stage over the past few decades. This is especially obvious through historical development, economic importance, subsectors, and the challenges and opportunities it faced in an era of rapid digital transformation. In the United Kingdom, the creative industries emerged as a pivotal policy mechanism, fostering economic growth, cultural enrichment and international influence. With a keen recognition of the sector's potential, the UK government implemented a range of supportive policies and initiatives aimed at nurturing creativity and innovation. These policies encompass funding for cultural organisations, tax incentives for creative businesses and investments in educational programmes to develop talent within the creative industries (Flew & Cunningham, 2010). Additionally, the UK's commitment to intellectual property protection and copyright enforcement bolstered the global reach of British creative products, from music and film to fashion and design. As a result, the creative industries became an integral part of the UK's economic and cultural identity, contributing significantly to its standing as a global creative powerhouse.

Beyond the policy and cultural economy aspects, the roots of the creative industries can be traced back to the cultural and artistic pursuits of humanity throughout history. From the creation of visual art to the performance of music and theatre, creative expression has always been an integral part of human society (Cunningham, 2002). The Industrial Revolution in the eighteenth and nineteenth centuries marked a significant turning point for the creative industries. The advent of mass production techniques allowed for the replication and distribution of creative works on a scale previously unimaginable. This period saw the emergence of publishing, music recording and cinema as prominent creative sectors. The aftermath of World War II witnessed the rapid growth of the creative industries, driven by increased consumer demand and advancements in technology. Television, advertising and fashion became prominent subsectors, contributing to the cultural and economic fabric of societies worldwide.

The creative industries evolved into a significant driver of economic growth in many countries. They contribute substantially to national GDPs, providing employment and generating revenue through various channels, including cultural events, tourism and intellectual property licensing. The creative industries provide a diverse array of employment opportunities, spanning from artists and musicians to software developers and marketers. This sector often attracts individuals with specialised skills and talents, contributing to the overall dynamism of the workforce. Further areas of economic generation include painting, sculpture, dance, theatre and music. It also includes newer forms of creative expression, such as digital art and multimedia installations. Film, television, video games, and the music industry are integral components of the creative industries. The rise of streaming platforms and digital distribution has revolutionised how content is produced and consumed. Design encompasses various fields, including graphic design, industrial design and interior design. Fashion, on the other hand, spans clothing, accessories and luxury goods, contributing significantly to the global economy. The advertising and marketing sector plays a crucial role in promoting creative products and services. It combines creativity with strategic communication to reach target audiences effectively.

The digital age has transformed the creative industries, introducing both opportunities and challenges (Potts et al., 2008). Online piracy, changing consumer behaviour, and evolving distribution models have disrupted traditional revenue streams. Creative professionals must continuously innovate and adapt to stay relevant in a rapidly changing landscape. Embracing emerging technologies, such as virtual reality and artificial intelligence, can open new avenues for creativity and revenue generation. Many governments recognise the economic and cultural value of the creative industries and implement policies to support them. These policies may include grants, tax incentives, and intellectual property protection (Potts, 2009). The creative industries also play a role in cultural diplomacy, promoting a country's culture and values on the international stage (Flew, 2012). Cultural exports, such as films, music and fashion, can enhance a nation's global image. The creative industries represent a vibrant and multifaceted sector that continues to evolve in response to technological advancements and shifting consumer preferences. As this chapter has demonstrated, these industries have a rich historical legacy and a significant economic impact. To thrive in the digital age, creative professionals must navigate challenges through innovation, while policymakers can play a pivotal role in supporting and sustaining this vital sector. The creative industries are not only a source of economic prosperity but also a wellspring of cultural expression, making them an essential component of contemporary societies.

It is important to understand how the creative industries was shifting within a global context that is made of changing technologies, cultural adaptations of those and regulations to support them (Flew, 2013). Curtin (2020) argues how neoliberal deregulation, speculation and financialisation unleashed the unfathomable potential of global media, thereby disrupting prior assumptions about the scope, scale, and practices of media industries. In this article, Curtin explores the disruptive forces at work in today's media industries and cautions users to remain alert to facile presumptions of happy diversity and personal empowerment. This is a call to the unravelling of an American superpower within the 'global', emerging not as the singular accomplishment of a national hegemony but rather as the multifarious and capillary effects of power under the sign of shareholder value. It is here that we begin to see how the global creative industries are moving towards a personalisation approach to align with the emergence of platforms and thereby social media.

While mainstream accounts of the impact of Internet technologies on the music industry especially have emphasised the crisis of the major-dominated mainstream recording industry during this 2000s and 2010s, a more optimistic discourse was also promoted, emphasising the opportunities that the Internet created for independent musicians. These same new technologies, argued by Haynes and Marshall (2018), enable artists to reach new global audiences and engage with them in ways that can facilitate more stable, financially self-sustaining independent careers. This approach in the music industry is broadly applicable to what we have been referring to as the creative industries. This moment is the transformation from creative industries to bedroom superstars.

Ashton and Patel (2018) provide a compelling account of how bedroom superstars were trained and guided during this period to highlight the potential economical income one might produce from their online activities. Their work denounces notions that vlogging is something everyone can do by referencing a range of media sources to examine the increasing public visibility of vlogging as a cultural work career. Of particular note is the curiosity around vlogging as a commercially viable undertaking and the how-to guidance materials that have emerged to steer would-be YouTube entrepreneurs onto a successful path. Through analyses of the social media presence of vloggers, they address how signalling-expertise strategies may be tailored to suit multiple platforms and multiple audiences. The research highlights that associations of vloggers with other vloggers formed an important part of how they signalled their expertise and helped to attract more fans. They also argue the ways in which expertise is signalled through the staging of authentic vlogging identities and locations. The authenticity includes the multiple processes that occur around a seemingly 'polished' final video, particularly vloggers' strategies to engage their audience by interacting with fans and collaborators, and the skills required to stage a relatable authenticity. Finally, they argue that vloggers possess a certain amount of expertise in their area, which is crucial to their success.

It is at this point that we begin to see a significant turn in the tide from bedroom stars towards sophisticated celebrities in their own right. These two decades clearly outline the shift in processes from solo efforts in the emerging social media spaces, towards quite sophisticated business approaches. It is at this point that the role of external agencies becomes increasingly important as masses of individuals begin to collectively explore their own rise to infamy on social media platforms. Before we arrive at the section that highlights the rise of this moment and how individuals begin to collaborate their efforts with other content creators and the agencies that work with these individuals, it's important to unpack the idea of celebrity. Specifically, we need to unpack the idea of Internet celebrity as Crystal Abidin (2018) has positioned this thinking. Then, through the moment of agencies and multichannel networks, we begin to see how new Hollywood types of celebrity models emerge, which shift how social media is used and how audiences shift and change to integrate social media into new and emerging aspects of their lives.

## The New Hollywood Model

By borrowing the work of Abidin (2018), we can (importantly) broaden our understanding beyond the concept of influencers alone. While influencers are significant and incredibly important to this moment of social media, this is not the only form of celebrity online, which enables us to extend our exploration of this new Hollywood model of celebrity through social media where users do not necessarily have to be 'influencers'. In talking about the Chinese model of celebrity, Abidin points to wanghong which roughly translates to red on the Internet to distinguish their specificity of high attention on the Internet. What is important here is to highlight that celebrity is not only an Anglocentric concept, but more diverse and broader than influencers alone. For example, through wanghong, Abidin (2018, p. 3) notes, 'In other words, these users are assigned celebrity status not for any variety of demonstrable talent, but for their specific ability to attract attention on the internet within the vast ecology of Chinese users'. The idea of drawing attention is important to keep in mind as we progress through this section.

The concept of 'celebrity' has a history within media studies, where Boorstin (1962, p. 57) notes on one of the first studies of celebrity, that it is a measure of understanding "the person who is known for his well-knownness". This approach towards well-known folk is based on the Hollywood 'star rating' system which emerged from the developing screen industry from the 1920s through to the 1960s. In essence, the idea of a 'star' was a way that ordinary folk could associate themselves with those portrayed on the big screen of the cinema. Feeley (2012, p. 468) observes the interest that has been displayed by media and cultural studies scholars within the broader media industries, where celebrity studies have developed, is an approach to understand "entertainment figures as transmitted via the twentieth century mass media". From within these two frameworks, we can see that the concept of celebrity is located within the mass media system and is a way for ordinary folk to make a connection with famous, popular and well-known individuals.

Turner (2004) develops this concept further to align with the popular media format of the early twenty-first century, specifically reality television. It is through this popular media format that the blurring begins between the two distinctive groups of 'celebrity' and 'ordinary folk'. Turner develops the idea that through reality television, ordinary folk can become celebrity, within a framework he defines as the 'demotic turn' (Turner, 2010). The demotic turn is "a means of referring to the increasing visibility of the 'ordinary person' as they turn themselves into media content through celebrity culture, reality TV, DIY websites, talk radio and the like" (p. 153). What is of significance here is that Turner refused to connect increased democratic influence with celebrity, a notion Hartley (1999) focused on through his democratainment concept. Within the portmanteau of democracy and entertainment, Hartley highlights that democratainment and DIY Citizenship is one manifestation of how television cultures play an important role in educating citizens about their societal environments. The fusion of politics with celebrity and entertainment provides the opportunity to revisit this scholarly debate, through the lens of network celebrity.

At its core, the notion of celebrity, whether in cinema, broadcast, or digital media, is primarily concerned with influence. What we are observing in its current form is the scale and speed at which celebrity can be built and utilised to mobilise large audiences. This observation becomes obvious through Senft's (2008) work on cam-girls as a form of online community building, where the collision of personal and political attributes merge to produce one's 'branded self'. In her 2008 publication, Senft brings together the two concepts of celebrity and capital, where she notes "the former exists to prop up the latter" (p. 25). She suggests the increase in popularity in online spaces that is focused on one's self identity and branding, can be thought of as a form of micro-celebrity, where "micro-celebrity is best understood as a new style of online performance that involves people 'amping up' their popularity over the Web using technologies like video, blogs and social networking sites" (p. 25). In 2013, Senft extends this idea around a central branding exercise, or a phenomenon she refers to as the 'branded-self'. The branded self refers to not only how online users identify themselves (race, gender, nationality, language, etc.) but also by what they do online (lurking, writing, performing, etc.). As such, the concept of the branded-self suggests microcelebrity is "the commitment to deploying and maintaining one's online identity as if it were a branded good, with the expectation that others do the same" (2013, p. 346). Thus, we see the emergence of individuals branding themselves through not only who they are but also by what they do to become key influential actors within online social networks.

This influential idea gains significant traction through the work of Abidin (2015, 2016) as she explores the concept of digital influencers. In her work that focused on digital influencers within the Singaporean fashion scene, Abidin defined the role of digital influencers as "everyday, ordinary Internet users who accumulate a relatively large following on blogs and social media through the textual and visual narration of their personal lives and lifestyles, engage with their following in "digital" and "physical" spaces, and monetise their following by integrating "advertorials" into their blogs or social media posts and making physical paid-guest appearances at events" (2016, p. 3). Here we begin to see the broader ecology of influence emerge from not only within social media, but also across the offline space through commercialisation. Through one's actions as a microcelebrity, they can influence large groups of consumers to purchase products and services, to also belong to a higher profiled group of social capital entrepreneurs. These individuals are building influence across a broad range of social media users in how they:

- communicate with particular languages ("Hey guys, today I'm going to show you how I get amazing eyelashes"),
- engage with users through positives interactions ("Hey guys, I need to tell you something really important"),
- display high media literacy skills using jump-cuts in their video editing and integration of cutting-edge technology like drone videography for example, and
- interface as cultural intermediaries between audiences and brands and services by acting as a knowledge conduit between audiences and topics.

We argue that a digital influencer plays an important gatekeeping function for the dissemination of ideas, values and calls to action. Borrowing from theories of French sociologist Pierre Bourdieu (1984), network influencers are 'cultural intermediaries' that translate knowledge and expertise between disparate cultural groups. Building further on Negus' (2010) re-appropriation of cultural intermediaries within the music industry as marketing agents for large audiences, Hutchinson (2017) describes cultural intermediaries as capital exchange agents that have the capacity to translate value between numerous cultural marketplaces. For example, an art agent has the expertise to translate fringe creativity within the visual art scene (cultural capital), for example, to those who would purchase those creative endeavours (economic capital). This framework can be applied to all cultural intermediaries, especially those operating in 'gatewatching' (Bruns, 2005) capacities in online environments.

With this as a backdrop, we move from the theoretical understanding of celebrity and fame online towards a case study that demonstrates how social media celebrities have been incredibly influential in the past ten years or so. While a duo of white American males, the Paul brothers (Jake and Logan) attract mixed emotions when they are brought into discussion spaces. While acknowledging that they are controversial, they have also pushed the limits of social media celebrity, making them a helpful case study for this section on social media celebrity.

### From Disney to Boxing: Celebrity, 'It's Everyday Bro'

Standing in front of large houses, multiple sports cars, Los Angeles colours, girls and tattoos of machine guns (hmmm hmmm), Logan Paul has his crew of fellow YouTubers 'wrapping' about how this celebrity thing is 'everyday bro'. Essentially, he's describing the life of an influencer that has moved beyond the bedroom towards that has multiple influencer friends who have purchased large properties so they can all live in these spaces to constantly make content for their multiple channels. In these spaces, every minute of these young people's lives are broadcasted to the world to demonstrate how cool they are and to portray a lifestyle that others should aspire to. This attracts brand deals, high view counts, commerce beyond the YouTube monetisation and a foray of celebrity status. It also forged its own industry to support this kind of business venture in this new Hollywood model of celebrity. It was a late 2010s model, and after the Paul brothers finished exploited this for all they could, many users likely reflected on how troublesome this kind of work really was (Fig. 5.1).

As a social media personality, Jake Paul shot to fame on Vine in 2013 orchestrating risky stunts with a dose of (bad) humour. Before Vine shut down/discontinued, he amassed over 5 million followers and accumulated 2 billion views. In 2014 he launched his YouTube channel (and has more than 20 million subscribers) where he engages in risky stunts and criminal activity (criminal trespassing and unlawful assembly after videos on social media showed Paul and friends engaging in looting during the BLM protests). Paul has a chequered past including:

- He has been accused of scamming his followers more than once (as part of his business deal ventures)
- He has been accused of domestic violence and emotional and mental abuse
- The FBI executed a federal search warrant of Paul's mansion (affidavit sealed)

**Fig. 5.1**  Jake Paul and Tam10 at the height of their social media success

- He was accused of sexual assault by two women. One of them filmed a disturbing YouTube video, describing a night with Paul in 2019 during which he forced her to perform oral sex on him.

Beyond these horrible accounts of a young man with no boundaries, he produced a lot of sexual and violent content. In January 2018, for example, Paul uploaded a vlog called "I lost my virginity", which initially had a thumbnail of Paul and then-girlfriend Erika Costell posing semi-nude. Paul has posted content telling his kid subscribers that education isn't important, since he didn't do well in school but became rich and famous, and other kids should follow his lead. He did, however, spruce his own education courses about becoming and influencer and getting paid for it. "Edfluence" was launched in 2018, and it was supposed to be a series of videos fan could unlock for just $7 that would give them a "roadmap" to success as an influencer. Except, it didn't unlock all videos, provided a 'teaser', where the teaser content included basic tips like 'own a phone'. The other videos cost $57. Edfluence no longer exists. In 2020, he launched a new platform, "Freedom Financial Movement" (subscription based) which turned out to be the same premise as Edfluence.

Paul's first major career accomplishment was a role on the Disney Channel series "Bizaardvark", in 2015 where he played Dirk, host of a video segment on a YouTube-esque series called "Dare Me Bro". In this role, his character took dare requests which was reasonably common across media including traditional media ecosystems. He was fired during season two (2017) after his neighbours went public with complaints about him. Around this time, he had launched "Tam 10" and his stunts included backyard fires and dirt bike stunts, even leaking his home address publicly which led to crazed fans storming his West Hollywood address, leaving his neighbours less than impressed.

His brother, Logan Paul is also a YouTube personality turned boxer. Like his brother, he started on Vine posting sketches such as dares, pranks and 'comedy'. He later created the Logan Paul Vlogs channel on August 29, 2015, which has since become his most subscribed YouTube channel, amassing 22 million subscribers. Both brothers launched incredibly successful merchandise lines, which became the standard for most social media content creators. Logan launched Impaulsive podcast in 2018 after losing popularity in the YouTube space after producing videos that were less than tasteful. Logan made several appearances in TV and film, including Law & Order: Special Victims Unit. He is broadly controversial like his brother, but the clincher was certainly visiting the *Aokigahara* forest, (suicide forest) in Japan, reputed to be a place people went to commit suicide, where he filmed his encounter with a corpse, sparking outrage that ended his YouTube career.

To revive his failed career as his fans began to wise up to the negativity of the Paul brother's characters, they launched their boxing league, in a way to challenge the UFC (Ultimate Fighting Championship). This has been somewhat successful for them, but what is important to acknowledge through the chaos of the Paul brothers is the new business models they pioneered through platformed media, specifically through social media. While monetisation was the primary source of income for many online content creators, these influencers were very much at the forefront of generating income from multiple sources. Brand deals, new platforms, merchandising, events and many other methods may have been in existence prior to these two brothers, but these two certainly brought them to the forefront of how online content creators could make a career beyond content alone. As would be expected, as the income models shifted, so too did the industry, paving the way for multichannel networks (MCNs) to ensure the new Hollywood model entrenched existing models of media industries.

## AGENCIES AND MULTICHANNEL NETWORKS (MCNS)

It is with agencies that individuals become incredibly visible. A multichannel network (this term will be abbreviated as MCN henceforth) is any entity or organisation that works with or directly produces a variety of content and performs commercial and marketing functions through the platform on which that content is distributed (Gardner & Lehnert, 2016). The term "multichannel network" was first used by YouTube, the platform used by most networks that are working with creators and platforms. MCNs are a type of creative agency that works directly with online content creators and will often have direct connection with the platform providers. This is beneficial for all concerned stakeholders as the MCNs can broker the conversation between online content creators and platform providers. As conversations shift and change through cultural uses, MCNs can ensure the content being produced is suitable for the platforms and that the platforms providers are up to date with the most relevant content creators. They occupy a unique position and have a particular role in the industrial model for social media and the industries that surround it that emerged during the rise of influencers and social media content creators that have been described in detail above.

MCNs act as important digital intermediaries (Hutchinson, 2023) that ensure the exchange of cultural production occurs between a broad variety of stakeholder groups, for example audiences and users of digital content. As an example, an MCN is like the A&R person of the music industry: they are there to find new and emerging talent and ensure they are signed to the record label. In the social media world, this is similar in that they are looking at the emerging online content creators to understand who they are and how they operate, what their audiences are like, and what the potential for them might be. Lobato (2016, p. 348) highlights how these are critical players within the media industries beyond screen industries alone: 'MCNs are a new breed of intermediary firm that link entrepreneurial YouTubers with the advertising, marketing and screen production industries'. Here we see how MCNs are very much at the centre of online content creation and form a bridge between limited audiences and new and expansive groups of interested viewers.

Gaenssle and Budzinski (2021), provide a compelling review of this agency period by reviewing existing theories of the economics of celebrities originally developed for 'stars' in traditional media, and discuss whether they are still applicable for Internet celebrities. They systematically analyse potentially new and additional factors for creating superstardom in social media that may contribute to the specific aspects of social media. These scholars conclude that the economics of superstars remain applicable and relevant for social media stars, although the occurrence, scale and scope of the effects contain social media specifics: network and commonality effects considerably gain relevance due to the specific economics of the digital environment. Several (allegedly) new 'star' factors in social media turn out to be either not radically new or only partly different to factors concerning classic media stars. Social media celebrities are not just "ordinary", their achievements should not be easily dismissed and, thus, the star-world remains hierarchical even in social media. Some elements that are relevant for social media superstardom, not captured by traditional superstar theories, and literally new in the digital environment, e.g. highly functional algorithms and recommender systems are significant in social media as we previously discussed.

In Gardner and Lehnert's study of how multichannel networks work with content creators, the mechanism of the MCN model emerged to manage new media phenomena. This can provide help to understand the mutually beneficial relationship between MCN institutions and video creators beyond the Western model alone. It also addresses the need for MCN guidance from creators in the growing consumer culture of short videos, as these MCN organisations provide a valuable way for creators to reach potential customers (Gardner & Lehnert, 2016). The two-way relationship between creators and the agencies is important not to understate in how they symbiotically operate together, which has been seen through many social media influencers (Troy Syvanne and Amplify, MoeZilla and Sprout Social, among countless others). In a recent study in China, Yunlun Ma and Yue Hu studied the combination of successful business models of TikTok software, providing consumers with a new way to create value (Ma & Hu, 2021). Moreover, they also noted that ByteDance and TikTok showed how organisations from transition economies could quickly and successfully transform TikTok's business model in the Chinese market by replicating elements of a successful business model (Ma & Hu, 2021). These findings will help to understand TikTok's business model transformation process better as one of the key platforms of the contemporary era.

The MCN mode of short video originated from the United States, but after localisation in China, it is still significantly different from foreign MCN mode. However, the MCN mode has not been emerging in China for a long time, and the concept is relatively new. There are not many books that conduct in-depth research and analysis on short videos and MCN mode. On the other hand, the existing domestic MCN institutions are still exploring the development direction in the development process. As for the analysis and research of the short video, the transmission process is a vast field, and the research in this aspect is quite diverse. As a product of the rapid development of short videos in China in recent years, TikTok is also the leading platform for innovation in the development of MCN. It is essential to study its business model and analyse the advantages and disadvantages brought by MCN to provide enlightenment and suggestions for developing short videos in the future.

## 'LIKE AND SUBSCRIBE': THE ETERNALLY ON LABOUR OF ONLINE CONTENT CREATORS

We have spoken about the online content creators in this industry, previously we discussed the audiences, and in the later part of this chapter we explored MCNs and the sorts of agencies that enable social media content creators larger audiences. What we haven't unpacked yet is the eternal drain on the creators in their 'always on' lifestyle (boyd, 2012), where one of the key aspects of rising above all the other creators depends on the amount of content one publishes.

A useful way to frame this work is to embed the activities of online content creators as a form of labour—an exchange of capital for services. Two ways in which this has been described previously include emotional labour (Hochschild, 1983) and relational labour (Baym, 2018). Emotional and relational labour are especially helpful for understanding the kind of work that occurs in online content production as it is typically undertaken by one (or a few) individuals who have a strong sense of the identity of their audiences. In both instances, these labour practices are the ways in which online content creators commodify their personalities in their work practice. From YouTubers welcoming their audience to another video through a "Hey guys, welcome to this week's video" approach, to other content creators who might entirely engage in conversations with their audience as they work for 'gifts' across a range of genres, the translation of one's personality into a labour practice is the foundation for online content creation.

Each platform has its own way of integrating labour practices, and as demonstrated below, it can be undertaken in several ways beyond the act of creating the content itself. In fact, in many cases, the content is the by-product of labour process—think here especially of cam girls and the wide variety of pornography genres, ask me anything (AMA) sessions with creators, or watching a gamer livestream via their Twitch account. In each of these examples, it is clear to understand how relational and emotional labour translates through the act of personality, or creativity, and into online content creation.

### Twitch TV x DJs

Twitch TV has a history of dynamic interaction with its audience, which in many ways builds on existing social media platform communication but has evolved specifically to align with gaming cultures. Figure 5.1 below highlights the Twitch TV interface for the #ClubQuarantine DJ session from Gabriel and

Dresden—a moment during the lockdowns of 2019 and 2020. There are common communication mediums most social media users would recognise such as the chat box on the right-hand side, a user-follow mechanism and a channel-subscribe option to the bottom right-hand side. A user can see how many people are viewing the channel (the number in red) and how long the creator has been live on the stream. The chat function is slightly different in that the content producer can implement a 'must follow' rule to engage in conversation, or delays between your first comment appearing in the stream. These actions tend to limit spam and hate speech as only those who genuinely wish to engage with the online content creator will proceed (Fig. 5.2).

What emerged in this space was the departure of gaming culture alone and the introduction of other complimentary creator cultures, for example live music and digital first personalities (Hutchinson, 2023). Music labels especially took to Twitch TV during the COVID-19 isolation era to not only make people aware of their cultural products but also to provide a space that replicates 'the club' as a space of socialisation and relaxation. A lead record label in this space was the dance label *Desert Hearts Records*, and increasingly clubs such as Poof Doof and One Six One in Melbourne were using the space in new and innovative ways to engage their audiences. These are unique examples of how online content creators took the always on lifestyle to a new level, where their homes became their workplaces during this period.

The platformed integrated approach has impacted on the creator culture of this space in a few key methods. First the creators can communicate in real time with their audience either through text comments, or some creators implement the live microphone for live 'shout-outs'. Often this is to thank people for being there, to say thanks for the financial support, or to generally communicate with their fans. One hangover from gaming culture is the concept of

**Fig. 5.2**  The #ClubQuarantine DJ set by Gabriel and Dresden, where content creators are using their relational labour in exchange for their creativity

'raids', which signifies as one artist channel winds up, the audience will transfer to another creator's channel (Jarrett & Murphy, 2023). This is especially significant to support collaborative ventures, and to maximise exposure from one artist, or group of, to another. These sorts of communication examples are unique to the digital first personality as they have an intimate communication process with their online only audience, that can transfer to other spaces—back to the club after COVID-19, while maintaining a strong audience relationship with the online space.

One specific always-on creator culture to emerge during COVID-19, is *plamping*. The recent phenomenon of 'plamping' (portmanteau of plant and lamp to describe the DJ's mise en scène) has emerged as a socialisation technique that is rapidly evolving to the mainstream—this combination of the lamp and plant is commonplace in DJ sets and is visible in Fig. 5.1. But this is more than a set dressing. When one is 'plamped' they are ready to socially engage with others by tuning in to a live DJ set on Twitch TV and interacting with other audience members in a 'hosted' Zoom room. This is the online equivalent of paying your entry fee to the club and hanging out with your mates. As users engage with each other via the chat functionality on the Twitch channel's stream, users build relationships. Twitch has its own style of communication, for example through the use of platform specific emojis such as WutFace, HotPokket and a host of unlockable emoticons. As the party kicks into gear, someone is likely to ask: 'still plamped? [insert Zoom Meeting ID] [Insert Zoom Meeting Password]'. Participants in these spaces often talk about music tastes, drug usage and other cultural interests. It is also a mechanism to facilitate Twitch TV 'raids' for online content creator channels.

### *YouTube Always On*

Questlove is the drummer from The Roots, a popular groove band from the USA. During the Black Lives Matter protests which were occurring alongside the COVID-19 isolation period, Questlove held a fundraising session on YouTube Live. The idea is that Questlove uses the YouTube Live platform to attract an audience and walks people through mixes and insights into the production of several songs from the groove genre. He is also highlighting key Black musicians and talking through several injustices from within the entertainment industry. While this live conversation is underway, there are tickers rolling along the bottom to promote the National Bail Fund Network, and below the video are several links to donate to certified organisations such as Food Hub:

> '*I'm raising money to support Food Hub to provide NYC students who depend on school meals who no longer have access. Let's party. But let's also help our fellow man. ANY AMOUNT can help'.*

Questlove's livestream is in many ways similar to the sorts of practices that occur on the YouTube live space—it is a key example of the always-on lifestyle. Although an artist such as Questlove is not likely to be on their all the time because of his other creative ventures, this luxury isn't afforded to other, less popular online creatives. The model he is engaging in, though, is incredibly typical of the ways in which online content creators engage the livestreaming aspect of content.

The live interaction on YouTube is limited to the chat box on the right-hand side, which includes a number of platform-specific emojis, of which users can either integrate from a signed in state or anonymously. If users wish to donate, they are directed to external sites to undertake this practice, as YouTube often state: 'Sorry, you can't donate in this country or region yet'. The online content creator does have the option of interacting with their audience, however much of the production in this livestream platform is one-way, traditional media oriented (Fig. 5.3).

What is interesting on this platform is the apparent difference of the traditional celebrity and the digital first personality. A large number of existing celebrities turn to YouTube Live as their preferred livestreaming platform, which is significantly different to the Twitch TV iteration. The stark difference here is the user interactivity. On Twitch TV, the users are acknowledged more frequently and integrated in the performance, whereas on YouTube Live, the users are more of a traditional audience. They are there to consume content and can chat amongst themselves, but that is frequently the extent of interaction here. This is representative of the content creator culture differences between those who are 'born' within the livestream space, and those traditional celebrities who move into this space.

This is especially obvious in the *PE health* genre on the YouTube Live platform. The traditional fitness instructors are focussed on talking at the participants, whereas those who have built their businesses on streaming platforms

**Fig. 5.3** Questlove from The Roots running a fundraiser on the YouTube Live platform

tend to communicate with the audience. The Body Coach TV often integrates the communication with his audience into the workout sessions. In Fig. 5.3 below, they can be seen exercising, yet they are also engaging in trivia with the audience by asking questions such as 'who is the vegetarian character on The Simpsons?', to which people respond in the comments to the right of the screen. At various points they call comments out and laugh along with the fitness participants. More traditional styled fitness instructors will acknowledge their participants at the beginning and end of the session, but typically only talk at the audience during the routine.

One strategic engagement technique Joe from The Body Coach employs during break sessions includes 'shout outs' to their fans. To do this, they put ear buds in and are likely in conversation with their social media manager who is feeding a collection of names to them. As Joe starts to call out people, the chat explodes with users wanting to be acknowledged live on the channel. This is the livestream version of audience members holding a sign up at the window behind the news presenter on the live news broadcast (Fig. 5.4).

The COVID era was especially problematic for online content creators who engage the always-on lifestyle. While it is useful to point towards to understand how online creatives embody their relational labour, it also highlights how incredibly difficult it was for these creators to separate their work lives from their personal spaces. In these examples, we see three successful online content creators who were able to maintain a presence in the wash of, or over-saturated digital media spaces. Whether that is through their ability to embody the digital first personality, or to embark on new and innovative approaches to online content creation, they were pushing the extremities of overloading the always-on lifestyle of these creators.

One helpful feminist studies critique of the relational labour of the online content creation industry comes from the feminist media scholar, Zoë Glatt

**Fig. 5.4**  Joe from The Body Coach TV instructing his audience through their workout

(2022). After conducting a multi-year ethnographic research project looking at creator cultures in the Northern hemisphere, her observations through her research found:

> *that the working lives of most content creators are fraught with stress and burnout, and smaller creators in particular are subject to algorithmic discrimination in an industry where visibility is key to success. Contrary to highly celebratory discourses that position online content creation as more open and meritocratic than traditional cultural industries, this is an advertising-driven industry that propels the most profitable creators into the spotlight, resulting in the closing down of mobility (p. 3853).*

Here we see a very different picture to the relational and emotional labour that has been described earlier. In fact, if the realities of these spaces are not new, and are a snapshot into understanding how and why users allow themselves to fall into these of precarity and excessive labour. TikTok has generated an entire new model, with the emergence of so-called livestreaming farms where people will live stream for hours on end, often in seemingly undesirable conditions (Fig. 5.5).

**Fig. 5.5** TikTok user @ JettyJamez often livestreams for hours from his house

Human computer interaction scholar Franziska Zimmer (2018) undertook a content analysis of livestreamers and observed 7667 livestreams. In this content, they found that the highest form of content by a long way (87%) was chatting, and this is how content creators earn their incomes. Sadly, social media platforms have created an environment where users need to be livestreaming constantly, creating content daily if not multiple times in a day, and the life cycle of a creator is often at the mercy of the regulatory and monetisation rules of the platform, along with the desire of their audiences. The once converted role of being a YouTuber is certainly not as glamorous as once thought.

## References

Abidin, C. (2015). Micromicrocelebrity: Branding Babies on the Internet. *M/C Journal, 18*(5). Retrieved from http://journal.media-culture.org.au/index.php/mcjournal/article/viewArticle/1022

Abidin, C. (2016). "Aren't These Just Young, Rich Women Doing Vain Things Online?": Influencer Selfies as Subversive Frivolity. *Social Media + Society, 2*(23), 1–17.

Abidin, C. (2018). *Internet Celebrity: Understanding Fame Online*. Emerald Publishing.

Ashton, D., & Patel, K. (2018). Vlogging Careers: Everyday Expertise, Collaboration and Authenticity. In S. Taylor & S. Luckman (Eds.), *The New Normal of Working Lives: Critical Studies in Contemporary Work and Employment* (pp. 147–169). Springer International Publishing.

Baym, N. (2018). *Playing to the Crowd: Musicians, Audiences, and the Intimate Work of Connection*. New York University Press.

Boorstin, D. (1962). *The Image: A Guide to Pseudo—Events in America*. Vintage.

Bourdieu, P. (1984). *A Social Critique of the Judgement of Taste* (1st ed.). Routledge.

boyd, d. (2012). Participating in the Always-On Lifestyle. In M. Mandiberg (Ed.), *The Social Media Reader* (pp. 71–76). New York University Press.

Bruns, A. (2005). *Gatewatching: Collaborative Online News Production*. Peter Lang Publishing, Inc.

Cunningham, S. (2002). From Cultural to Creative Industries: Theory, Industry, and Policy Implications. *Media International Australia, 102*, 54–65.

Curtin, M. (2020). Post Americana: Twenty-First Century Media Globalization. *Media Industries (Austin, Tex.), 7*(1).

Feeley, K. (2012). Gossip as News: On Modern U.S. Celebrity Culture and Journalism. *History Compass, 10*(6), 467–482.

Flew, T. (2012). *Creative Industries: Culture and Policy* (Vol. 1). Sage Publications Ltd.

Flew, T. (2013). *Global Creative Industries*. Polity.

Flew, T., & Cunningham, S. (2010). Creative Industries After the First Decade of Debate. *The Information Society, 26*(2), 113–126.

Gaenssle, S., & Budzinski, O. (2021). Stars in Social Media: New Light Through Old Windows? *Journal of Media Business Studies, 18*(2), 79–105.

Gardner, J., & Lehnert, K. (2016). What's New About New Media? How Multichannel Networks Work with Content Creators. *Business Horizons, 59*(3), 293–302. https://doi.org/10.1016/j.bushor.2016.01.009

Glatt, Z. (2022). "We're All Told Not to Put Our Eggs in One Basket": Uncertainty, Precarity and Cross-Platform Labor in the Online Video Influencer Industry International. *Journal of Communication, 16*(2022), 3853–3871.

Hartley, J. (1999). *Uses of Television*. Routledge.

Haynes, J., & Marshall, L. (2018). Beats and Tweets: Social Media in the Careers of Independent Musicians. *New Media & Society, 20*(5), 1973.

Hochschild, A. R. (1983). *The Managed Heart: Commercialization of Human Feeling*. University Press of California.

Hutchinson, J. (2017). *Cultural Intermediation and Audience Participation in Media Organisations*. Palgrave Macmillan.

Hutchinson, J. (2023). *Digital Intermediation: Unseen Infrastructures for Cultural Production*. Routledge.

Jarrett, J., & Murphy, D. (2023). Genealogy of a Hate Raid Paper presented at the DiGRA, Seville Spain.

Lobato, R. (2016). The Cultural Logic of Digital Intermediaries: YouTube Multichannel Networks. *Convergence, 22*(4), 348–360.

Ma, Y., & Hu, Y. (2021). Business Model Innovation and Experimentation in Transforming Economies: ByteDance and TikTok. *Management and Organization Review, 17*(2), 382–388.

Negus, K. (2010). The Work of Cultural Intermediaries and the Enduring Distance Between Production and Consumption. *Cultural Studies, 16*(4), 501–515.

Potts, J. (2009, August 2009). Introduction: Creative Industries & Innovation Policy. *Innovation: Management, Policy & Practice, 11*(2), 138.

Potts, J., Cunningham, S., Hartley, J., & Ormerod, P. (2008). Social Network Markets: A New Definition of the Creative Industries. *Journal of Cultural Economics, 32*(3), 166–185.

Senft, T. (2008). *Camgirls: Celebrity & Community in the Age of Social Networks*. Peter Lang.

Senft, T. M. (2013). Microcelebrity and the Branded Self. In J. B. John Hartley & A. Bruns (Eds.), *A Companion to New Media Dynamics* (pp. 346–354). Wiley-Blackwell.

Turner, G. (2004). *Contemporary World Television*. Springer.

Turner, G. (2010). *Ordinary People and the Media: The Demotic Turn*. Sage Publications Ltd.

Zimmer, F. (2018). *A Content Analysis of Social Live Streaming Services*. Paper presented at the Social Computing and Social Media. User Experience and Behavior, California.

## CHAPTER 6

# Social Media, News and the Public Sphere

## INTRODUCTION: THE NEW PUBLIC SPHERE

The Irish economist and philosopher Edmund Burke once famously declared journalism to be the political 'fourth estate'. It was Burke's assertion that journalism is the fourth and last pillar of politics, alongside those representing the commoners, nobility and the church. Journalists as such are responsible for advocating for the people while holding the parliament's political representatives to account—but what does this mean in the social media era? This understanding of the value of journalism and the news media as a fourth estate in society has been an important idea for both industry and policymakers. Indeed, it is the premise from which notions of journalistic freedom and editorial independence are also derived but western democracy has changed in the years since Burke's claim. In the digital age, notions of peasants and nobility are rarely expressed, while a strong shift towards secularism in the West also calls into question the role of the church as a dominant political power. Still, journalism and news media remain, and in many ways, they are more important than ever. The ubiquity of smartphones and social media apps means the public has unprecedented access to a broad range of high-quality news. At the same time, technological innovation and the removal of barriers to entry into media production mean that anyone can become a news producer on social media. The sheer size of popular platforms such as Facebook, X, TikTok and Reddit, also means that their owners have opted to delegate editorial responsibility to algorithms that are ill-equipped to decipher fact from fiction or determine what is in the public interest.

The new paradigm for news production on social media amplifies an ongoing tension between the economic and democratic value of media. The media and news are big businesses, capable of attracting huge amounts of audience attention and advertiser revenue. Social media platforms have afforded even greater access to news for many global citizens, as well as a range of

J. Hutchinson et al., *Social Media in Society*, https://doi.org/10.1007/978-3-031-66360-4_6

perspectives outside of the confines of their national discourse. At the same time, advertising revenue for news producers has declined as ad spending has redirected towards digital intermediaries such as Facebook and Google News (Australian Competition and Consumer Commission, 2019). At this point, we must ask which of these is more important: the profitability of the firms or the public interest. Furthermore, should social media companies share the same legal responsibilities as traditional news providers? Facebook founder and CEO, Mark Zuckerberg, has tried to distance his company from this issue of journalistic responsibility, claiming during congressional testimony that Facebook is not a media company but a technology company (Castillo, 2018). At the same time, Twitter owner, Elon Musk has referred to his platform as the new "public town square" (Pariser, 2022), which recognises the important role of digital platforms as a medium for political communication. If social networking sites aren't media companies but instead are technology firms, what is their relationship to news and democratic notions of the public sphere?

These questions are important when we consider how much news is now consumed via social platforms. According to the Pew Research Centre (2022), approximately 31% of US American adults regularly get their news from Facebook. By comparison, 25% got their news from YouTube, 14% from Twitter and 13% from Instagram. This data shows, that at least in a US context, social media is now one of the largest components of the news diet of adult citizens. Likewise, the University of Canberra's Digital News Report (Park et al., 2022) shows that 44% of Australian adults say they regularly get their news on social media, although only 19% said it was their primary source of news. The same research found that while television remains the primary source of news for most Australian adults, social media now comes in second place, outpacing other news media products such as newspapers and radio by a significant margin. The public's interest and demand for news on social media platforms were initially met with enthusiasm from news media companies. Cross-referencing the Public Interest Journalism Initiative's newsroom database with active pages on Facebook shows a rapid uptake of Facebook by Australian newsrooms from 2009 to 2011, and steady growth in the years since. A slight increase can be seen again at the start of the coronavirus pandemic. This brings into focus the significance of social media as a source for current events compared to traditional channels for news (Fig. 6.1).

Research has also shown that UK audiences who get their news from social media, search engines and news aggregators have more diverse news repertoires (Fletcher et al., 2021). At the same time, users from digital intermediaries were more likely to consume partisan news than those finding their news from the original source.

Numbers aside, there is also a significant qualitative difference in how people interact with and consume news on social media compared to traditional media systems. News on social media is unique for a number of reasons, this includes the ability of audiences to create and disseminate stories of their own (Roberts, 2019), the ability for users to respond to outlets and journalists in

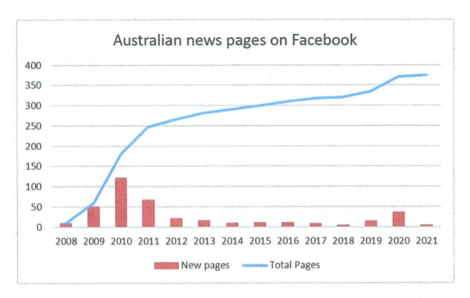

**Fig. 6.1**  A combination graph showing the uptake of new pages with Australian news content and a line showing their cumulative growth

real-time and have those comments seen by the public, the ability for users to share and be active in the dissemination of news from outlets, and the influence of user data in determining how algorithms recommend some stories over others (Martin & Dwyer, 2019).

In this chapter, we consider the changing landscape of news and the public sphere considering the social media revolution. We will examine the changing role of news producers in the face of algorithms, citizen journalists and misinformation. We also consider the distinction between being a platform and a publisher and its ramifications for policy and practice. Finally, we consider the meaning and shape of the new public sphere and what this means for democratic citizens. Core to this discussion is recognising that on social platforms, the audience has become far more involved in the creation and distribution of news which has been facilitated by a lowered barrier of entry to media production. This paradigm shift creates challenges for the traditional gatekeepers and institutions of the media who wish to remain economically viable while still acting as a democratic safeguard.

## DID FACEBOOK BURY THE EDITOR?

The editor used to be considered the gatekeepers and the agenda setters of the newsroom (DeVito, 2017). Working alongside journalists, editors and sub-editors' tasks involve choosing headlines, organising the story order for publication, proofreading and editing story structure, fact checking, delegating leads to journalists, and selecting images to go with stories. Their role in many ways was packaging the stories written by journalists so they were ready for the reader and the printing press. As twenty-first-century information and communication technologies emerge though, the task of curating news has become increasingly diffuse. Social media companies provide what is referred to as "distributed access", a category of distribution because of platform technologies which also includes news aggregators and search engines (Fletcher et al., 2021). These intermediaries have their own logic for organising content, which due to the scale of the platforms and the sheer number of stories posted each day, cannot be curated by individuals in a way that is economically viable. Instead of humans organising news stories on social media platforms such as Facebook, YouTube and Twitter, this function has been delegated to recommender systems, a specific class of machine learning algorithm that determines what content users see on their feeds based upon their individual interests. Distributed access is in many ways an upheaval of the way news is consumed and so with it the role of editors in curating the news agenda. This also raises new questions though about the role of editorial responsibility and accountability for tech firms and reporters.

In 2016, Mark Zuckerberg was asked about the role of Facebook as a news editor during a live Q&A with members of the public. The CEO remarked, "No, we are a tech company, not a media company" (Fiveash, 2016; Segreti, 2016). He would go on to present a similar line of argument to the US Congress two years later when pressed by the House Energy and Commerce Committee, insisting that they are foremost, a technology company not a publisher (Castillo, 2018). Why make this distinction? Why try to deny the media of a social media company? Some argue that this is a necessary step to ensure the company doesn't become legally treated like a publisher. In many Western democracies, media publishers are afforded several journalistic freedoms. At the same time, they are still also liable for the content they produce, including whether their content infringes on copyright, or if the content is considered inappropriate for public consumption. Furthermore, in countries like Australia media firms are also obliged to produce a certain amount of local content. For technology companies, being recognised as a hosting service for user-generated content, rather than a publisher for news, limits some of these responsibilities (Napoli & Dwyer, 2018; Vaidhyanathan, 2018, p. 218). But is this a fair distinction to make? Facebook, Google and Twitter don't have newsrooms in a traditional sense, but they are still active in the distribution of news. Their recommender systems are responsible for organising millions of stories every day for an audience that numbers in the billions.

According to Karimi et al. (2018) the primary function of a recommender system is to "filter incoming streams of information according to the users' preferences or to point them to additional items of interest in the context of a given object". They do so through two primary inputs, data they have about the content that is posted online and data about users. These machine learning algorithms make assumptions about the content being posted based on a range of data points such as the text in a post, hashtags and the account that posted it. It also makes assumptions about users and their interests based on what they like and follow, location data and what their friendship circle likes and follows. These inputs, combined with the amount of engagement a piece of content has received, allow the algorithm to suggest content that might be of interest to the user. For instance, your browsing history might be used to recommend content from the same news outlet or on similar topics. Alternatively, your local data might be used to recommend local content when you visit a new country or city. These algorithms also give priority to content that is new, comes from popular accounts, or has received a higher level of engagement than average.

This kind of process can be useful for users and platforms. If everything goes to plan, for users it means that they are more likely to see content they like. There is also a stronger chance they will end up seeing the same content that their friends or the people they follow are seeing too. Depending on the platform, this can also help ensure people see content that is local and relevant to them. For platforms, the benefits are extensive. First, there is so much new content being produced every minute that some form of filtering system is required to organise it all. Furthermore, without a recommender system, irrelevant content might easily drown out the content users actually want to see. Finally, by giving users the content they want, the recommender system also helps to keep users on the site longer, which means more advertising revenue and a more profitable platform.

These systems are not without problems though. Brake (2017) suggests that algorithmic interventions in news can lead to what they term "implementation bias", where the practice and behaviours of journalists may change because of technology. Examples of this kind of change could include a bias towards covering certain kinds of stories which are more likely to receive high engagement at the cost of others. Algorithms can also depend upon correlations to curate content which, unlike editors, means they lack a profound understanding of what the content means or the implications for its dissemination (DeVito, 2017, p. 757). These are what DeVito (2017) describes as "algorithmic values". These biases mean that social media companies, and other platforms for distributed access which use algorithms, have a curatorial effect on the consumption of news that is akin to the activities of an editor. This in turn, puts into question their claims that they are merely a technology company or if they are indeed publishers of media.

At its crux, we can see that there has been a diffusion of editorial power for news producers in the social media paradigm. At the level of primary access, editors still exist and help to curate stories while setting the news agenda, but when distribution and access is moved to social platforms, that process is subjugated to the influence of algorithms. These recommender systems in turn replace journalistic instinct with the logics of the data commodity. This is of particular relevance when we consider how much of our news diet is derived from these platforms and the inherent biases that come with these technologies. Furthermore, these distributors don't have the same regulatory responsibilities as news producers, nor the same overhead costs. It is at this point then we should turn our attention to affect this might be having on journalistic practice and how the news media industry has responded to this new paradigm.

## 'TWEET OR BE SACKED': CHANGING NORMS FOR JOURNALISM ONLINE

Just like editors, the role of journalists is changing. Media and communication scholar, Diana Bossio (2017) suggests that journalistic norms—which are the established practices, expected behaviours and codes of conduct that society comes to expect from practitioners—are having to adapt to social media's popularity as a news source. Bossio (2017, p. 25) contends that for journalists, objectivity, verification and professional autonomy were once thought of as "indispensable" standards or practice but are now being challenged by new norms such as authenticity, transparency and collaboration. A shift away from objectivity as a journalistic norm in favour of authenticity on social media may represent a move away from the institutional ivory tower of journalism towards a more relational practice that attempts to bring news producers closer to their audience. Bossio suggests that verification's challenge from the emerging norm of transparency on social media may come in the form of "presenting or explaining the processes of news source selection, or justification for the particular representation of a news event" (Bossio, 2017, p. 34). As such, journalists are attempting to be more open about their decision making, and in a way that means a writer's relationship to a story continues well after its publication.

These shifts see journalists frequently engaging with their audiences and one another online, but this practice is not without its risks. Engaging with social media has also meant that journalists have become the targets of attacks (Lawrence & Napoli, 2022, p. 4). Research has shown that most journalists in the US experience some kind of harassment online and that this kind of behaviour disproportionately affects women (Lewis et al., 2020). This kind of harassment typically manifests as name calling or attempts to embarrass reporters, but in more extreme cases involves threats of violence and sexual harassment. At the same time, journalistic institutions seem to be struggling to keep up with these developments. Interviews with journalists have shown that responses from management at news organisations have been lacking (Holton et al., 2023). Writers are expected to engage with their audience, but any extreme backlash from users is deemed to be part of the job.

These matters play into another unique aspect of social news, which is the numbers game of online journalism. Engagement metrics are an important input for most recommender systems and therefore the performance of stories on platforms. Martin and Dwyer (2019) identify the "rise of the metadata commodity". This paradigm refers to the active role that engagement metrics play in influencing journalistic practice. A 2022 study which interviewed journalists from 16 US newspapers affirmed this notion, suggesting that newsrooms are increasingly looking to engagement metrics to help decide what kind of content to pursue (Walters, 2022). Newsrooms are also pursuing strategies to make stories go viral and compete with other high engagement content. Research has shown users are often motivated to share stories either out of a perceived altruism—wanting to break the story first—or out of an emotive, or knee jerk reaction to the content and its presentation (Denisova, 2023). News producers are aware of this and produce a range of soft news to cater to this kind of consumption including visual journalism, short videos and clickbait.

If we return to Burke's argument of journalism as the fourth estate in society, these changes to journalistic practice demarcate a dramatic shift in how we see their endeavour and the relationship of journalists to society. As the fourth estate, objectivity is long thought to be a necessary step to distance the reporter from the individuals in the story and those whom it affects—although notably this was already a heavily contested notion prior to the social media period (S. Maras, 2013). A shift towards authenticity and transparency sees the journalist becoming much closer to their audience online. At the same time, the shift towards metadata as a commodity also means that the audience is having a greater influence on the construction of stories and the news agenda as a whole. While some have suggested that social media is a *fifth* estate, there is reason to rationalise the fourth estate having lost some of its independence and becoming more immersed in the lives of the people it once watched from an ivory tower.

## From Citizen Journalism to Twitter Paparazzi

While technology and audience engagement have been a driving factor for change, the proliferation of user generated content has been another important influence on the social media news-scape. Social media enables everyday users to contribute to the production and dissemination of amateur news. Platforms such as YouTube, Twitter, Facebook and TikTok lower the barrier of entry for broadcasting which allow citizen journalists to cultivate their own audiences in these online spaces. The advent of citizen journalism is facilitated also in part by the introduction of smartphones and other smart devices which provide users with inexpensive production tools for the recording and editing of content (Ali & Fahmy, 2013).

Social media platforms are also free to the public and lack editorial gatekeeping of traditional broadcast media. At the same time, the network power (Castells, 2011) of these platforms provides users a reach that was also unattainable in the broadcast era. It has been argued that this development is of benefit to society as it is more democratic compared to traditional media systems. Citizen journalism on social media does so by enabling users to create and share stories that might not normally be covered by institutional journalists. This includes topics that might not be allowed due to government censorship, issues that are counter to the commercial interests of the media owners, or topics that are too niche to be considered of the public interest. Citizen journalism is also thought to be an important tool for whistleblowing, exposing corruption and malpractice within private institutions and government (Mutsvairo & Salgado, 2022).

Bellingcat is an example of one of the more prominent citizen journalism groups online and on social media today. This collective of "open source" investigative reporters use social media to publicise their new stories which are simultaneously published both on their official website and promoted through their official Twitter channel (Cooper & Mutsvairo, 2021). The group rose to prominence in the 2010s for their coverage of topics such as the downing of flight MH17 in Eastern Ukraine, the illegal trade of wildlife to the UAE, and state violence in Columbia. The group has proven themselves to be able to operate at a level that is comparable to trained, institutional journalists. The group has been proactive in fact checking misinformation as it is spread on social media (Anderson, 2022). They will also crowdsource fact finding by inviting community members to verify images and identify their location. A common feature of their work has been to investigate the activities of bad actors online by sifting through their social media accounts. In one such example, Bellingcat had reported on an alleged Russian spy who tried to infiltrate the International Criminal Court in the Hague. As part of their investigation, they showed how their fake social media accounts had been developed to provide cover for their activities (Bellingcat, 2022). This work highlights how citizen journalism can make effective use of social media not only for dissemination but also for the fact-finding process and the sourcing of leads.

Coverage of the Arab Spring in 2011 also proved to be pivotal for social media use and citizen journalism. Ali and Fahmy (2013) contrast three case studies of citizen journalism in the Middle East and North Africa from that period: the 2009 Iranian election protests, the 2011 overthrowing of Egyptian president Hosni Mubarak, and the 2011 overthrowing of the former president of Libya, Muammar Gaddafi. Their studies showed how the gatekeeping role of mainstream media outlets was circumvented by citizen journalists who were documenting protests on social media and using smartphones to produce audio-visual content of events as they unfolded. Over several weeks and months, citizens of Iran, Egypt and Libya were able to witness the scale of protests in the street, while these matters were absent from their nation's newspapers and televisions. At the same time, international newsrooms also relied on this footage and commentary from citizen journalists to inform their own coverage of these events, a task usually performed by foreign correspondents. Ali and Fahmy (2013) suggest that, while citizen journalism was facilitated by social media, it still required the adoption of their stories by larger, traditional media systems to extend their stories to a wider audience.

Citizen journalism usually isn't considered a direct threat to mainstream journalism. Instead, it is often used to add dimension to stories produced by institutional journalists or as the basis for soft news and puff pieces (Ali & Fahmy, 2013). There are also some areas of the world where institutional journalism isn't economically viable, and amateur writers are able to provide volunteer coverage. Locals, armed with smartphones and cheap recorders can cover stories in conflict zones and help document events as they happen in real-time. As global newsrooms become smaller, the viability of long-term investigative journalism has also been challenged. As such, some volunteer citizen journalist groups have risen to prominence as they help to fill the niche left behind by declining institutional reporting. Conversely, citizen journalism may offer a valuable counterpoint to mainstream or institutional journalism. In countries where there is a degree of distrust for mainstream journalism, citizen reporting has been shown to be a preferred alternative (Carr et al., 2014).

Christian Fuchs (2010, p. 178) promotes citizen journalism's potential as a counterpoint to commercial mass media. Citizen journalists who produce alternative media are less likely to be compromised by the large-scale economic interests of the mainstream press. Historically, traditional media producers have had issues balancing ideas that are in the public interest with large commercial enterprises who pay for advertising space. It has also been argued that mainstream capitalist mass media is often produced by class elites who perpetuate the inherent ideology of the status quo. As such, 'alternative media' is better able to provide critical perspectives and alternate viewpoints without the influence of corporate shareholders and advertising partners. In later work, Fuch's (2017) also acknowledges the exploitation of content producers on platforms such as Facebook. Content creators, such as citizen journalists, often provide unpaid labour to a platform while their content is used to help sell advertising space. This transaction isn't entirely one sided, as citizen journalists find value in the reach these platforms provide through their large audience base. Some platforms such as YouTube, TikTok and more recently X (formerly Twitter) provide monetisation opportunities to some users, providing they meet certain criteria. But while the barrier for entry onto these platforms is low, the barrier to monetisation is much higher.

There are a number of critical issues that emerge from citizen journalism, these pertain to accuracy of the journalism and the knowledge of ethics from amateur reporters. There are also questions of exploitation from the perspective of critical political economy, and to what benefit are user producers provided and to what extent are they reimbursed or empowered through their actions. The issues previously highlighted show how fundamentally different social media is as an arena for news, truth telling and the sharing of ideas, and that the guardrails governing traditional media and institutional news don't apply in the digital wild west.

## Fake News, Post-truth and Deep Fakes

The proliferation of false information online has been a grave concern for platforms, regulators, journalists and scholars. The diminished role of the news media as gatekeepers of information has allowed citizen journalism to flourish, but social media platforms are also fertile ground for fake news, conspiracy theories and other forms of misinformation. For the producers of news, this is particularly alarming, as professional reporters competing with false information can be shared with the same speed and weight that true ideas can be. It has been said by some that we are living in a 'post-truth' era, where facts are no longer agreed upon. Another term for this is 'information disorder'.

Scholars distinguish between three types of information disorder, these are misinformation, disinformation and malinformation (Wardle & Derakhshan, 2018). Misinformation refers to false information or misleading content which has been produced in a haphazard way, but not with the intent to harm others. This could include things such as conspiracy theories, misrepresented facts, or reporting which is relying on previously refuted information. The most egregious example of misinformation in recent years would be the proliferation of COVID conspiracies on social media including rumours regarding its origins and the safety of vaccines. A 2020 study examining COVID misinformation of social media analysed the spread of both false and accurate information on Twitter, Instagram, YouTube, Reddit and Gab (Cinelli et al., 2020). One of the more interesting findings to come from this study was that both misinformation and accurate information spread in much the same way, although patterns of distribution did vary from platform to platform. This kind of data suggests that platforms might be agnostic to fact or fiction, but some platforms may serve as more effective vehicles for spreading information regardless of its accuracy.

One of the more egregious forms of information disorder comes in the form of 'astroturfing'. Astroturfing is a name for coordinated inauthentic behaviour which seeks to give the appearance of a groundswell of public support for a particular issue (Keller et al., 2020). This behaviour mimics grassroots support for a campaign or issue, hence the name astroturfing. Coordinated inauthentic behaviour is enacted using bots or disposable accounts which will push a political perspective through posts, comments and fake engagement. This kind of manipulation can be detected by similar patterns of behaviour. Astroturfing campaigns tend to manifest as a short burst of high volume posting which quickly dissipates (Ratkiewicz et al., 2010). The coordinators will copy the same post or distribute variations on the same content at scale and then proceed to aggressively upvote, like, share and comment. Many platforms attempt to detect and defend against this kind of behaviour, but it's still possible for some incursions to break through.

Alongside this coordinated network activity, another concern of the post-truth era has been regarding the proliferation of 'deepfakes'. Defined as "intentionally deceptive synthetic videos created with the use of Artificial Intelligence" (Hameleers et al., 2022, p. 1), deepfakes have risen to prominence with the widespread availability of generative artificial intelligence tools. Among the concerns raised has been the use of widespread propaganda, blackmailing and cyberbullying (M.-H. Maras & Alexandrou, 2019). In early 2023, the use of generative AI for deepfakes caught the imagination of reporters and the public

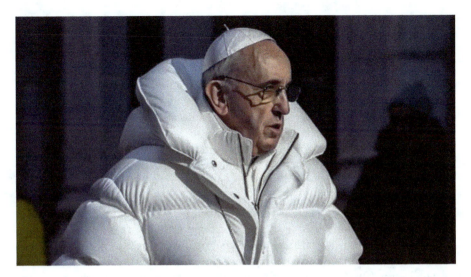

**Fig. 6.2**  A viral image of Pope Benedict XVI made by Pablo Xavier using Midjourney

when a convincing image of Pope Benedict XVI was circulated wearing a Balenciaga jacket (see Fig. 6.2 above).

It has been theorised that this technology could be deployed as part of a coordinated disinformation campaign by imitating political leaders or members of the public. While these concerns are real, emerging research has suggested that the current technology isn't able to produce content that is as persuasive as authenticated news (Hameleers et al., 2022). Nor do the deepfaked videos appear to be as effective as text-based content.

## PUBLIC SPHERE AND PUBLIC OPINION

Alongside the 'fourth estate' the other key common arguments for the value of news media in society is 'the public sphere'. Popularised by Jürgen Habermas, he asserts that, ideally there is a shared space which is essential to democratic life by which citizens have access and are free to debate issues as equals (Habermas et al., 1974). This is to say that for democracy to be enacted, people must have a place by which to communicate and debate ideas, be it in coffee shops, town halls or public squares. A true democracy, it is argued, is not possible without free debate and instead interest groups would be forced to operate in silos. In 1974 they asserted that "this kind of communication requires specific means for transmitting information and influencing those who receive it. … newspapers and magazines, radio and television are the media of the public sphere" (Habermas et al., 1974, p. 49). Today, in the digital era, social media has become a new space for public debate. We can see this idea echoed by Elon Musk in 2022 ahead of his acquisition of Twitter, where they referred to the platform as "the de facto public town square" (Pariser, 2022).

On social media platforms, establishing public opinion is a tricky issue. While these sites offer a much greater exposure to the voices, features of the platform and the norms associated with posting can still lead to biases when it comes to the observation of public opinion. Journalists frequently quote users from social networking sites as a form of vox populi, i.e. 'the voice of the people' (Ross & Dumitrescu, 2019). This allows writers to add colour and dimension to stories and give a sense of what the general public feels is important in relation to a matter. This is not a new tradition either. Prior to social networking sites, it was common to see journalists and reporters venture out into public spaces to gather insights from the general public. Nowadays, this is done by trawling through comments and posts and finding choice quotes to add to news stories. At first glance, this seems like an innovation. The turnaround on stories can be much quicker, as reporters need not venture outside their office to obtain public opinions. News producers can also report on public engagement with an event in real-time and it is not uncommon to see social media posts used as material during rolling coverage of live sports events or elections.

McGregor (2019) observes though, that users don't accurately reflect the electorate, and for political issues this is problematic. Their studies show that journalists tend to have highly curated feeds on Twitter which leads to an inherent bias that favours the social circles of the reporter. Brake (2017, p. 33) contends that "to the extent that journalists focus on what is trending on social media because it is easy to measure…they may also end up devoting a disproportionate amount of attention to issues of interest to social media users… and cover issues from their perspective using quotes drawn from social media because they are easy to find". Furthermore, McGregor (2019) argues, using social networks for vox populi adds to the illusion that social media is legitimate representation of the public and therein further entrenching the social and political power of social media companies.

The proliferation of bots and fake community voices on social media also calls into question the legitimacy of social media comments as a source for public opinion. One such example in Australia was observed in a study by Hobbs et al. (2020). Their research identified that as an Indian resource magnate, the Adani Group, petitioned to produce a coal mine in the Australian north, a surge of inauthentic posts emerged in support of the development. Posts were found to be suspiciously similar with one another, with the implication that they might have been produced by a public relations firm to provide the impression that there was a groundswell of support for the resource project. The authors concluded though that these tweets are few and far between and as such likely to have had little impact on the debate. In comparison, during the 2016 US Presidential election, bots and fake accounts were found to have been used on Facebook and Twitter by a Russian troll farm, the Internet Research Agency, as a form of election interference. It has been identified that a wave of inauthentic accounts was created to promote fake stories or create dissent, typically in favour of Donald J Trump. A study published in Nature Communications found that these posts were mostly speaking to the converted, with a heavily concentrated audience of exposure who strongly identified as Republican voters (Eady et al., 2023). Furthermore, they found that there appears to be no clear relationship, at a statistical level, between exposure and voting behaviour.

The challenges of bots, trolls and fake news not only undermine the integrity of election campaigning and create a thorn in the side of authentic democracy, but they also create challenges for researchers in trying to identify community opinion. Harris (2023) argues that the threat of bots and trolls online constitute three dilemmas. The first is the threat of deception, whereby unknowing individuals might believe stories that are untrue and possibly made with malintent. The second threat is scepticism, which is to say that fake accounts not only spread disinformation but also help to establish a climate of distrust online. The third is the epistemic threat, whereby information disorder diminishes our previous capability of discerning fact from fiction. For researchers and journalists, simple verification techniques such as checking someone's bio is no longer sufficient. The once steadfast 'blue tick' on Twitter has also lost its efficacy as a verification symbol since its new owners turned it into a subscription service (Biggs, 2023). In any study of political discourse, we must now assume that at least *some* of the communication is inauthentic.

## Conclusion: Regulation and the Path Forward

The intersection of social media and journalism presents both opportunities and challenges relevant to the public sphere, as evidenced by the research presented in this chapter. Social media companies have been revolutionary in lowering the barrier to content creation, but in turn, this has had significant impacts on news and the journalism industry. The democratisation of content creation allows everyday users to not only consume news but also to be active in producing it. As such, the journalism industry now finds itself in an unprecedented competition not just for audience share, but in defining what is considered truth in the public sphere.

This shift has benefited society in certain aspects, with previously unheard or marginalised voices now having a platform to share their perspectives. Additionally, citizens now enjoy broader access to high-quality news on channels of distributed access such as Facebook (Fletcher et al., 2021). However, with the spread of fake news and disinformation, the accuracy of information circulating on platforms is not a given. The vast inventory of content available has compelled social media firms to rely on algorithm-based recommender systems to manage information. This delegation of editorial responsibility to algorithms has fundamentally altered journalistic practices and introduced new dynamics into the news economy. These algorithmic recommender systems, while efficient, are not fool proof. Vulnerable to exploitation they can allow misinformation to spread rapidly, often with little safeguards for accuracy. In critical areas like public health and politics, the potential consequences are severe and far-reaching. This has been evidenced by the proliferation of misinformation during the COVID pandemic and the 2016 US Presidential Election.

Looking ahead, several key stakeholders—regulators, tech companies, journalists, and the public—play pivotal roles in shaping the future of social media and journalism. Governments and regulatory bodies worldwide are foremost grappling with the challenge of managing the flow of information on social media while upholding principles of free speech and preventing censorship. The policies and frameworks they develop significantly influence the landscape of online news and information dissemination, but overreach has become an issue in its own right.

Media and law scholar Donato Vese (2022) contrasts various international regulatory responses to fake news on social media. In China, social media companies must only link to registered news organisations, and platforms must also respond to inaccurate stories on their sites. By comparison, US regulations have required digital intermediaries such as Facebook and Google News to catalogue all advertising on their sites and make them publicly available via a content library. In Australia, governments have used public-facing critical information campaigns to help promote election integrity as well as enacting national security laws aimed at preventing foreign interference. These interventions are indicative of the strong and divergent ideological traditions of their respective nations. Vese (2022) also notes that in some countries, laws designed to prevent misinformation can be, and have been, used to restrict freedom of expression or censor political dissent. Also known as 'chilling effects', this kind of censorship and dissuasion is counter to democratic notions of a marketplace of ideas.

The sustainability of waning news markets has also been a policy consideration. Australia has been at the forefront of trying to maintain the viability of news media in the face of migrating advertising revenue towards digital intermediaries. The *News Media Bargaining Code* caught global attention as a first of its kind legislation that requires digital platforms to enter into revenue-sharing agreements with news producers active on their sites (Bossio et al., 2022). In Canada, similar legislation under the *Online News Act* has also required digital intermediaries to enter mandatory bargaining with news producers. In both instances, Alphabet has swiftly come to agreements with news producers, while Meta has chosen to cease publishing news. While Meta's news blackout in Australia only lasted a few days—at the time of writing, Canadian Facebook still doesn't allow the sharing or publication of news stories on their site.

This response is characteristic of the libertarian worldview still maintained by many of Silicon Valley's technology companies (see Chap. 3). Rather than direct regulation from governments, these companies prefer platform-centric solutions. For example, Meta has initiated its own measures such as providing grants to fund public interest journalism in Australia (Meta, 2021) as well as the Facebook Oversight Board, an independent body established to oversee content moderation decisions on their platforms. Meta's approaches would firmly rest within what Flew (2021) classifies as corporate-lead regulation, which coexists alongside state-led and NGO-led initiatives, illustrating the multifaceted nature of digital platform regulation. Such an environment is unique in its scope, encompassing national, regional and global dimensions (Flew, 2021).

And so, the contest between democratic and commercial interest for news production has continued well into the social media era. New technology has always posed a threat to existing institutional powers and while the format has changed, many of the core issues are the same. As evidence, one need only read the concerns levelled at radio broadcasters in the 1920s whereby newspapers thought broadcasters would pirate their stories (Jolly, 2016). At the same time, journalists and media companies are adapting to this new environment through changing journalistic practices and leveraging regulatory power to maintain their economic interests. Users for the most part seem to have benefitted from this transition with greater access to diverse news and more opportunities to have their voices heard. There is also evidence to suggest that younger generations, at least in Australia, might be making a shift to print news while reducing their commitment to social news (Park et al., 2023, p. 76). With generative AI technologies now adding a further disruption to this industry, there is even more uncertainty to be had. This emerging technology could exacerbate many of the existing problems currently felt within the industry or offer a new opportunity for efficiency and scale that can meet the demands of the social media paradigm.

## REFERENCES

Ali, S. R., & Fahmy, S. (2013). Gatekeeping and Citizen Journalism: The Use of Social Media During the Recent Uprisings in Iran, Egypt, and Libya. *Media, War & Conflict, 6*(1), 55–69.

Anderson, T. (2022). Stopping Attacks on Health Care. *World Health Organization. Bulletin of the World Health Organization, 100*(8), 470–471.

Australian Competition and Consumer Commission. (2019). Digital Platforms Inquiry.

Bellingcat. (2022, 16 June 2022). *The Brazilian Candidate: The Studious Cover Identity of an Alleged Russian Spy.* Retrieved from https://www.bellingcat.com/news/americas/2022/06/16/the-brazilian-candidate-the-studious-cover-identity-of-an-alleged-russian-spy/

Biggs, T. (2023). *Twitter's Seussian Blue Tick Saga Eroded Trust, Without Boosting Subs.* Retrieved from https://www.smh.com.au/technology/twitter-s-seussian-blue-tick-saga-eroded-trust-without-boosting-subs-20230425-p5d352.html

Bossio, D. (2017). *Journalism and Social Media: Practitioners, Organisations and Institutions.* Springer.

Bossio, D., Flew, T., Meese, J., Leaver, T., & Barnet, B. (2022). Australia's News Media Bargaining Code and the Global Turn Towards Platform Regulation. *Policy & Internet, 14*(1), 136–150.

Brake, D. R. (2017). The Invisible Hand of the Unaccountable Algorithm: How Google, Facebook and Other Tech Companies are Changing Journalism. *Digital Technology and Journalism: An International Comparative Perspective,* 25–46.

Carr, D. J., Barnidge, M., Lee, B. G., & Tsang, S. J. (2014). Cynics and Skeptics: Evaluating the Credibility of Mainstream and Citizen Journalism. *Journalism & Mass Communication Quarterly, 91*(3), 452–470.

Castells, M. (2011). Network Theory | A Network Theory of Power. *International Journal of Communication, 5*, 15.

Castillo, M. (2018). *Zuckerberg Tells Congress Facebook is not a Media Company: 'I Consider Us to be a Technology Company'*. Tech. Retrieved from https://www.cnbc.com/2018/04/11/mark-zuckerberg-facebook-is-a-technology-company-not-media-company.html

Cinelli, M., Quattrociocchi, W., Galeazzi, A., Valensise, C. M., Brugnoli, E., Schmidt, A. L., et al. (2020). The COVID-19 Social Media Infodemic. *Scientific Reports, 10*(1), 1–10.

Cooper, G., & Mutsvairo, B. (2021). Citizen Journalism: Is Bellingcat Revolutionising Conflict Journalism? In *Insights on Peace and Conflict Reporting* (pp. 106–120). Routledge.

Denisova, A. (2023). Viral Journalism. Strategy, Tactics and Limitations of the Fast Spread of Content on Social Media: Case Study of the United Kingdom Quality Publications. *Journalism, 24*(9), 1919–1937.

DeVito, M. A. (2017). From Editors to Algorithms: A Values-Based Approach to Understanding Story Selection in the Facebook News Feed. *Digital Journalism, 5*(6), 753–773.

Eady, G., Paskhalis, T., Zilinsky, J., Bonneau, R., Nagler, J., & Tucker, J. A. (2023). Exposure to the Russian Internet Research Agency Foreign Influence Campaign on Twitter in the 2016 US Election and its Relationship to Attitudes and Voting Behavior. *Nature Communications, 14*(1), 62.

Fiveash, K. (2016). *"We're a Tech Company, We're Not a Media Company," says Facebook Founder*. Retrieved from https://arstechnica.com/tech-policy/2016/08/germany-facebook-edit-hateful-posts-zuckerberg-says-not-media-empire/

Fletcher, R., Kalogeropoulos, A., & Nielsen, R. K. (2021). More Diverse, More Politically Varied: How Social Media, Search Engines and Aggregators Shape News Repertoires in the United Kingdom. *New Media & Society, 25*, 14614448211027393. https://doi.org/10.1177/14614448211027393

Flew, T. (2021). *Regulating Platforms*. Wiley.

Fuchs, C. (2010). Alternative Media as Critical Media. *European Journal of Social Theory, 13*(2), 173–192.

Fuchs, C. (2017). The Power and Political Economy of Social Media. In *Social Media: A Critical Introduction* (2nd ed., pp. 121–152). Sage Publications.

Habermas, J., Lennox, S., & Lennox, F. (1974). The Public Sphere: An Encyclopaedia Article (1964). *New German Critique*, (3), 49–55.

Hameleers, M., van der Meer, T. G., & Dobber, T. (2022). You Won't Believe What They Just Said! The Effects of Political Deepfakes Embedded as Vox Populi on Social Media. *Social Media + Society, 8*(3), 20563051221116346.

Harris, K. R. (2023). Liars and Trolls and Bots Online: The Problem of Fake Persons. *Philosophy & Technology, 36*(2), 35.

Hobbs, M., Della Bosca, H., Schlosberg, D., & Sun, C. (2020). Turf Wars: Using Social Media Network Analysis to Examine the Suspected Astroturfing Campaign for the Adani Carmichael Coal Mine on Twitter. *Journal of Public Affairs, 20*(2), e2057.

Holton, A. E., Bélair-Gagnon, V., Bossio, D., & Molyneux, L. (2023). "Not Their Fault, but Their Problem": Organizational Responses to the Online Harassment of Journalists. *Journalism Practice, 17*(4), 859–874.

Jolly, R. (2016). *Media Ownership and Regulation: A Chronology Part One: From Print to Radio Days and Television Nights.* Report. Parliamentary Library (Australia). Retrieved from https://apo.org.au/node/61193

Karimi, M., Jannach, D., & Jugovac, M. (2018). News Recommender Systems–Survey and Roads Ahead. *Information Processing & Management, 54*(6), 1203–1227.

Keller, F. B., Schoch, D., Stier, S., & Yang, J. (2020). Political Astroturfing on Twitter: How to Coordinate a Disinformation Campaign. *Political Communication, 37*(2), 256–280.

Lawrence, R. G., & Napoli, P. M. (2022). *News Quality in the Digital Age.* Taylor & Francis Group.

Lewis, S. C., Zamith, R., & Coddington, M. (2020). Online Harassment and its Implications for the Journalist–Audience Relationship. *Digital Journalism, 8*(8), 1047–1067.

Maras, S. (2013). *Objectivity in Journalism.* Polity.

Maras, M.-H., & Alexandrou, A. (2019). Determining Authenticity of Video Evidence in the Age of Artificial Intelligence and in the Wake of Deepfake Videos. *The International Journal of Evidence & Proof, 23*(3), 255–262.

Martin, F., & Dwyer, T. (2019). The Numbers Game: Social News Analytics. In F. Martin & T. Dwyer (Eds.), *Sharing News Online: Commentary Cultures and Social Media News Ecologies* (pp. 61–90). Palgrave Macmillan.

McGregor, S. C. (2019). Social Media as Public Opinion: How Journalists Use Social Media to Represent Public Opinion. *Journalism, 20*(8), 1070–1086.

Meta. (2021). *Facebook Announces AU$15 Million News Fund and Begins the Phased Launch of Facebook News in Australia.* Retrieved from https://www.facebook.com/journalismproject/facebook-invests-in-australia-news-fund-and-launches-facebook-news

Mutsvairo, B., & Salgado, S. (2022). Is Citizen Journalism Dead? An Examination of Recent Developments in the Field. *Journalism, 23*(2), 354–371.

Napoli, P. M., & Dwyer, D. L. (2018). US Media Policy in a Time of Political Polarization and Technological Evolution. *Publizistik, 63*(4), 583–601.

Pariser, E. (2022, October 28). *Musk's Twitter Will Not Be the Town Square the World Needs.* Retrieved from https://www.wired.com/story/elon-musk-twitter-town-square/

Park, S., McGuinness, K., Fisher, C., Lee, J. Y., McCallum, K., & Nolan, D. (2022). *Digital News Report: Australia 2022.* News and Media Research Centre.

Park, S., McGuinness, K., Fisher, C., Lee, J. Y., McCallum, K., Cai, X., et al. (2023). *Digital News Report: Australia 2023.* News Media Research Centre, University of Canberra.

Pew Research Centre. (2022). Social Media and News Fact Sheet. In *Social Media & the News.* Retrieved from https://www.pewresearch.org/journalism/fact-sheet/social-media-and-news-fact-sheet/

Ratkiewicz, J., Conover, M., Meiss, M., Gonçalves, B., Patil, S., Flammini, A., & Menczer, F. (2010). Detecting and Tracking the Spread of Astroturf Memes in Microblog Streams. *arXiv preprint arXiv:1011.3768.*

Roberts, J. (2019). Citizen Journalism. In *The International Encyclopedia of Media Literacy* (pp. 1–10).

Ross, A. R., & Dumitrescu, D. (2019). 'Vox Twitterati': Investigating the Effects of Social Media Exemplars in Online News Articles. *New Media & Society, 21*(4), 962–983.

Segreti, G. (2016). Facebook CEO says Group will not Become a Media Company. *Internet News.* Retrieved from https://www.reuters.com/article/us-facebook-zuckerberg-idUSKCN1141WN

Vaidhyanathan, S. (2018). The Incomplete Political Economy of Social Media. In *The SAGE Handbook of Social Media* (pp. 213–229).

Vese, D. (2022). Governing Fake News: The Regulation of Social Media and the Right to Freedom of Expression in the Era of Emergency. *European Journal of Risk Regulation, 13*(3), 477–513.

Walters, P. (2022). Reclaiming Control: How Journalists Embrace Social Media Logics While Defending Journalistic Values. *Digital Journalism, 10*(9), 1482–1501.

Wardle, C., & Derakhshan, H. (2018). Thinking About 'Information Disorder': Formats of Misinformation, Disinformation, and Mal-information. In *Journalism, 'Fake News' & Disinformation* (43–54).

## CHAPTER 7

# Social Media and Politics

## INTRODUCTION: ARE CAMPAIGNS WON ON SOCIAL MEDIA NOW?

Does social media support or harm democracy and the public sphere? The function of social media campaigns that support and maintain political and social changes has been well documented, often presented as affordances for democracies, or conversely as challenges that confront our political systems and thereby our societies. What we do notice is the role that social media campaigns play within these spaces and moments of voter direction towards specific candidates. While not new—politics and media has been at play since Aristotle times—these particular social and political changes are a result of social media platforms as a more participatory media arrangement than that of traditional media. Social media offers a variety of opportunities for citizens to communicate their personal opinions, thoughts and articulations that demonstrate individual expressiveness within socio and political participation. One aspect of these communication processes is to sustain democratic systems as well as to engage and collaborate for policymaking processes. The other side of the debate is that social media is derailing our trust in institutions and communication mechanisms which have become responsible for the current state of chaos within many geopolitical regions.

## SOCIAL MEDIA AS INFLUENCE CAMPAIGNS

Social media offers multiple tools, strategies and content for supporting civic engagement and political participation, as well as options for accessing, creating and distributing information, organising, decision-making and building a shared identity—the kinds of participatory actions needed by online activism (Castells, 2015; Kavada, 2010; Porta & Mosca, 2009). However, social media enables low-cost participation, making this approach perhaps less influential in

J. Hutchinson et al., *Social Media in Society*, https://doi.org/10.1007/978-3-031-66360-4_7

defining participation (Earl & Kimport, 2011). Personal participation and digital media usage have established powerful relationships (Bakker & De Vreese, 2011; Vaccari et al., 2015; Vromen, 2007) to identify and distribute information about the community and political concerns (Vaccari et al., 2015; Vromen, 2007).

Creating alternative content and participating in social and political change has become an important function of social media. It is an affordable and accessible tool to improve a social movement's capability for communication and coordination (Bennett & Segerberg, 2012) and mobilise public participation (Denning, 2001). Extensive research has shown that digital activists are more than capable of creating alternative media and public sphere through social media. This approach effectively circumvents mainstream gatekeepers, allowing for direct communication of counter-narratives to stakeholders' digital media activism serves as an alternative media as these arguments have been supported by Downing (2010) and Gutiérrez (2018), and alternative public sphere as a new way for ordinary people to express and unite against dictatorial power structures which creates counter publics (Edingo, 2021). Also, social media can be used to counter the dominant narratives (Downing, 2010; Poell & Borra, 2012; Feltwell et al., 2017; Gutiérrez, 2018; Indranila, 2022). Therefore, social movements can use social media to expand the digital public sphere and strengthen political activism.

A social movement's success or failure depends on its ability to mobilise resources and exploit political chances to achieve its purpose (Martin, 2015), and its achievements rely on the effectiveness of its information production and distribution. Social movements must therefore be sensitive to changes in the impacts of political, organisational, and tactical situations (Maher et al., 2019), and change their social media strategies as a protest cycle develops, which in turn will create changes in the external environment (Martin, 2015). For example, movement actors might adopt a more political logic as it focuses on policy and long-term consequences, rather than political events (Kriesi et al., 2013) to negotiate with people in authority or power at the same time as the movement itself encourages society to participate via social media. Through this process which includes online strategies that positively influence the effectiveness of the movement and often result in the campaign being embraced by a political system.

In many cases, social media has provided people with a voice and awareness, enabled them to call for action and allowed them the freedom to express themselves and participate in social movements. The recent types of activism enable individuals to utilise social media to advocate for social and political change by managing movements and facilitating collective declarations created and reinforced by civil society. Therefore, social media platforms have evolved to be a vital instrument for social and political change, playing essential roles for the Occupy movement (Castells, 2015) and the Arab Spring (Guesmi, 2021), as well as more youth-driven movements like the Umbrella movement (Lee & Chan, 2015). These political shifts also reflect the practices of global movements, for example Black Lives Matter (Freelon et al., 2016) and #MeToo movements (Lee & Murdie, 2021), or Indonesian anti-corruption movements such as the Save KPK 2014 movement (Jamil & Doktoralina, 2016; Suwana, 2019; Wijayanto et al., 2022), and Malaysian social movement for proper elections like the Bersih movement (Johns & Cheong, 2019; Azlan, 2020). In other words, social media can support influence campaigns across large cohorts of users and has established a method of driving public engagement that can drive genuine political change.

## REVOLUTIONS ON SOCIAL MEDIA

### *The Arab Spring*

The Arab Spring was a sequence of pro-democratic revolution and activist movements that began in 2011 and primarily affected Muslim countries, including Egypt, Morocco, Tunisia and Syria. It was one of the first activist movements in modern culture to be formed via social media platforms, and the influence of digital media on the activists' work was evident in their social media usage, for example Facebook, Twitter and texting messages during those uprisings. Social media platforms are robust, speedy, and relatively low-cost, allowing activists to organise and communicate information about protests (Castells, 2015; Guesmi, 2021; Tufekci, 2014) and drive the communication and influence campaigns around socio-political changes. Throughout the Arab Spring movement, as individuals used digital media to create large-scale collective action while ensuring personalised action stayed at the vanguard (Bennett & Segerberg, 2013), protestors and activists demonstrated the connective logic of crowd and organisationally enabled networks.

During the Arab Spring movement, government censorship was a significant concern and a severe issue. One crucial change was the opening of Facebook usage in Egypt and Tunisia as this allowed civil society to access social media platforms, particularly after the option of language translation from English into Arabic was introduced in 2009 (Tufekci, 2014). The local networks used Facebook and Twitter especially to alert the rest of the world of the civil unrest in these Arab nations. Facebook and Twitter became significant social media platforms for planning and organising labour strikes and protesting harsh political and economic conditions in Egypt and Tunisia (Guesmi, 2021; Tufekci, 2014). These platforms also enabled protestors to share photos and videos of demonstrations as they happened, virtually connecting with and engaging people from different parts of the globe. The speed and scale of the user-led communication via social media platforms was unprecedented for 2011.

It was, however, not only activists who understood social media; it became increasingly clear that governments could also utilise its mass communication and immediacy affordances to control populations. The Egyptian government closed the Internet to stop further broadcasting of the protests, preventing

**Fig. 7.1** Illustration showing the Facebook logo during the Arab Spring Movement (Source: Time.com Cartoon of the Week)

anyone outside the country from seeing what was unfolding (Tufekci, 2014), and counterattacked by hacking into activists' emails and social media accounts and shutting those down too (Tufekci, 2014). However, some citizens illegally bypassed Internet blocking software to enable social media access temporarily. This digital battle indicates how both individuals and institutions can access and utilise social media to distribute information and mobilise people to support or resist political and social change.

The Arab Spring also highlighted digital media's potential to transform a shared vision. This Arab movement started led to a trend of social media outlets seizing the opportunity to brand themselves as platforms that could be good for use in political activism and resistance. Now, the Arab Spring is often credited and referred to as a 'Facebook Revolution' or 'Twitter Revolution' that would not have seen as great a success in its efforts without social media (Guesmi, 2021; Wolfsfeld et al., 2013). There is pushback against this perspective that more accurately reflects that platforms did not *drive* the revolutions as such, but were essential tools to shore up the efforts of those already active in the uprisings (González-Bailón et al., 2011). The illustration below embodies this moment that describes how the Facebook logo was repurposed for 'freedom' for the Arab Spring (Fig. 7.1).

### The Save KPK 2015 Movement

Indonesia has an anti-corruption movement, the 2015 Save KPK movement, which helps and protects the Indonesian Corruption Eradication Commission (the KPK) from being criminalised by the Indonesian National Police. The

KPK institution was formed on December 27, 2022, to eliminate corruption, primarily corruption cases concerning prominent people or elites (Tapsell, 2015), but this institution has been weakened several times include attempts by Indonesian politicians to weaken its authority, legislative proposals to amend its law, and allegations and police cases against KPK commissioners (Suwana, 2018, 2019; Wijayanto et al., 2022). The movement arose in 2015 due to efforts by other groups, including the police, to further undermine the KPK power, and Indonesian society fought this situation and gained support for the KPK via social media. Indonesian civil society assembled in person and online to provide their support to the KPK, and the Save KPK movement was an example of digital activism to maintain the Indonesian democratic system.

This 2024 movement was an online movement to support KPK as its commission, Bibit Samad Rianto (chairman) and Chandra Hamzah (deputy chairman), were charged by Police with suspected bribery as part of corruption case (Mahditama, 2012; Soebagjo, 2015; Suwana, 2018). This campaign also took place on social media and websites, including Facebook pages (Save KPK and Save Indonesia), Twitter (#SaveKPK), and the website Change.org (Suwana, 2018). However, the movement period in 2015 with hashtag #akuKPK or #SaveKPK differed from the former Save KPK movements. The difference is because the 2015 movement combined offline and online activism and maximised social media usage to invite more individuals from across society and its external networks to participate, with social media effectively supporting offline mobilisation (Freedom House, 2012). The movement was also visible on social media globally, and, as a result, the hashtag #saveKPK emerged as a global trending topic several times from January 23 to 24 in 2015 (Rahutomo et al., 2020; Freedom House, 2015; Hidayat, 2015) (Fig. 7.2).

As previously noted, individuals participate in digital activism based on emotional relations (Juris, 2012; Castells, 2015; Papacharissi, 2015). This digital activism means that people who participate can refrain from engaging with the intricacy of political alliances correlated with the communal ideology, as they can communicate their personalised ideas utilising social media platforms like Twitter (Papacharissi, 2015). Participants produced, disseminated and rallied online information through social media platforms during the movement. They used the #saveKPK2015 hashtag on Facebook and Twitter (while Instagram and TikTok were not popular yet), which became an online instrument to organise activists, religious leaders, professionals, scholars and political actors to support the KPK organisation (Clough, 2015), and also ordinary Indonesian civil society, including pro-democracy activists and non-government organisation actors (Suwana, 2018; Savirani, 2015; Wijayanto et al., 2022), labour organisations, and higher degree education students (Suwana, 2018: Gabrillin, 2015). The Indonesian civil society for that movement has included pro-democracy activists, professionals, religious or community leaders, academics or scholars and politicians gathered and protested

**Fig. 7.2**  Illustration of the Save KPK Movement (Sources: Liputan6.com)

in the Indonesian parliament building to promote the sustainability of the KPK as an institution.

Traditional collective action requires centralised information, organisational structure and goal direction. The collaboration groups in the 2015 Save KPK movement instead had weaker social connection of networks and acted voluntarily, with no leaders, demonstrating the attributes of Connective action, which relies on individualised messages and online coalition as part of the connective action logic (Bennett & Segerberg, 2012). Bennet and Seggerberg's connective action logic has become evidence in how the Save KPK participants developed coalition groups via personalised free expression online (e.g. tweets, hashtags, and status updates), communication, and voluntary coordination without an organisational structure or leadership. They employed social media to communicate and coordinate their strategies and to enact them. Social media also helped activists in Jakarta to communicate and coordinate with activists in other provinces. In other words, social media enabled strategic campaign tools that promoted the Save KPK movement to distribute knowledge about the situation so that the weakening of the KPK became an Indonesian national issue and to organise information and people to oppose it.

## *The #MeToo Movement*

The #MeToo movement initially launched as a movement to raise attention to female violence and sexual harassment and primarily to support victims of sexual crimes. Although the hashtag had been trending for some years, the movement gained international media traction in 2017 when there was a case of sexual assault allegations from an American female actress (initiated by Alyssa Milano) against Harvey Weinstein, a movie mogul who became an influential figure in Hollywood as the cofounder and co-chairman of Miramax Films and later the Weinstein Company (Quan-Haase et al., 2021; Lee & Murdie, 2021). The campaign supports women who expose and call out inappropriate sexual behaviour in the media entertainment industry. #MeToo became dependent on social media resources and platforms to highlight the issue to the public. Hashtags are a consistent form of social and political engagement, as individuals can use them to support movements as part of digital activism (Quan-Haase et al., 2021). Utilising a hashtag for a specific issue generally takes less effort than organising or participating in a protest. However, the use of hashtag #MeToo movement involves sharing personal stories of sexual violence as this enables significant insights into the potential of digital feminist activism in raising feminist consciousness and promoting solidarity among women (Mendes et al., 2018). Therefore, hashtags are distinct from forwarding a status, tweet or comment. Still, the emotional, psychological and functional barriers that produce variant experiences and legitimise some women's voices, opinions, and involvement with others while women's participation in digital activism can be costly at a personal and professional level.

Nevertheless, a study in 2018 by the Pew Research Centre highlighted the use of the hashtag *#MeToo* was utilised within around 19 million tweets. This was a direct result that followed Alyssa Milano's initial post on Twitter about the sexual allegation issue, which resulted in more than 55,000 uses of the hashtag per day (Brown, 2019). Social media enabled the hashtag to spread fast and extensively which attracted support from other sexual violence survivors (Quan-Haase et al., 2021). The two words "Me Too" have also been used as a meme globally, including in an Instagram post by celebrity Evangeline Lilly, who shared the meme with her 2.1 million followers (Bleznak, 2018). In the context of this movement, and as a strategy for campaigns more broadly, online memes have become successful when their context is diverse, quickly shared and easily understood. The #MeToo movement highlighted the critical issue of a safe working environment free from sexual harassment, was able to spread awareness about this issue and started a global conversation about sexual harassment in society by utilising social media platforms.

The #MeToo movement has since migrated to the other social media platforms that shifted the issue from the US alone and on to a global stage (Lee & Murdie, 2021; Quan-Haase et al., 2021). However, while activists use social media to support digital activism, they are often dependent on the degree of media freedom within their country. While Internet technologies are

**Fig. 7.3** The creative emoji and nickname "Rice bunny" in Chinese (Sources: The Conversation/Marcella Cheng)

networked globally, governments can regulate access to the Internet and its content through a variety of cybersecurity mechanisms. Similarly, activists also can use creativity to circumvent government censorship of online content. For example, in China, the extension of nicknames and online emojis is not just a public relations strategy designed to increase a campaign to become more popular but a strategic way to overcome online censorship (Zeng, 2020). When the Chinese government attempted to censor the #MeToo movement, the public who wanted to engage in the #MeToo movement in China adopted the creative use of emojis and connotations for calling out sexual harassment claims (Fig. 7.3).

Figure 7.3, for example, became an alternative, coded hashtag that symbolised the MeToo movement in China, is known as 'Rice Bunny' because the word for 'rice', 'mi', sounds like 'me', and the word for 'rabbit', 'tu', sounds like 'too' (Zeng, 2019). This innovative cultural coding enabled women to circumvent state censorship and prohibitions on free speech (Zeng, 2020), and take part in the more significant global movement. Social media has tools and features, such as emojis and hashtags which can further help society—especially women in this case—to participate in social movements, and the creativity of their content and narratives can help the community bypass censorship and take part in politics.

### The Occupy Movement

Another global collective movement is the Occupy Movement, which protested for economic and social justice following the financial sector collapse in

September 2008 with the collapse of Lehman Brothers (Merle, 2018). The anti-capitalist movement Adbusters, a Canadian media activist group, initiated the #OccupyWallStreet protest. These activists aimed to highlight how the powerful elite (1% of the population) collectively own more than the sum owned by the remaining 99% and to draw attention to corruption in the financial sector and corporate influence on governments (Gerbaudo, 2017).

On September 17, 2011, protestors occupied one of the financial districts in New York—Zuccotti Park, in response to the US Government's decision to provide financial support and prop up big business at the personal cost of millions of Americans. The Occupy movement's usage of social media facilitated a crucial part in rapidly distributing updates regarding that profession and rallying participants about the occupation and mobilising participants. Based on its connective actions (Bennett & Segerberg, 2013), which are meditated in its online networks, the Occupy movement is an example of a crowd-enabled network, with the participants in the movement being more inclusive, flexible, and adaptive than organisations.

The Occupy movement utilised Facebook and Twitter (Conover et al., 2013) to mobilise the public, gain member feedback and build solidarity (Kavada, 2015). Activists organised mass protests through Tumblr, Twitter and Facebook (Gerbaudo, 2017), as they were live-streamed during the two-month occupation of Wall Street, with more than 1000 cities in the world participating in the protests using the hashtag #OccupyWallStreet (Constanza-Chock, 2012; Gerbaudo, 2017). The Occupy hashtag grew to become a meme as ordinary people adopted it and incorporated the message into their accounts of economic disadvantaged (Castells, 2015; Gerbaudo, 2017). The merger of text and images used to support the growing Occupy movement included digital posters and memes (Fig. 7.4).

Social media was employed by the Occupy Movement to distribute and amplify the information and protests that usually occur offline. Several features of social media platforms, including comments and likes, were beneficial metrics of the movement's dynamic (Kavada, 2015), enabling key actors and activists to reflect on its personality and improve its attractiveness to society (Kavada, 2010, 2015). Social media users also provided essential emotional support for the core activists participating in offline action through solidarity messages and more tangible actions such as material support (Kavada, 2015). This support demonstrates that social media users are a critical element of social movements (Bräuchler, 2020; Lim, 2017; Suwana, 2018) and that social media use can amplify a movement's capacity to conduct actions that support social and political change. Therefore, digital media literacy is necessary for society to have critical thinking, analytical and evaluation skills, creating accurate information daily. In other words, society needs its members to have suitable digital media literacy skills to partake in socio and political change.

**Fig. 7.4**  Occupy movement poster designs (Source: Inspiration Feed)

## SWINGING THE VOTERS: ELECTIONS IN THE PHILIPPINES AND THE US

Movements are important across social media as described above, but one of these particular movements is the conversations that surround political elections. These events have significant results, i.e. the election of incumbents, and as such should have public debate as a crucial part of democratic systems worldwide. In this section we will especially focus on two key case studies: the Philippines, and the United State. While each country has a unique political landscape, voters' sentiments and strategies to sway voters can vary. Let's explore some key aspects of elections in these countries.

### Philippines

The Philippines has a government structure with a presidential system in which the people directly elect the president. The 1987 Philippine Constitution states that both the president and the vice president must meet multiple requirements, such as being born a native of the Philippines, being registered as voters, and being at least forty years old and having lived in the Philippines for at least ten years before the election in which they stand (Haryanto, 2022). However, in Philippines presidential elections, unlike those of other countries, the president and vice president are not elected as one package or coalition, but separately (Haryanto, 2022), although presidential candidates may campaign with a vice-presidential candidate as their running mate (Haryanto, 2022). Recently, presidential elections in the Philippines have been lively and highly competitive and have often involved well-developed social media strategies

(Arugay, 2022; Quitzon, 2021). For example, strategies to sway voters have in the past involved political campaigns in which candidates engaged in extensive campaigning, including via protests, public appearances and media advertisements. However, In 2016 President Rodrigo Duterte won the presidential election in part thanks to an innovative social media campaign which used disinformation tactics to attack other candidates (Ong & Cabañes, 2018; Quitzon, 2021). In this election, voters were divided among four presidential candidates, and this strategy to sway voters brought Duterte victory in a way like those of past Philippine presidents who have come to power on the backs of a minority of voters (Arugay, 2022; Wong, 2022).

The development of digital technology has allowed electoral candidates' words, actions and thoughts to be promoted directly to society by social media. As political campaigns in the Philippines address essential issues, social media are now also being utilised to grasp attention and votes, publicise campaign promises, and appeal to voters' emotions. It is unsurprising that electoral campaigns have taken to using social media, as these new media platforms can influence and affect voters. A swing voter is one who could go either side: while some voters are robust, prominent and loyal supporters of one or another candidate, some individuals or groups also used other new methods of micromedia manipulation to sow political messages among distinct and separate groups of unsuspecting voters who continue with candidate doubt up until election day (Mayer, 2008). The swing voter has been growing in the Philippines political context.

In the Philippines, the advantages social media platforms offer for mobilising political support have become particularly evident during national and local elections. During the 2016 polls, for example, the 'cyber army', or dedicated social media followers of Rodrigo Duterte, launched a vigorous social media campaign that helped catapult him to the presidency (Arugay, 2022; Wong, 2022). The Duterte campaign employed a volunteer-driven strategy that relied on social media influencers to spread its populist message to their many followers (Teehankee & Thompson, 2016). Some specific groups applied new micromedia manipulation techniques to spread political messages among certain groups of voters without their knowledge. One such method was the design of a more diffuse network of social media influencers, who appear as harmless online public figures or celebrities for specific audiences, designed to pass under the radar and evade detection (Ong et al., 2019). Another form of manipulation is the creation of an organised network of electronic trolls or troll armies— as these are a misinformation army, even if they are not even real people (Quitzon, 2021).

Key opinion leaders in the Philippines include celebrities and online public figures with large numbers of social media followers who support political campaigns such as Rodrigo Duterte's election campaign in 2016. Duterte has a strong image as a revolutionary and a stranger from the elite group, which the Duterte camp developed during the presidential election campaign 2016 (Reynaldo, 2021; Wong, 2022). Some macho action movie stars, including

Cesar Montano, Mocha Girls, Philip Salvador, Robin Padilla also endorsed Duterte and posted about him on their social media profiles (Reynaldo, 2021). These celebrity, public figure or influencer endorsements were able to significantly impact voters' opinions and sway their support to Duterte, in the presidential election of 2016. Social networks can also enable vote buying, a process in which candidates or their supporters offer money or favours to voters in exchange for their votes, and this remains a challenge in some areas (Cruz, 2019).

Foreign influence in the media landscape of the Philippines is neither covert nor significant. Under the Duterte administration, the Presidential Communications Operations Office oversees public television and radio stations and has signed formal media agreements with Chinese providers (Han & Elemia, 2022), but the audiences of these Chinese state-run media outlets are much smaller than those of their private-sector competitors. Nevertheless, the social media disinformation campaigns discussed above expose cracks in Philippines society that hostile foreign actors could exploit. Should it be in the interest of a foreign power to influence an election, it would be sufficient for that power to support the disinformation campaign of its preferred party and undermine that party's opponents using established disinformation warfare tactics. For example, a 2020 Graphika report on a China-based online disinformation campaign found that it supported the presidential campaigns of Duterte-aligned politicians Sara Duterte and Imee Marcos (Nimmo et al., 2020; Han & Elemia, 2022). Another research showed that a specific network constructed five significant investments in the Philippines between March 2018 and March 2019 and designated fake social media profiles during that time (Nimmo et al., 2020). This network glorified Duterte, his family, and his political partners while criticising opponent figures and crucial independent Philippines media (Han & Elemia, 2022). Another critical juvenility of posts is concentrated on supporting the great things that have been conducted by China (Nimmo et al., 2020). This campaign collected a moderately extensive online audience in the Philippines.

Facebook and Instagram have taken down or restricted many accounts run by strident Duterte supporters and supporting groups both inside and outside the government, on the grounds of coordinated inauthentic behaviour or violations of Facebook's community standards. Work on state-based foreign interference in the Philippines is underdeveloped, given the predominant focus on local political disinformation and communications and media studies scholars; however, the Duterte administration's embrace of China is increasing political and media interest in possible Chinese interference in the Philippines (Bradshaw et al., 2021). Opportunities thus exist to support anti-disinformation campaigns, including digital media literacy programmes, particularly in the result of the Philippines presidential elections and around the COVID-19 situation in 2022, which struck the Philippines vigorously (Internews, 2021). Therefore, there could be scope to support a greater focus in the Philippines on foreign state-based disinformation and interference campaigns by improving digital media literacy.

In recent years, social media platforms have gained immense influence and emerged as a potent tool for political campaigns and propaganda in the Philippines, as Filipinos are heavy Internet and social media users (Quitzon, 2021). According to 2019 data, they spend approximately 10 hours and 2 minutes daily in cyberspace, and 71% of the population uses social media, including Facebook, Twitter and Instagram (Kemp, 2020). Also, the research data stated Filipinos spend 4 hours and 12 minutes on social media per day (Kemp, 2020). Political candidates are thus utilising social media, for example Facebook, Instagram, Twitter and YouTube, to engage with voters, share their messages, and mobilise political support. As noted above, online influencers took an essential role in the Philippine media atmosphere (Han & Elemia, 2022). While some influencers can be key opinion leaders in election campaigns, others are anonymous. These anonymous operators have orders to transform distinctive political campaigns into viral political propaganda and social media influence. A further condition of this is that the Marcos Dynasty needed to represent their favourable public image in the eyes of the nation to influence public opinion (Wafiq, 2023). Dark accounts of economic plunder and human rights transgressions had to be glossed over by a counter-narrative that spoke instead of a golden age of history under the Marcos regime, spread through an enormous propaganda and disinformation drive waged by social media influencers, websites, Facebook pages and groups, and YouTube channels (Teehankee, 2023). Social media distributed fake content that systematically denied corruption and abuse while simultaneously exaggerating the achievements made during the Marcos years, and denigrating critics, rivals, and the mainstream press alike (Mendoza, 2022).

This deliberate effort to paint a glorious depiction of martial law for political ends was facilitated through networked disinformation. Disinformation refers to the organised political deception creation in which commitments are allocated to various or loose affiliated groups of hierarchised online workers (Ong & Cabañes, 2018). Also, disinformation is entrenched as an organised industry, in which major marketing and strategic communications players provide political consultancy services in Philippines (Bradshaw & Howard, 2018). The practice of spreading disinformation on social media is very systematic, and some political clients from other countries are tapping into these practices and services offered by Filipino firms.

The architecture of disinformation globally is directed by prominent advertising, marketing and public relations firms dealing with political clients. These unrecognised hands deftly direct operations to achieve political strategies anchored in social media and big data. Investigative reports have identified how data analytics firms such as Cambridge Analytica have been able to harvest online data from digital platforms such as Facebook to develop new election strategies and tactics (Cadwalladr & Graham, 2018). Big data analytics are being used to rebrand electoral candidates in ways that appeal to voters. Social media planners recently centralised and combined the across-the-board political campaigns of nominees from every level, with public relations methods charging from USD 100,000 for nationwide campaigns to USD 1000 for regional campaigns (Ong et al., 2019). Populist leaders have engaged in social media platform disinformation campaigns to disseminate their anti-establishment narrative, which includes a refusal of the legality of succeeding democratic regimes, the discharge of traditional media, and allegations of corruption made against independent organisation that fight for civil and human liberties (Persily, 2017). Following the disinformation process through social media has further reinforced personality-based politics and weakened rules-based governance.

### The United States

This chapter also discusses social media users' attitudes towards the potential or actual influence social media can have on election campaigns and political content, and how these vary according to political partisanship. Two affordances of social media—visibility and spreadability—heavily impacted the US presidential elections in 2016 and 2020 as they were how disinformation and misinformation were disseminated to the public. This misinformation and disinformation widened the scope for potential political partisanship via political information bias, ultimately impacting the election outcome in both years.

The term 'affordance' refers to what an environment offers an individual or a concept: that is, what it can deliver or supply, whether for right or wrong (Osiurak et al., 2017). One social media scholar danah boyd has stated, there are four affordances of social media including persistence, visibility, spreadability and searchability and these form multiple mediated atmospheres formed by social media platforms (boyd, 2014). In this context, persistence refers to the durability of expressions and content, visibility is the possible audience who can handle the viewer, spreadability is the comfort of content sharing, and searchability is the capacity to discover content (boyd, 2014). Spreadability acts as an affordance for the growth of the digital world, opening an extensive range of opportunities and challenges, and visibility allows people to quickly disseminate content with a diverse audience and access it, ultimately improving the possible perceptibility of a certain political message (boyd, 2014).

Political campaigning in the 2016 and 2020 US elections was used to create alternative election narratives designed to affect citizens' political perceptions and orientations. Visibility allowed these narratives to be successful, as being shared through digital networks made them public by default, meaning they were viewed and interpreted by many. For example, in 2016, 77% of the United States population actively used social media networks (Richter, 2021). Visibility, the affordance representing the potential audience exposed to online content, allowed society to view disinformation regarding the presidential candidates. This is significant because as social media is a digital and social media collection designed to expand and improve digital media communities for information dissemination and networking (Osborne-Gowey, 2014), when the viewing of misinformation and disinformation increases in social media platforms, so does its believability, and this has negative repercussions for the public.

Spreadability, another affordance of social media (boyd, 2014), is designed to help people spread information. This can be done in many ways, as the majority of what is posted online can be spread in just a few seconds. As boyd (2014) has highlighted, one social media characteristic is that the information that can be shared online is unrivalled, as social media are both solid and complicated. The evolution of news consumption on social media reflects an overriding of traditional news media, in which people believe information that is spread by their 'friends' online regardless of its ultimate source (Mazoyer, 2020). The spreadability of information online is a result of clustering and homophily. One scholar, Aral (2020), explains that social networks are characterised by triadic closures, which tend to form triangles or triads, between three individuals within social networks. A triadic closure leads to clustering among similar people and creates groups that are densely connected within a cluster but weakly connected across clusters. People with similar socioeconomic status, interests and ideas populate the densely connected clusters, which are typically connected by weak ties that string from one cluster to another. For example, in the 2016 US election, pro-Trump supporters formed one network of clusters in the same way that pro-Clinton supporters formed another. These clusters also form because social networks are clustered and homophilous. The term 'homophily' refers to how people tend to associate with people who are like themselves, in this case regarding political ideology (Aral, 2020). Homophilous ties ease communication and make it easier for people to trust one another. Combined with how easy it is to spread information on social media, these clusters and homophilous groups had the power to significantly impact the rate at which disinformation spread during the presidential election.

Regarding the frequency with which American social media users post about or discuss political topics with their social media networks, it was revealed that only 9% of adult social media users claimed to post or share information about socio and political topics on social media platforms, based on a Pew Research Centre survey (Mcclain, 2021). The social media active users in the United States at this time were 248 million. This indicates that approximately 64 million Americans were actively discussing the 2016 presidential election on social media, with another 60 million Americans potentially weighing in on the conversations. The growth of misinformation on social media has been vast and research suggests that social media users are 'tempted to follow recommendations from their peers' (Heuer & Breiter, 2018). This research explains why fabricated news articles spread far and wide across all social media platforms: because they constantly fell into the hands of those who wanted to believe them. For example, people within pro-Trump clusters seized the opportunity to spread fake news stating that Pope Francis was endorsing Donald Trump's presidency (Allcott & Gentzkow, 2017). They also seized the opportunity to spread the fake news that an FBI agent doubted in Hillary Clinton's email leaks was found dead in an alleged murder-suicide (Allcott & Gentzkow, 2017). As a result of their clustered and homophilous networks, every time disinformation was liked, shared, commented on etc., then family and friends on social media networks who felt the same way were inclined to do the same. This explains why the magnitude of spreadability on social media in this election campaign was so high.

Disinformation was thus unwittingly spread by people whose views were validated by fabricated stories, or who feel strongly about them. The circulation of this kind of information created a fraudulent campaigning process during the 2016 US election, which genuinely affected its outcome (Wardle & Derakhshan, 2018). Without the visibility and spreadability of social media creating an environment in which disinformation could thrive, the repercussions would have been much less significant. The election was a 'cataclysmic' event in which Republican Donald Trump won against Democrat Hillary Clinton, with Trump's victory taking many by surprise (Cillizza, 2016). Additionally, the election challenged conventional political frameworks, as social media and disinformation were thoroughly combined into the nationwide campaign tactics of both parties for the first time as an untraditional and controversial notion (Gillies, 2018). The situation was also escalated by the skyrocketing presence of fake news, automated bots and the proliferation of paid commentators worldwide, all of which contributed to the spreading of disinformation. These mass viewing numbers are evident in statistics published by Tankovska (Richter, 2021), which display the Facebook engagement for the top 20 mainstream and fake election narratives in the 2016 election, sorted by several actions. These statistical data show mainstream news stories developed 12 million actions on the website, compared to only fake news which generated only 3 million actions between February and April 2016 (Richter, 2021). Moreover, between August 2016 and election day, however, fake news engagement increased, generating around 9 million Facebook actions, while mainstream news stories dropped to also generating 9 million actions (Richter, 2021). These numbers represent the extent to which the public engaged with misinformation and disinformation online around the US election, as it grew more demanding and challenging for each political party but thankfulness to the growth of social media platforms.

And these numbers are representative of one social media platform only. While Facebook was a notably popular site in the 2016 election, Instagram and Twitter are recorded as having an even higher percentage of users in the United States (Richter, 2021). This potential is made possible by the visibility affordance of these platforms, as it is clear how content is accessed and viewed in such broad contexts. The impact of this affordance on the US election was controversial, as the disinformation was viewed so widely—particularly regarding Hillary Clinton—and is thought to have swayed and manipulated voters' opinions. And while the United States was already heavily exposed, social media visibility also allowed other countries to contribute to online campaigning, including Russia and China. One disinformation campaign was instigated by a group of young Macedonians who spread many pro-Trump fake news stories to make money from social media advertising (Hasen, 2017). For example, just one story generated by one of the Macedonians, which stated that Hillary Clinton would face an indictment in 2017, was shared over 140,000 times on Facebook, resulting in a genuine belief in the article and thus considerable revenue for the Macedonians (Hasen, 2017). Another fabricated narrative widely known as "Pizzagate" resulted in serious violence: a 28-year-old man read a viral social media story that suggested Comet Ping Pong in Washington DC ran a child sex ring and was being used by Hillary Clinton's associates. He therefore drove for six hours to reach the venue and fire an AR-15 rifle at it and its occupants (Kang & Goldman, 2017). Less violently, many people formed negative opinions of Hillary Clinton, resulting in the creation of swing voters. As Heuer (2021) explains, the visibility of social media leads to these dangerous outcomes because the more widely something is viewed, the more believable it becomes.

Visibility and spreadability, two of the affordances of social media, certainly created challenges regarding the disinformation uncovered during the US presidential election in 2016. The power of disinformation would have been insignificant if not for these affordances, as they provide social media and its users with a seamless environment in which to quickly fabricate narratives that are viewed and shared by a massive number of people. During the presidential election, this created havoc and manipulated the choices and opinions of many—and most importantly, of American voters. The portrayal of Hillary Clinton in particular was unfair. At the time, it was not recognised that she was the target of a serious disinformation campaign during the election.

The relationship between the affordances of visibility and spreadability and the spread of disinformation about election candidates reveals the potential for using social media to facilitate favourable attitudes among the supporters of each party. When analysing the bigger picture of these affordances in partnership with disinformation and their effect on the US presidential election, it becomes evident that they possess significant influence and power over the public, as many people tend to believe and distribute information on social media platforms. Social media, such as Facebook, Twitter, YouTube and Instagram, is now society's primary source of news or information, where misinformation and disinformation can spread on these platforms.

## Is There Social Media After Cambridge Analytica? The Implications of Data and Politics

The Cambridge Analytica scandal, which emerged in 2018, revealed how a particular company had leveraged the personal data of millions of Facebook users for political purposes without any consent. The scandal had significant implications for how people perceive and use social media, and for the regulation and oversight of data and politics. For example, Cambridge Analytica revealed that during the 2016 UK Referendum to leave the European Union and the 2016 US presidential election, people received false information and targeted advertisements based on their social media activity and profiles to influence their decisions and sway their opinions (Carmi et al., 2020). These were designed to influence their political decisions regarding the 2016 US Presidential Election and the UK Brexit Referendum on leaving the European Union in 2016 (Carmi et al., 2020). The scandal raised widespread concerns about privacy, data security, and the manipulation of political processes through social media, and brought greater public attention to the issues of data privacy, consent and social media power. It also increased online users' awareness of the extent of data collection and its potential misuse and prompted governments and regulatory bodies worldwide to act towards stricter online regulation (Hu, 2020). For instance, the US Federal Trade Commission resolved the Cambridge Analytica–Facebook scandal; it ordered Facebook to adopt new privacy standards. Meanwhile, one strong digital regulation is General Data Protection Regulation (GDPR) that launched by the European Union in 2018, therefore strengthening data protection rules and giving individuals more control over their private data is critical (Suwana, 2018). The response to the Cambridge Analytica–Facebook scandal drew upon multiple law and policy reforms (Hu, 2020), as other countries also implemented or proposed similar regulations to protect user privacy and regulate data usage.

Social media platforms, including Facebook, have made efforts to enhance transparency and improve user privacy controls. They introduced new policies and tools to give users more information about data usage and greater control over their personal information (Hu, 2020). The Cambridge Analytica scandal also contributed to distrust and scepticism among online users regarding social media platforms and their handling of personal data, so some individuals have become more prudent about the information they share, strengthening their privacy settings or reducing their online presence on specific digital platforms. The Cambridge Analytica scandal resulted in calls for improved Facebook platform regulation and cessation of platform use (Lang, 2018).

The calls for accountability and oversight that the scandal prompted led to hearings and inquiries by governments and regulatory bodies, in which tech executives were questioned about their data practices, algorithmic transparency and potential political influence. Moreover, the Cambridge Analytica scandal drew awareness that social media utilises algorithms to curate content as well as target users. Social media platform companies should take user data protection more seriously and deal with this issue more transparently (Schneble et al., 2018). Making the information exchange transparent will be increasingly important in building trust for the public institution to provide the right information to the society. The clarity and accountability of these algorithms have been questioned, particularly in the context of political content and potential biases. The need for algorithmic transparency and an examination of the algorithms' impact on democratic processes gained prominence in public discourse.

Finally, the Cambridge Analytica scandal sparked discussion of the psychographic profiling of US and UK voters who posed a threat to the electoral process. This practice should be contextualised as a challenge to democratic institutions extensively. As a practical example, online privacy issues and data protection are listed in the terms and conditions of every social media, but the explanation needs to be easier to comprehend by online society (Schneble et al., 2018). Therefore, conversations about digital media literacy and the need for individuals to be informed and critical users of online information have been growing as the scandal highlighted the importance of digital media literacy and an understanding of the collection of personal data and online usage in empowering individuals to make more effective decisions and protect their digital privacy.

## 'Platform Democracy': The Case of Taiwan

Civic tech activists are experimenting with and innovating in the areas of public engagement, deliberation and collaboration with digital media platforms. Taiwan has gained recognition as a notable case study in "platform democracy" due to its innovative and inclusive approach to utilising digital platforms for public participation and engagement in policy making processes. The Taiwanese government has successfully leveraged technology and social media to foster direct communication between citizens and policymakers, allowing for more transparent and participatory governance with digital media technology. Some critical aspects of Taiwan's platform democracy that we will discuss further are drawn from the Sunflower movement, the g0v (pronounced "gov-zero") movement, and the vTaiwan movement.

### *The Sunflower Movement*

Taiwan's Sunflower movement and platform democracy have demonstrated online engagement with digital and data activism that led to a possible political change from social media movements to party politics. The transition of Taiwanese activists to participation in formal establishments happened because of the citizens' desire for authentic democracy, which drove the Sunflower movement (Ho, 2018). Audrey Tang, a vital member of the Sunflower and g0v (civic tech community) movements, joined the government and became the country's Minister of Digital Affairs (Miller, 2020). In this case study, the merging of power and politics started integrating digital activists and digital media technologies in new forms that enable them to create political decisions and political positions in the government (Miller, 2020). However, the resourcefulness of civic technology participants has increased without any indication that they have formed a closer connection with government officers (Postill, 2018). Further evidence that combines digital technology and activism from Sunflower movement, which is currently one of the global vibrant civic technology communities that collaborate with the government, they have remained involved in several projects pressuring the government for more transparency and clarity in their decision.

## The g0v Movement

The g0v movement is a civic tech or digital activist community that emerged in Taiwan due to a perceived lack of government transparency. It was founded in 2012 by Taiwanese activists, online hackers, and open data enthusiasts (Miller, 2020; Sandman & Gregori, 2020) who organised a leaderless movement. The g0v also created vTaiwan, an open-source platform for a hybrid deliberation process that aids citizens, government organisations and civil society in coming to agreements on contentious issues (Sandman & Gregori, 2020). Also, Audrey Tang, a member of g0v, became the country's digital minister and this showed the integration between power and politics through digital technology in an unprecedented way to create a new political decision-making approach (Miller, 2020). The movement emerged in response to concerns about government transparency and accountability. It aims to bridge the gap between citizens and government by leveraging technology to provide access to government data. It also encourages collaboration between the public and government officials, as it advocates for open government, open data and citizen participation. The members of the g0v community develop and maintain various digital platforms and tools that enable citizens to access and analyse government data, collaborate on policy issues, and contribute to public decision-making.

The members of g0v actively contribute to various open-source projects related to open data, civic engagement and accountability. These collaborative projects often require the creation of tools and platforms to help people better understand government data. This allows citizens to take part in governance more effectively. For example, the g0v community developed a platform that makes information from the Accounting and Statistics Office in Taiwan easily accessible to the public. The platform is highly engaging and user-friendly, enabling the Taiwanese public to review every item in the government budget (Tang, 2019). This initiative set a new standard for active civic technology communities and is recognised as a world-class example for civic engagement (Ho, 2018; Tang, 2019). Overall, the g0v movement in Taiwan is a testament to how technology and citizen collaboration can promote transparency, accountability and participatory governance (Fig. 7.5).

## vTaiwan

Taiwan provides an online consultation platform, vTaiwan, which was developed to engage citizens in policy making. It started when a former minister without portfolio, Jaclyn Tsai visited a g0v hackathon event and urged the development of a digital media platform that can enhance collaboration and communication between citizens and the government (Ho, 2020). Taiwanese digital activists responded quickly, producing the vTaiwan platform (v stands for virtual), which allows governmental agencies to open ongoing disputes for public deliberation (Ho, 2020). Since the development of the platform, the discussion of issues goes through a process of opinion-collecting, reflection and

**Fig. 7.5** The g0v Venn
Diagram (Source:
https://g0v.asia/)

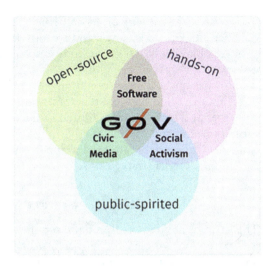

then legislation. The vTaiwan platform is software designed to collect and interpret multistakeholder consensus, integrated with the digital tool of politics and it enables Taiwanese users to put forward policies transparently, involve multiple stakeholders in the deliberation process, and propose suggested political changes (Sandman & Gregori, 2020). It employs a deliberative approach, combining online and offline discussions to address complex societal issues (Ho, 2020; Sandman & Gregori, 2020), such as the regulation of Uber, Airbnb and online alcohol sales, and allows citizens, experts, industry representatives, and government officials to collaborate and find consensus on policy matters (Ho, 2020). With its support for these digital platforms, Taiwan has been forward-looking in terms of using digital governance to gain support for politics.

Taiwan has shown significant strides in digital governance by embracing open data initiatives, developing digital infrastructure and promoting e-participation (Ho, 2020; Tang, 2019; Schneider, 2019). Another current Taiwanese initiative is investment in education technology, as national education reforms have transformed the idea of digital or media literacy, preferring instead to digital or media competence in which citizens become co-creators (Ministry of Digital Affairs, 2023). This initiative could bring multiple learnings together with the advancement of digital media technologies such as resource transfer and collaboration to learn digitally (Ministry of Digital Affairs, 2023). These digital affordances in Taiwan present the capability of digital media platforms to support a more participatory and inclusive democratic system. By leveraging technology and engaging citizens through social media, the vTaiwan platform is software designed to collect and interpret multistakeholder consensus, integrated with the digital tool of politics. The government has created opportunities for dialogue, bridged the gap between policymakers and the public, and incorporated diverse perspectives into decision-making processes.

Taiwan's experiment offers valuable lessons for other countries seeking to enhance citizen participation and trust in democratic governance through digital media platforms. This case study emphasises the use of fast and secure technologies for broad civic and political involvement. Cyber warfare and disinformation have been continuing to threaten democracy systems globally, but Taiwan is one country that can share the civic and political engagement strategies and tactics it has adopted in the battle against misinformation, disinformation and repression. Further allies with the same reasoning and intentions need to collaborate to develop a resilient global neighbourhood using such digital media strategies.

## CONCLUSION

This chapter has demonstrated the significance of social media within the political space. Social media and its platforms have grown from periphery tools that are used in communication spaces and have moved towards an integral communication strategy of political leaders. As the case studies have shown, the use of social media has applied from politically motivated events (Occupy, MeToo, etc.) and for political elections themselves. This has been helpful with spreading information and gaining traction, but as we've also seen, it is problematic when misinformation, disinformation and political interference are included in the process. In this scenario, we move from the egalitarian capacity of public communication tools and towards the inhibition of democracy through lies and manipulation. There are also positive humanity traits as described through the Taiwan case, where social media has encouraged positive engagement with politics and government.

The common ground to emerge from this exploration of social media within politics is that the concept of the border or region disappears quite quickly. In the US and UK moments, international political interference has been proven. For The Occupy and MeToo movements, for example, they attracted significant international attention, pushing these causes onto the main stage. In the following chapter, we unpack the internationalisation of social media further, specifically looking at international relations.

## REFERENCES

Allcott, H., & Gentzkow, M. (2017). Social Media and Fake News in the 2016 Election. *Journal of Economic Perspectives, 31*(2), 211–236.

Aral, S. (2020). *The Hype Machine: How Social Media Disrupts Our Elections, Our Economy, and Our Health—And How We Must Adapt*. Crown.

Arugay, A. A. (2022). *Stronger Social Media Influence In The 2022 Philippine Elections*. ISEAS-Yusof Ishak Institute.

Azlan, N. A. (2020). The Hashtag Game: Disrupting Dissent during the Bersih 4 Protest. Asiascape: Digital. *Asia, 7*(1–2), 69–87.

Bakker, T. P., & De Vreese, C. H. (2011). Good News for the Future? Young People, Internet Use, and Political Participation. *Communication Research, 38*(4), 451–470. https://doi.org/10.1177/0093650210381738

Bennett, W. L., & Segerberg, A. (2012). The Logic of Connective Action: Digital Media and the Personalization of Contentious Politics. *Information, Communication & Society, 15*(5), 739–768. https://doi.org/10.1080/1369118X.2012.670661

Bennett, W. L., & Segerberg, A. (2013). *The Logic of Connective Action: Digital Media and the Personalization of Contentious Politics.* Cambridge University Press.

Bleznak, B. (2018). *Ryan Gosling and More Hollywood Men Who Have Spoken out Against Harvey Weinstein.* Cheatsheet.

Boyd, D. (2014). *It's Complicated: The Social Lives of Networked Teens.* Yale University Press.

Bradshaw, S., & Howard, P. N. (2018). Challenging Truth and Trust: A Global Inventory of Organized Social Media Manipulation. In *The Computational Propaganda Project* (Vol. 1, pp. 1–26).

Bradshaw, S., Campbell-Smith, U., Henle, A., Perini, A., Shalev, S., Bailey, H., & Howard, P. N. (2021). *Country Case Studies Industrialised Disinformation: 2020 Global Inventory of Organised Social Media Manipulation.* Oxford Internet Institute.

Bräuchler, B. (2020). Bali Tolak Reklamasi: The Local Adoption of Global Protest. *Convergence, 26*(3), 620–638.

Brown, N. E. (2019). Me Too Political Science: An Introduction. *Journal of Women, Politics & Policy, 40*(1), 1–6.

Cadwalladr, C., & Graham H. E. (2018). How Cambridge Analytica Turned Facebook 'Likes' into a Lucrative Political Tool. March 18, 2018. *The Guardian.* Retrieved from https://www.theguardian.com/technology/2018/mar/17/facebook-cambridge-analytica-kogan-data-algorithm

Carmi, E., Yates, S. J., Lockley, E., & Pawluczuk, A. (2020). Data Citizenship: Rethinking Data Literacy in the Age of Disinformation, Misinformation, and Malinformation. *Internet Policy Review, 9*(2), 1–22.

Castells, M. (2015). *Networks of Outrage and Hope: Social Movements in the Internet Age.* Wiley.

Cillizza, C. (2016). President-elect Donald Trump's Cataclysmic, History-Making Upset. *Washington Post.* Retrieved July 20, 2020, from https://www.washington-post.com/news/the-fix/wp/2016/11/09/how-donald-trump-pulled-off-an-upset-of-cataclysmic-historic-proportions/

Clough, J. (2015, February 18). KPK vs Polri: Children of Light and Children of Darkness. *The Jakarta Post.* Retrieved from http://www.thejakartapost.com/news/2015/02/18/kpk-vs-polri-children-light-and-children-darkness.html#sthash.sGBz0k5D.dpuf

Conover, M. D., Ferrara, E., Menczer, F., & Flammini, A. (2013). The Digital Evolution of Occupy Wall Street. *PLoS One, 8*(5), e64679.

Constanza-Chock, S. (2012). *Preliminary Findings: Occupy Research Demographic and Political Participation Survey 2012.* Occupy Research.

Cruz, C. (2019). Social Networks and the Targeting of Vote Buying. *Comparative Political Studies, 52*(3), 382–411.

Denning, D. E. (2001). Activism, Hacktivism, and Cyberterrorism: The Internet as a Tool for Influencing Foreign Policy. In *Networks and Netwars: The Future of Terror, Crime, and Militancy* (pp. 239, 288).

Downing, J. D. (Ed.). (2010). *Encyclopaedia of Social Movement Media*. Sage Publications.

Earl, J., & Kimport, K. (2011). *Digitally Enabled Social Change: Activism in the Internet Age*. MIT Press.

Edingo, D. B. (2021). Social Media, Public Sphere and Counterpublics: An Exploratory Analysis of the Networked Use of Twitter During the Protests Against the Citizenship Amendment Act in India. *The Journal of Social Media in Society, 10*(2), 76–101.

Feltwell, T., Vines, J., Salt, K., Blythe, M., Kirman, B., Barnett, J., et al. (2017). Counter-Discourse Activism on Social Media: The Case of Challenging "Poverty Porn" Television. *Computer Supported Cooperative Work (CSCW), 26*, 345–385.

Freedom House, F. H. (2012). *Indonesia Freedom on the Net 2012*. Freedom House.

Freedom House, F. H. (2015). *Indonesia Freedom on the Net 2015*. Freedom House.

Freelon, D., McIlwain, C. D., & Clark, M. (2016). *Beyond the Hashtags: # Ferguson, # BlackLivesMatter, and the Online Struggle for Offline Justice*. Centre for Media & Social Impact, American University, Forthcoming.

Gabrillin, A. (2015, January 28). Save KPK! Sehatkan Polri! Jokowi di Pihak Siapa? (Save KPK! Cleanse POLRI! Jokowi in which side?). *Kompas*. Retrieved from http://nasional.kompas.com/read/2015/01/28/13315301/.Save.KPK.Sehatkan.Polri.Jokowi.di.Pihak.Siapa

Gerbaudo, P. (2017). Social Media Teams as Digital Vanguards: The Question of Leadership in the Management of Key Facebook and Twitter Accounts of Occupy Wall Street, Indignados and UK Uncut. *Information, Communication & Society, 20*(2), 185–202.

Gillies, J. (2018). "Feel the Bern": Marketing Bernie Sanders and Democratic Socialism to Primary Voters. In *Political Marketing in the 2016 US Presidential Election* (pp. 97–112).

González-Bailón, S., Borge-Holthoefer, J., Rivero, A., & Moreno, Y. (2011). The Dynamics of Protest Recruitment Through an Online Network. *Scientific Reports, 1*(1), 1–7.

Guesmi, H. (2021). The Social Media Myth about the Arab Spring. *Aljazeera*. Retrieved December 22, 2023, from https://www.aljazeera.com/opinions/2021/1/27/the-social-media-myth-about-the-arab-spring

Gutiérrez, M. (2018). Proactive Data Activism. In *Data Activism and Social Change* (pp. 49–105). Palgrave Pivot.

Han, B. C., & Elemia, C. (2022). *Beijing's Global Media Influence*. Philippines, Freedom House. Retrieved from https://freedomhouse.org/country/philippines/beijings-global-media-influence/2022#footnote44_7qejo0l

Haryanto, A. (2022). Bagaimana Sistem Pemilihan Presiden di Filipina & Apa Bedanya? (What is the Presidential Election System in the Philippines and What is the Difference?). May 11, 2022. Tirto.id. Retrieved August 24, 2023, from https://tirto.id/grWm

Hasen, R. L. (2017). The 2016 US Voting Wars: From Bad to Worse. *William & Mary Bill of Rights Journal, 26*, 629.

Heuer, H. (2021). Helping People Deal with Disinformation—A Socio-Technical Perspective. In *Workshop Human Aspects of Misinformation at CHI 2021, May 08–13, 2020, Yokohama, Japan*. ACM, New York, USA.

Heuer, H., & Breiter, A. (2018, September). Trust in News on Social Media. In *Proceedings of the 10th Nordic Conference on Human-Computer Interaction* (pp. 137–147).

Hidayat, R. (2015, January 24). Setelah #SaveKPK, Kini #SavePOLRIKPK Mencuat Di Twitter. *ANTARAKALTENG News*. Retrieved April 20, 2024, from https://kalteng.antaranews.com/berita/237545/setelah-savekpk-kini-savepolrikpk-mencuat-di-twitter

Ho, M. S. (2018). From Mobilization to Improvisation: The Lessons from Taiwan's 2014 Sunflower Movement. *Social Movement Studies, 17*(2), 189–202.

Hu, M. (2020). Cambridge Analytica's Black Box. *Big Data & Society, 7*(2), 2053951720938091.

Indranila, A. (2022). Social Media As A Counter Space For The Motherhood Community In Creating Counter-Hegemony. *Jurnal Komunikasi Indonesia, 11*(2), 4.

Internews. (2021). Disconnected: Information Dynamics in BARMM during the COVID-19Pandemoc: An Information Ecosystem Assessment by Internews. *Internews*, February 2021. Retrieved from https://internews.org/sites/default/files/2021-02/Internews_Information_Ecosystem_Assessment_BARMM_Philippines2.pdf

Jamil, A., & Doktoralina, C. M. (2016). The Save KPK Movement: A Framing Analysis of Coverage in Indonesian News Media Surrounding the KPK and Police Dispute. *Mediterranean Journal of Social Sciences, 7*(3 S1), 229.

Johns, A., & Cheong, N. (2019). Feeling the Chill: Bersih 2.0, State Censorship, and "Networked Affect" on Malaysian Social Media 2012–2018. *Social Media + Society, 5*(2), 2056305118821801.

Juris, J. S. (2012). Reflections on# Occupy Everywhere: Social Media, Public Space, and Emerging Logics of Aggregation. *American Ethnologist, 39*(2), 259–279.

Kang, C., & Goldman, A. (2017). In Washington Pizzeria Attack, Fake News Brought Real Guns. *New York Times, 5*, A1.

Kavada, A. (2010). Activism Transforms Digital: The Social Movement Perspective. In M. Joyce (Ed.), *Digital Activism Decoded: The New Mechanism of Change* (pp. 101–118). International Debate Education Association.

Kavada, A. (2015). Creating the Collective: Social Media, the Occupy Movement and its Constitution as a Collective Actor. *Information, Communication & Society, 18*(8), 872–886.

Kemp, S. (2020). *Digital 2019: Philippines. We Are Social and Hootsuite*. Retrieved May 20, 2022, from https://datareportal.com/reports/digital-2019-philippines

Kriesi, H., Lavenex, S., Esser, F., Matthes, J., Bühlmann, M., Bochsler, D., & Esser, F. (2013). Mediatisation as a Challenge: Media Logic Versus Political Logic. In *Democracy in the Age of Globalization and Mediatization* (pp. 155–176).

Lang, C. (2018). 'It's Not Good.' Mark Zuckerberg Discusses the #DeleteFacebook Campaign. Time. Retrieved February 20, 2023, from https://time.com/5210799/mark-zuckerberg-addresses-delete-facebook-campaign-after-cambridge-analytica/

Lee, F. L., & Chan, J. M. (2015). Digital Media Activities and Mode of Participation in a Protest Campaign: A Study of the Umbrella Movement. *Information, Communication & Society, 19*(1), 4–22. https://doi.org/10.1080/1369118X.2015.1093530

Lee, M., & Murdie, A. (2021). The Global Diffusion of the# MeToo Movement. *Politics & Gender, 17*(4), 827–855.

Lim, M. (2017). Freedom to Hate: Social Media, Algorithmic Enclaves, and the Rise of Tribal Nationalism in Indonesia. *Critical Asian Studies, 49*(3), 411–427. https://doi.org/10.1080/14672715.2017.1341188

Mahditama, I. (2012, November 30). Taking it to the Internet: People Power 2.0. *The Jakarta Post*. Retrieved April 6, 2024, from http://www.thejakartapost.com/news/2012/11/30/taking-it-internet-peoplepower-20.html

Maher, T. V., Martin, A., McCarthy, J. D., & Moorhead, L. (2019). Assessing the Explanatory Power of Social Movement Theories across the Life Course of the Civil Rights Movement. *Social Currents, 6*(5), 399–421.

Martin, G. (2015). *Understanding Social Movements*. Routledge.

Mayer, W. G. (Ed.). (2008). *The Swing Voter in American Politics*. Rowman & Littlefield.

Mazoyer, B. (2020). *Social Media Stories. Event Detection in Heterogeneous Streams of Documents Applied to the Study of Information Spreading across Social and News Media* (Doctoral dissertation, Université Paris-Saclay).

Mcclain, C. (2021). 70% of U.S. Social Media Users Never or Rarely Post or Share About Political, Social Issues. *Pew Research Centre*. Retrieved August 20, 2024, from https://www.pewresearch.org/short-reads/2021/05/04/70-of-u-s-social-media-users-never-or-rarely-post-or-share-about-political-social-issues/

Mendes, K., Ringrose, J., & Keller, J. (2018). #MeToo and the Promise and Pitfalls of Challenging Rape Culture Through Digital Feminist Activism. *European Journal of Women's Studies, 25*(2), 236–246.

Mendoza, M. E. H. (2022). Philippine Elections 2022: TikTok in Bongbong Marcos' Presidential Campaign. *Contemporary Southeast Asia: A Journal of International and Strategic Affairs, 44*(3), 389–395.

Merle, R. (2018). A Guide to the Financial Crisis—10 Years Later. *Washington Post*. September 10, 2018. Retrieved November 11, 2023, from https://www.washingtonpost.com/business/economy/a-guide-to-the-financial-crisis%2D%2D10-years-later/2018/09/10/114b76ba-af10-11e8-a20b-5f4f84429666_story.html

Miller, C. (2020). How Taiwan's Civic Hackers Helped Find a New Way to Run the Country, Guardian Newspaper, 27 September 2020.

Ministry of Digital Affairs, Ministry of Digital Affairs. (2023). *Interview with Reuters—Andrius Sytas and Taiwan Ministry of Digital Affairs—Audrey Tang*. Updated on January 25, 2023. Retrieved from https://moda.gov.tw/en/press/background-information/3639

Nimmo, C., Eib, S., & Ronzaud, L. (2020). Operation Naval Gazing: Facebook Takes Down Inauthentic Chinese Network. *Graphika*. Retrieved from https://public-assets.graphika.com/reports/graphika_report_naval_gazing.pdf

Ong, J. C., & Cabañes, J. V. A. (2018). Architects of Networked Disinformation: Behind the Scenes of Troll Accounts and Fake News Production in the Philippines. Architects of Networked Disinformation: Behind the Scenes of Troll Accounts and Fake News Production in the Philippines.

Ong, J., Tapsell, R., & Curato, N. (2019). *Tracking Digital Disinformation in the 2019 Philippine Midterm Election*. Public report available at www.newmandala.org/disinformation

Osborne-Gowey, J. (2014). What is Social Media. *Fisheries, 39*(2), 55–55.

Osiurak, F., Rossetti, Y., & Badets, A. (2017). What is an Affordance? 40 Years Later. *Neuroscience & Biobehavioral Reviews, 77*, 403–417.

Papacharissi, Z. (2015). *Affective Publics: Sentiment, Technology, and Politics*. Oxford University Press.

Persily, N. (2017). Can Democracy Survive the Internet? *Journal of Democracy, 28,* 63.

Poell, T., & Borra, E. (2012). Twitter, YouTube, and Flickr as Platforms of Alternative Journalism: The Social Media Account of the 2010 Toronto G20 Protests. *Journalism, 13*(6), 695–713.

Porta, D. D., & Mosca, L. (2009). Searching the Net: Web sites' Qualities in the Global Justice Movement. *Information, Communication & Society, 12*(6), 771–792. https://doi.org/10.1080/13691180802109063

Postill, J. (2018). Populism and Social Media: A Global Perspective. *Media, Culture & Society, 40*(5), 754–765.

Quan-Haase, A., Mendes, K., Ho, D., Lake, O., Nau, C., & Pieber, D. (2021). Mapping# MeToo: A Synthesis Review of Digital Feminist Research Across Social Media Platforms. *New Media & Society, 23*(6), 1700–1720.

Quitzon, J. (2021). *Social Media Misinformation and the 2022 Philippine Elections.* Centre for Strategic and International Studies.

Rahutomo, R., Budiarto, A., Purwandari, K., Perbangsa, A. S., Cenggoro, T. W., & Pardamean, B. (2020, August). Ten-Year Compilation of# Savekpk Twitter Dataset. In *2020 International Conference on Information Management and Technology (ICIMTech)* (pp. 185–190). IEEE.

Reynaldo, K. M. T. (2021). *Tracing the Roots of Disjunction: Dutertismo and the Discourse of Liberal Democracy in the Philippines* (Doctoral dissertation, Lingnan University).

Richter, F. (2021). Statista. Disinformation and Manipulation Is Rife on Social Media, Statista, Felix Ritcher, viewed 14 June 2021. https://www-statista-com.access.library.unisa.edu.au/chart/11831/manipulation-tactics-on-social-media/

Sandman, J., & Gregori, B. (2020). How Tech Tools Helped Taiwanese Activists Turn a Social Movement Into Real Policy Change. New America. October 1, 2020. Retrieved from https://www.newamerica.org/weekly/how-tech-tools-helped-taiwanese-activists-turn-social-movement-real-policy-change/

Savirani, A. (2015). Jokowi's Supporters are Starting to Doubt the 'Indonesian Obama'. Retrieved November 11, 2014, from http://theconversation.com/jokowis-supporters-are-starting-to-doubt-the-indonesian-obama-37843

Schneble, C. O., Elger, B. S., & Shaw, D. (2018). The Cambridge Analytica Affair and Internet-Mediated Research. *EMBO Reports, 19*(8), e46579.

Schneider, F. (2019). Digital Democracy in Taiwan: The Sunflower Movement and its Legacies. *Taiwan Fellowship Report,* 1–20.

Soebagjo, N. (2015). Indonesia's Political Elites Drive Anti-graft Agency into Jeopardy. Australia. Retrieved from http://theconversation.com/indonesias-political-elites-drive-anti-graft-agency-into-jeopardy-37364

Suwana, F. (2018). *Digital Media and Indonesian Young People: Building Sustainable Democratic Institutions and Practices* (Doctoral dissertation, Queensland University of Technology).

Suwana, F. (2019). What Motivates Digital Activism? The Case of the Save KPK Movement in Indonesia. *Information, Communication & Society,* 1–16.

Tang, A. (2019). Inside Taiwan's New Digital Democracy. March 12, 2019. *The Economist.* Retrieved July 31, 2023, from https://www.economist.com/open-future/2019/03/12/inside-taiwans-new-digital-democracy

Tapsell, R. (2015). Indonesia's Media Oligarchy and the "Jokowi Phenomenon". *Indonesia,* (99), 29–50.

Teehankee, J. C. (2023). *Beyond Nostalgia: The Marcos Political Comeback in the Philippines*. Saw Swee Hock Southeast Asia Centre London School of Economics and Political Science (LSE).

Teehankee, J. C., & Thompson, M. R. (2016). The Vote in the Philippines: Electing a Strongman. *Journal of Democracy, 27*(4), 125–134.

Tufekci, Z. (2014). Big Questions for Social Media Big Data: Representativeness, Validity and Other Methodological Pitfalls. In *Proceedings of the International AAAI Conference on Web and Social Media* (Vol. 8, No. 1, pp. 505–514).

Vaccari, C., Valeriani, A., Barberá, P., Bonneau, R., Jost, J. T., Nagler, J., & Tucker, J. A. (2015). Political Expression and Action on Social Media: Exploring the Relationship Between Lower-and Higher-Threshold Political Activities Among Twitter Users in Italy. *Journal of Computer-Mediated Communication, 20*(2), 221–239.

Vromen, A. (2007). Australian Young People's Participatory Practices and Internet Use. In *Young Citizens in the Digital Age* (pp. 111–127). Routledge.

Wafiq, N. H. (2023). *Media Manipulation and the Marcos Dynasty*. Modern Diplomacy. Retrieved February 2, 2023, from https://moderndiplomacy.eu/2023/05/15/media-manipulation-and-the-marcos-dynasty/

Wardle, C., & Derakhshan, H. (2018). Thinking about 'Information Disorder': Formats of Misinformation, Disinformation, and Mal-information. In *Journalism, 'Fake News'& Disinformation* (pp. 43–54).

Wijayanto, Suwana, F., & Sardini, N. H. (2022). Cyber Terror, the Academic Anti-corruption Movement and Indonesian Democratic Regression. *Contemporary Southeast Asia, 44*(1), 31–55.

Wolfsfeld, G., Segev, E., & Sheafer, T. (2013). Social Media and the Arab Spring: Politics Comes First. *The International Journal of Press/Politics, 18*(2), 115–137.

Wong, A. C. (2022). Philippine Elections and the Politics Behind It. *The Interpreter*.

Zeng, J. (2019). You say# MeToo, I say# MiTu: China's Online Campaigns against Sexual Abuse. In *# MeToo and the Politics of Social Change* (pp. 71–83).

Zeng, J. (2020). # MeToo as Connective Action: A Study of the Anti-sexual Violence and Anti-sexual Harassment Campaign on Chinese Social Media in 2018. *Journalism Practice, 14*(2), 171–190.

## CHAPTER 8

# Social Media and International Relations

## INTRODUCTION

The role of social media across governments has many different faces—internal, external, positive, negative and everything in between. When looking at international relations, it's important to examine the role social media plays for government officials, how it might take a position between government and other governments, and its tactical deployment within times of war. As with all social media use, there are several categories of users including government officials, countries, individuals, and of course user citizens, each with their unique perspective on the role social media should play and how it can be harnessed for that perspective. And building on the last chapter, the role that dis and misinformation plays in the communication process.

In the first section of this chapter, we build on the concept introduced in Chap. 7 to unpack international relations. We begin by examining the role social media plays within interference campaigns within politics.

## INTERFERENCE CAMPAIGNS

Interference campaigns are organised efforts to manipulate or disrupt political, social or economic processes in a foreign country, often to advance the interests of another country or group. These campaigns can take many forms, but typically involve using disinformation, propaganda, and other forms of covert influence to shape public opinion, sow division, or create chaos. Propaganda and disinformation activities are produced and disseminated by trolls or paid Internet users who are individuals or groups that publish inflammatory, counterfeit, or deceptive information by social media chat channels, online discussion forums, and comment parts on other platforms and sites (Tolmach et al., 2023; Paul & Matthews, 2016). These messages produce enormous amounts and disseminate across many channels via traditional and online media.

J. Hutchinson et al., *Social Media in Society*, https://doi.org/10.1007/978-3-031-66360-4_8

One form that interference campaigns can take is social media manipulation. This manipulation involves using trolls, bots, fake accounts and other techniques to spread false information or amplify specific messages on social media platforms. They also involve many layers and components, as running a foreign interference campaign is more intricate than just purchasing $100,000 in Facebook ads to activate a few lines of computer code or buying a network of fake Twitter accounts to make topics trend and influence online discourse (Jankowicz, 2020; McCombie et al., 2020). One case study we will examine in this chapter is Russia's use of information warfare, which started in the United States in 2014, intensified after the 2016 election, and continues today.

In 2016, at the beginning of the 58th US presidential election campaign, social media platforms were bombarded with posts originally from the Internet Research Agency (IRA), a commercial trolling farm which conducts online operations in the name of the Russian government (Prier, 2020). The IRA aimed to influence the election and achieve the ascent of Donald Trump by promoting radical groups and spreading misinformation. Its posts were widespread, coordinated and often false, using inauthentic accounts, misleading memes, and the mobilisation of discontentment—tactics which were applied in Ukraine before they were used on Americans (Patrikarakos, 2017; Dawson & Innes, 2019)—and with them, this troll farm changed the discourse of the 2016 US election. When Americans interacted with and shared the sensational, divisive, and groundless information they saw online during Trump's election campaign, they were in fact sharing content produced by and posted from fake accounts run by the IRA (Jankowicz, 2020), a point which highlights the vulnerability of the political process to outside influence and bad actors on social media. While the effect of the IRA's online campaign by Russia is difficult to measure, there is no doubt that it was able to impact the election result and was willing to move to significant spans to achieve that goal.

The IRA also ran another, similar disinformation campaign during the 2016 US presidential elections (Jacoby, 2018). This campaign aimed to create legitimate distrust between Americans. It also aimed to find genuine faults in American society and magnify them. Its primary focus was finding people who were open to this content and would promote it unthinkingly. It strategically utilised Facebook's advertising system and posted false and contrived advertisements on different social media platforms. The organisation did utilise the good and bad information through social media, like they uploaded fake political posts designed to position Hillary Clinton in a bad light, organised online rallies and rolled out hashtags (McCombie et al., 2020). Also, the campaign or posts targeted Hillary Clinton by leaking her emails and accusing her of cheating during the elections, and persuaded people to join fake community groups by arguing that she did not deserve the Black vote (McCombie et al., 2020). As polarisation targets fear and anger to gain engagement, time, and shares—and therefore increased advertising value—social media feed algorithms also promoted these posts, meaning that more people saw them.

The IRA controlled over 30,000 fake accounts across Facebook and Twitter (Robertson, 2018), and the company was found guilty by the US National Intelligence Council (2017) of using these accounts for 'the deployment of information warfare', illegal cyber operations, direct targeting of voters, and the creation of increased support for extreme and destabilising political movements. It exploited the mass communication enabled by social media or the shareability functions of social media sites to direct people's attention and foster their hatred on specific topics, including social and political ones. Thus, while Russia did not 'hack' the vote as has been claimed, they did influence voters to support the candidate they believed would demonstrate the weaknesses of the democratic system and create instability at the American political situation like that of other countries. For example, Russia employed social media platforms to enable conspiracy views and rumours and disseminate counterfeit news in some countries in Europe and America (Sampson, 2018). Interference campaigns have become more familiar in recent years, particularly in response to tensions between major geopolitical powers. These situations pose a significant threat to the integrity of the democratic process and can undermine trust in both institutions and the media. As a result, governments and other organisations need to detect and counter these campaigns, including covert efforts to influence critical actors or groups such as activists, educators, policy makers, politicians, reporters/journalists, and community and religious leaders to advance the interests of the campaigns' organisers.

Another form of interference campaigns involves the stealing and dissemination of sensitive information via hacking and leaks, to embarrass or undermine groups or individuals. In Estonia, as in the US, James Bond–style international intrigue was replaced by hackers and hard drives (Jankowicz, 2020). The fact that Estonia is the member in the NATO (North Atlantic Treaty Organization) and invokes article number five of its alliance with the issue from using force against it (Azad et al., 2023). Moreover, in 2007, Russia resorted to a grey zone fight, employing cyber war against Estonia in DoS (denial-of-service) bombards a server with traffic, making a website or resource inaccessible and DDoS (distributed denial-of-service) attacks multiple computers or machines to flood a targeted resource (Ottis, 2008; Azad et al., 2023), with several strategies employed, including User Data Protocol/UDP flood (a cyber-attack where a large number of UDP packets are sent to a server to crush its ability to process and respond), distorted web queries, email spam, etc. (Ottis, 2008).

However, Estonia prevailed against its attackers and became one of the great leaders in cybersecurity and Internet technologies, pioneering 'e-residency' for foreigners via Skype and enabling its citizens to vote, pay taxes, and bank online long before such practices were commonplace in other countries (Jankowicz, 2020), and Estonia's cyber invasions with more advanced networks that can be considered a national security threat (Ottis, 2008).

## War in the Grey Zone: The Social Media Weaponisation

The social media weaponisation involves using social media tools and platforms to manipulate public opinion, spread disinformation and influence social, political, and military outcomes. This phenomenon has been growingly recognised and studied recently and is known as 'grey zone warfare'. The term 'war in the grey zone' describes the tactics or strategies employed by government and non-government actors to exploit the ambiguity and non-attribution of cyber operations, including those conducted through social media platforms, and grey zone warfare strategies include using comprehensive and integrated campaigns to pursue political purposes, staying below the red line of escalation to a traditional conflict, and reaching steady movement towards an objective rather than scaling decisive campaigns to achieve immediate results (Azad et al., 2023). Grey zone warfare involves employing representatives and numerous tools in ambiguous strategies to achieve expected objectives (Azad et al., 2023), as the operations may not clearly cross the verge of war because of the ambiguity of international law, actions and attribution, or the effect of the actions does not explain a reaction (Dowse & Bachmann, 2019). Cyber warfare is preferable for players operating in grey zone warfare because it covers actions in a fog of disorder. At the same time, cyber warfare can also establish high-impact invasions with minimum resources (Poornima, 2020). In addition, the types of communication campaigns common in grey zone warfare rely on the digital media technologies, and many of communication tactics, as typical marketing, and advertising campaigns, which makes them particularly insidious and challenging to tackle.

As previously noted, Russia is one of the strategists for this form of cyber warfare, as it uses social media to directly influence people in other countries (Jankowicz, 2020; Prier, 2020). Russia has also weaponised social media to weaken its opposition, as indicated by its increased reliance on non-military tools to challenge the West in situations such as in the US (Chin, 2019), and its extensive usage of grey zone warfare opposed to Ukraine, which has included underground and destruction operations prepared to organise the foundation for a full-scale attack (Azad et al., 2023). Another example of a nation using disinformation to discredit its political opponents is Indonesia (Kwok, 2017; Tapsell, 2018): in the 2014 presidential election, due to a massive use of black campaigns and hostile information deliberately designed to deceive voters and reduce candidates' electability using digital media, people become aware of the capacity of online hoaxes to affect elections (Tapsell, 2018; Ong & Tapsell, 2020). For example, Indonesia had 'Saracen' as an organised campaign conducted by fake news factories (Smith & Perry, 2022) against political targets such as political parties, their supporters and opposition actors (Santosa et al., 2018; Ong & Tapsell, 2020). Cracking down on disinformation sources in some countries could be challenging, as these sources vary broadly.

Some key aspects of social media weaponisation, disinformation/misinformation and propaganda in the grey zone are social media platforms that provide powerful tools and features for spreading false information, propaganda, and conspiracy theories (Prier, 2020). Yet not all disinformation spreads via social media using paid Facebook advertising or Twitter bots. Much of this kind of material is also shared by members of civil society—ordinary citizens themselves—and this is aided by the increasing popularity of digital chat platforms like WhatsApp and Telegram (Baulch et al., 2022; Ong & Tapsell, 2020). Even ordinary news posts and social media trends can efficiently distribute a message to a broad group outside their social networks, and malicious players can use social media capability to spread messages using numerous media forms and on multiple social media platforms, aiming to garner coverage in the mainstream media (Prier, 2020). Controlling social media trends is a powerful way of spreading information. Techniques like search engine optimisation (SEO) and trends control will become standard in future cyber wars as practices of producing conflict, spreading false information and generating an opponent to change their course of action or results. Government and non-governmental actors can create and strengthen narratives to manipulate public opinion and advance their agendas. Thus, these online weapons could become a threat to democracy.

Disinformation is described as information that is intentionally fabricated to misinform other people, as the information is not only incorrect but that the individual or people spreading it knows it is false, so it is a deliberate, purposeful lie that points to people getting misinformed by malicious actors (Wardle & Derakhshan, 2017). In the past, disinformation campaigns have been fabricated to sow distrust and influence public opinion. They are propagated by groups or agencies that aim to manipulate information to convey specific, often political, ideologies, and utilise the clustering and homophilous properties intrinsic to social media to disseminate targeted false messages to clusters of people on social media platforms. The term 'clustering' describes the way in which social media platforms are made up of highly connected groups. These dense social media clusters are generally organised based on similar interests, socioeconomic backgrounds, and demographics (Sinan, 2020). Clustering relates to homophily in that one is the result of the other, with homophilous people forming highly connected clusters. Conversely, homophily reflects the adage 'birds of a feather flock together' (Sinan, 2020, p. 67), or more specifically, it reflects how people with similar interests and beliefs form ties. Clustering and homophily are prevalent on social media platforms featuring group communication including Twitter, Facebook and WhatsApp, and they are also observed in the geographic composition of nationalities within a region, like how ethnic groups cluster within neighbourhoods. These two key characteristics of social media are frequently exploited to spread disinformation and/or misinformation, which can lead to interference campaigns. As Sinan states, they explain why social media supports increased political polarisation, echo chambers, fake news distribution, and produces enormous returns on marketing assets (Sinan, 2020, p. 64). People who run disinformation campaigns using targeted false content use social media platforms' clustering and homophily characteristics. Their content gains popularity and credibility from those clusters and, as a result, is spread faster and more efficiently by them.

Another factor which makes disinformation more believable to social media users within a highly dense cluster is the way in which volume often creates an increased perception of credibility. The social media characteristics and the tendency of social media users have been manipulated and weaponised by various groups and agencies, including the IRA. Mejias and Vokuev (2017) stated that:

> Private ownership of the social media platforms used during protests can make it easy to co-opt and weaken social movements. More importantly, this analysis suggests that civil society can become an active participant in its own dis-empowerment by engaging in an excess of self-interested communication through the production and consumption of disinformation (p. 1029).

Moreover, the current discussion of the weaponisation of social media acknowledges that while people are not often persuaded to believe something contrary to their personal beliefs, those personal beliefs can be amplified, and people can be manipulated to act on them by social media posting or content. Regarding the Ukraine case, the IRA fabricated false information designed to paint the Ukrainian government and president in a poor light. This disinformation was spread through sheer volume, with inaccurate content being shared by sources that appeared trustworthy to the clusters the IRA targeted. Similarly, the IRA mimicked homophilous individuals on social media, sharing targeted clusters that would accept content it knew for the 2016 US presidential election. In both instances, the disinformation and propaganda divided individuals and undermined democratic processes. This case showed Russia employing psychological elements such as social connections on social media (homophily), reposting tweets by credible or prominent people, or accepting phone calls, individual texts, and emails that come from the networking circle to push their opponents to obtain incorrect information that becomes 'a truth' (Jakubowski, 2019). These examples demonstrate that social media has been influential in multiplying information warfare operations.

The IRA is still at work running disinformation campaigns; however, since the findings against them regarding the 2016 US presidential election, there is greater international awareness of how this agency operates and which propaganda techniques it utilises. Propaganda refers to disseminating narratives extensively and fast, which social media mainly enables through bots or apps that cause news items to become trends, increasing the probability they will leap to become news in mainstream media. Finally, the networked character of social media allows saturation in multiple media outlets, which lends credibility to false stories (Jakubowski, 2019). According to Watts, Russia is the first to incorporate the "entire social media ecosystem" into its information operations

(Watts, 2017). There is now an increased recognition of how clusters can serve as echo chambers to proliferate disinformation in an information vacuum.

Disinformation campaigns present a danger to an economy and even a nation, as "distortion of information erodes trust in the socio-political institutions that are the fundamental fabric of democracy: legitimate news sources, scientists, experts, and even fellow citizens" (Bliss et al., 2020, p. 1). The clustering and homophily typical of social media have been exploited by the IRA and organisations like it to spread disinformation to those clusters which are the most susceptible to being persuaded by it. Both clustering (i.e. the tendency for people to form highly connected groups) and homophily (i.e. the way people form groups based on similarity) are exploited by that IRA agency. The information disintegration of common perspective is continued throughout homophilous characters, and it is formed as a group—like the characteristics of online communities we explored in Chap. 4. People or individuals with similar views on social media sites grow to cluster into secluded networking elements of group polarisation. (Sinan, 2020; Sunstein, 2002; Zollo et al., 2017; Del Vicario et al., 2016). Homophily also enables the validation bias towards inaccurate claims that reinforce the group and prevent the discussion of disagreeing information (Zollo et al., 2017) and it can develop quickly through online (Aral et al., 2009).

The circumstance might initiate a demonstrative shift in networking in the accumulation of social media data, as agents who had followed primary news sources consult the information among their networks in a decentralised style (Bentley et al., 2023). The agencies fabricate disinformation to incite confusion and scepticism, but while they continue to spread disinformation using such means, their campaigns can be rendered less effective when others understand their concepts and tactics. In addition to the tactics described above, the IRA employed social media within Russia to encourage people to protest in support of Putin remaining president.

There are three ways in which the IRA operates in disinformation campaigns, like Cyber conflict and digital rights researchers argued that first, IRA operatives create fake activist organisations, pages, and community groups on social media. They create social media profiles for people who do not exist, and these accounts become members of the fake organisations they have set up and/or fans of their fake pages, so that they can like, comment on, and share the content those organisations and pages produce. Finally, the IRA produces social media profiles for fake regional news companies, which broadcast pieces that the fake organisations and social media profiles they have created above can share via social media platforms (Francois & Lin, 2021). In 2014, the IRA orchestrated its anti-Ukrainian-government campaign by spreading disinformation using various fake Facebook pages, statuses, comments, videos, photos, etc. Therefore, social media could be utilised by states for their actions to weaken those who oppose them, as these social media weapons could be more potent than military tools to interfere with other countries' political and social situation.

Political interference campaigns such as the one in which the IRA worked to create false perceptions of and defame Ukraine's President and government, the Ukrainian military, and other government officials (Jacoby, 2018; Bacio Terracino & Matasick, 2022) have been increasing. Social media provide grey zone actors with free access to platforms from which they can share any kind of misinformation and disinformation and it can be easily spread worldwide (Jacoby & Zuckerberg, 2018). In this example, the IRA implemented a strategy that included spreading memes and creating a high volume of social media page interactions in support of the Russian occupation of Crimea (Al-Rawi & Rahman, 2020).

Through social media posts, comments and shares, the IRA achieved not only the spread of disinformation, but cyber-attacks, terrorist actions and the intimidation of Ukrainian residents (MFAU, 2019). Social media was its primary tool due to the rapidity with which information can travel from one user's screen to another. This allowed the IRA to create a campaign that grasped the attention of a large-scale audience—predominantly one made up of Russian citizens in Russia as a point that demonstrates how information warfare aims, and works, to exacerbate pre-existing tensions and differences among citizens. This campaign led to its audience initiating action against the Ukrainian government and in favour of the Russian government (MFAU, 2019). The influence Russia gained over Ukraine via the IRA's social media campaigns was not something the world had ever seen before, and provided an initial demonstration of how effectively social media platforms are an instrument in political campaigns due to the features, dimensions, scale and advance information network systems and social media platforms configuration, which use emotional appeal to improve screen time, distribution and engagement with information or malicious disinformation.

## DEFENCE AGAINST INFORMATION WARFARE

As noted above, information warfare is a broad term encompassing the many different strategies and tactics that nations, organisations or individuals can apply to achieve strategic goals through the dissemination of information or disinformation. It can take many forms, including propaganda, cyber-attacks, social engineering, news and social media manipulation (Prier, 2020), and information manipulation to achieve a strategic or battlefield advantage over opponents during traditional warfare.

Furthermore, research suggests that the Internet enables information manipulation and interference approaches wherein information is weaponised to interrupt democratic social and political processes (Whyte, 2020). This process is explicitly worrying because short-term developments promise to support powerful interference operations (Whyte, 2020). Moreover, information warfare has demonstrated that effective activities targeted at democratic countries and their citizens happen mainly on social media platforms. Social media platforms are used by strategic key players to gain followers, from dedicated followers and neutral audience, develop their standpoints, and disseminate information that can tarnish opponents' reputation.(Singer & Brooking, 2018; Nissen, 2015). In other words, information warfare has influenced political decisions and activities in the social and political spheres.

The malicious influence activities considered online information warfare strategies could be encouraged in non-military environments like the news sources, social media platforms, and ordinary civilian discussions as they are not typically part of traditional military processes (Ventsel et al., 2023). Information warfare involves the participation of civil society who consciously or unconsciously disseminate and amplify the information through various social media channels, and it is often perceived as just international online activities (Jantunen, 2018, p. 37; Nissen, 2015). Social media influencers usually remain undercover, producing events such as demonstrations and meetings to achieve their expected outcome rather than publicising their messages directly (Ventsel et al., 2023). Many citizens felt that the efforts to deceive online users by information warfare violated the integrity of the democratic voting system and affected their confidence in the U.S. political system (Ross et al., 2022). Meanwhile, Trump supporters felt that the allegations of collusion between President Trump and Putin undermined his victory, constraining his ability to form relations with Russia and effectively govern. Therefore, the potential consequences of harmful information influencing activities in this way include increased instability and polarisation and decreased social cohesion among citizens.

Information warfare is interchangeable with other forms or warfare, such as political information warfare. While there are thoughts of activities beyond the hatred expressed between states (Whyte, 2020), some differences exist. For example, political warfare affects using the whole scope of instruments of state authority rather than army service power alone to ensure state interests in transnational affairs (Whyte, 2020). Information warfare, on the other hand, involves using ICT (information and communication technology) to disrupt or damage the reputation, credibility and operations of individuals, organisations and even nations. Therefore, there is a requirement from multistakeholder including civil society organisations, education organisations, business, government and platform technology companies to create changes and innovation, with the goal of creating a more secure political environment for online users. However, it remains essential to conduct personal verifications and investigations of information online to avoid being misinformed.

For the U.S. context, Facebook is a social networking service and social media company owned by the United States technology business, Meta, that also owns Instagram and WhatsApp. The development of algorithms and proliferation of sources on digital platforms can make it challenging to assess quality and trustworthiness of news and information. Moreover, these platforms have evolved to include the expansion tools to share information but also disinformation and information warfare (Boyd-Barrett, 2019). To avoid foreign interference utilising Facebook, this platform proposed to label political advertisements and enact a new paid ads system that required anyone conducting ads related to political campaigns, civil rights, the economy, immigration, and others to prove their U.S. residency by supplying social security and government-issued identification information (Boyd-Barrett, 2019).

Despite the changes that social media platforms have developed, the spread of correct information and disinformation will continue. The inability to distinguish between accurate and misleading news and information can rapidly spread harmful disinformation. This problem is further compounded by malicious entities intentionally distributing false and deceptive information whose sole aim is to damage individuals and society (ACMA, 2020). Therefore, verifying information online and recognising the signs of disinformation are essential. Bergstrom and West (2021) recommend that users question the source of information and consider how the source may know the information they are sharing. Other recommendations for identifying misinformation include being wary of unfair comparisons, evading verification bias (the tendency to accept information compatible with previous beliefs) and considering multiple explanations when seeking to understand a pattern or event. Lastly, the ability to analyse online content or information is essential. Fact-checking sources of information are also crucial to ensure the validity of information online and avoiding making decisions based on misinformation.

The reasonable deniability of civic actions in available information warfare, especially online operations, creates challenges regarding diplomatic responses to attacking states. For example, in its use of information warfare against Taiwan, the People's Republic of China aims to manipulate public opinion and psychology. Media is a crucial tool for exploiting public opinion, agenda setting, creating political views and political actors, and structure narratives in specific ways. Deception and manipulation occur mainly through media personnel. Furthermore, China's restricted control of its media drives its contestation of any international players to infiltrate and distribute the effect. Taiwan's unrestricted media region alongside the multiple Chinese news sources causes its citizens to be exposed to information warfare operations, in particular with the popular opinion and psychological propaganda campaigns by China (Haciyakupoglu & Ang, 2019; Nimmo et al., 2020) and IRA psychological warfare (Jakubowski, 2019). Social media combines psychological aspects of current situations as both the reality and the hyperbola are vital for information warfare operations. This combination is basically because people are triggered by desire and fear that could be activated by Information that includes religion, race and other worries in vulnerable audiences. America can be seen as a strong country because of its multiculturalism, technological advancement and dedication to freedom of speech, yet it is also vulnerable to information warfare as demonstrated through the continued efforts by Russia (Jakubowski, 2019).

Beijing's priority on attention and ability to transfer information across different countries is highly demonstrated by its growth of the People's Liberation Army of Strategic Support Force in China. These government services integrate digital technology, digital occupying and warfare conditions and have potentially influenced the complex conditions that complicate warfare for the Taiwan Ministry of National Defense (Grossman et al., 2017). Therefore, the 2017 Quadrennial Defense Review (QDR) by the Taiwan government focused on Taiwan's armed forces and its ability to problematise and prevent attack. However, Taiwan is continuing to leverage its democratic system, access to global social media, nationwide solidarity, and citizen-military associations to integrate its citizens as a powerful force against the Chinese information warfare campaigns (Haciyakupoglu & Ang, 2019). Thus, Taiwan has been enhancing its national defence capabilities to maintain their cyber security and counter information warfare.

Another example of information warfare from China that can broaden our awareness of information operations originating from China is Operation Naval Gazing. The areas in which China's information warfare unfolds include, most prominently, information manipulation via the power of traditional media owners, influencers, reporters and spying actions (Haciyakupoglu & Ang, 2019). Some of its content reflects Chinese messages openly or secretly regarding issues like life during COVID-19, Hong Kong demonstrations, and Taiwan's autonomy issues (Nimmo et al., 2020). Therefore, China's strategic use of invisible support has promoted its political content in those countries and cemented its position in international competition with the United States especially regarding territorial disputes in the South China Sea. China's People's Liberation Army (PLA) could also show a range of cyberspace, blockade and marketing campaigns designed to force Taiwan to comply with unification or push Taiwan's leadership to the negotiation table on the PRC's terms (Grossman et al., 2017). In any case, the PRC would seek to prevent potential United States intervention in any Taiwan contingency campaign (Grossman et al., 2017).

Chinese propaganda processes started in 2016 with online postings about Taiwan, with information specifically designed to attack President Tsai Ing-Wen (Nimmo et al., 2020). This attack presents a crucial situation for other foreign states: intentional misinformation or disinformation may be only part of a more comprehensive information warfare campaign that integrates online and offline strategies (Haciyakupoglu & Ang, 2019). These numerous conditions of information warfare create a substantial danger to Taiwan (Grossman et al., 2017), the country's ongoing defence strategy includes preparing to resist China invasion (Haciyakupoglu & Ang, 2019). However, countries targeted by information warfare campaigns may need to focus on prevention and response to their citizens rather than combating them.

Defending against information warfare requires nations to take a multifaceted approach that addresses both the technical and the non-technical aspects of the problem. Some potential strategies include improving citizens' digital media literacy, enhancing platform security and content moderation, promoting transparency in online advertising, and fostering international cooperation to establish norms and regulations regarding cyber operations.

The distribution of disinformation and misinformation is problematic nation-wide and worldwide as they attempt to damage democratic systems and pro-cesses (Suwana, 2021; Kahne & Bowyer, 2017; Carson & Titcomb, 2017). Exposure to various standpoints is also critical for maintaining the democratic system and society. At the same time, there are growing issues regarding the discriminatory condition of social and political conversations at regional, national and global levels (Kahne et al., 2012).

Digital media literacy skills are essential for handling information warfare. Citizens must, therefore, be equipped with the digital media literacy necessary to have critical thinking, analytical skills, evaluation and determine online information, and produce facts as part of everyday habits (Suwana, 2021). Further education could be organised and prepared in a method that encour-ages everyone to identify the primary classifications of misinformation and dis-information, critically analyse diverse type of media content and make informed decisions when they face possible misinformation and disinformation (Ventsel et al., 2023). Finally, addressing the weaponisation of social media requires a multi-faceted approach involving governments, social media platforms, civil society and individuals, all promoting and encouraging digital media literacy.

Responding to grey zone warfare by improving citizens' digital media liter-acy will train citizens to recognise and critically assess the news or content they consume and share. This ability will teach them to understand the different types of media bias, identify the sources of information and recognise when news or stories are being manipulated for political (or any other) purposes. As the arena of war and propaganda expands to encompass the digital environ-ment, therefore there is an urgency to enlighten society and equip them with the skills of digital media literacy (Wineburg & Reisman, 2015; Bjola & Pamment, 2016; Sanderson & Ecker, 2020; Aslam et al., 2020). Digital media literacy is helpful to distinguish between facts or information, misinformation, and disinformation. Therefore, the skill-based view of digital media literacy needs to be well developed. At the same time, media scholar Buckingham (2019) argues that the individual's ability to assess media content also relies on their knowledge of its content and understanding of the topics, not just how media present it. Buckingham (2019) also implies that a much more compre-hensive vision of media literacy focuses on developing critical thought about the media's economy, ideology and cultural proportions will be critical to countering information warfare rather than managing fake news or other types of misinformation as trends.

In another study of information warfare between Russia and Estonia, some researchers have found that enhancing digital media literacy for information warfare involves two elements which are skills and knowledge. Conversely, information warfare requires organising in citizens the same adaptable skills that encourage learners to navigate their daily news sources effectively; on the other hand, it expands citizens' knowledge of the qualities and diversity of the contemporary media sphere and makes them aware that this public sphere can be deceptive in the nationwide security context. (Ventsel et al., 2023). Thus, the state must implement digital media literacy education as part of the broader push towards developing and maintaining national security and resilience, not only as part of the education of citizens.

Collaboration with multistakeholders is also necessary, as no nation can defend against information warfare alone. Collaboration with other organisations, including government agencies, NGOs, and private companies, can enable groups to pool their resources, share information, and develop more effective online strategies to defend against information warfare (Suwana, 2021). The future of multistakeholder diplomacy to promote national online security will start with ongoing multistakeholder collaborations that will mature over years (Ciglic & Hering, 2021). As noted above, digital media literacy is required during the present age of increasing fake information and hybrid warfare (Aslam et al., 2020). Thus, multistakeholders must engage in arena of misinformation or disinformation, which enable multidisciplinary cooperation to tackle the current international crisis (Bulger & Davison, 2018). The multi-collaboration between multistakeholder should be facilitated to maintain endurable, adaptable national digital media literacy training programmes that respond to global society (Suwana, 2021). Responses to information warfare include the technological, the regulatory, and the social, but so far, they have focused on traditional national security and defence tropes, including deterrence, detection, denial, disruption, and destruction. Below, we catalogue some of these approaches based on government and research institute reports and critique them. We argue that digital media literacy and building trust and social cohesion must play a more significant role nationally, regionally, and globally to combat global information warfare and support digital diplomacy internationally.

## DIGITAL DIPLOMACY

Digital diplomacy is a new term referring to the creation of public diplomacy in which digital media technologies, such as social media sites and digital technology channels, are used to conduct diplomatic relations and advance foreign policy objectives. It has become increasingly important in recent years as digital media technologies have transformed how people communicate and interact. The definition of digital diplomacy has developed across several fields. Some definitions that state social media usage for diplomatic purposes are minimalistic. However, others are expansive, describing digital diplomacy as a method for operating change through digital media tools and online collaboration (Bjola & Pamment, 2016). Scholars have also stated that digital diplomacy as a concept should be expanded, both due to the digitalisation of public diplomacy (Manor & Pamment, 2019) and to emphasise how digital media affects all diplomatic practice strategies and how the process of digitising diplomacy occurs over time and includes trial and error (Spry, 2020).

There are several online mechanisms in digital diplomacy; one scholar stated that this mechanism is related to content creation, the sender's status, audience reception, frequency and online networking authority (Cassidy, 2018). As both a field of public diplomacy and a diplomatic technique, digital diplomacy also includes some essential tools and techniques. These include social media campaigns, online forums and discussion platforms, virtual meetings and conferences, data analysis and visualisation, and digital storytelling (Cassidy, 2018; Rashica, 2018). Governments and diplomats can also use digital media technologies to monitor and track public opinion, analyse trends and patterns, and identify potential areas of conflict or cooperation. The cumulative analysis showed that these mechanisms and practices operate as a form for creating standardisation that reflects the style of diplomatic signalling that enables the Minister of Foreign Affairs (MFA) to project their crisis messages most effectively and have authorised and unauthorised agents in the digital age (Cassidy, 2018). This situation shows how diplomatic processes signalling how diplomatic players currently employ social media during crises and they have developed due to social media usage and function as a beneficial instrument in evaluating.

Digital diplomacy is also helpful for other purposes, such as maintaining prestige (Manor & Pamment, 2019; Spry, 2020), promoting national interests, fostering international cooperation, engaging with foreign audiences (Rashica, 2018), and managing diplomatic crises using effective communication strategies (Cassidy, 2018). It can help governments and diplomats collaborate more comprehensively with multistakeholders. And it has become increasingly important in recent years as digital technologies have transformed how people communicate, interact, and engage with digital media. For example, given what we now know about Russian disinformation active actions, it is clear that the United States Information Agency was never truly prepared to engage in information warfare; thus, rather than operating a Russian style of online campaign using harmful propaganda, the agency has become a public diplomacy platform promoting a positive online message (Prier, 2020), suggesting that governments and diplomats can employ digital media technologies to monitor and track public opinion, analyse trends and patterns, and identify potential areas of conflict or cooperation.

Digital media usage by some governments and institutions can show actual transformations in the digital media use of other nations' Ministries of Foreign Affairs (MFA). Another example of situation is Russia's social media usage to distribute narratives that challenged the environment and occasions in Crimea Peninsula, which showed some MFAs embrace narrative techniques for public diplomacy online (Manor & Manor, 2019). Some issues are figures via social media to explain global events to digital citizens and connect diverse digital diplomatic initiatives to legible foreign policy (Manor & Manor, 2019). Overall, digital diplomacy has the potential to become a powerful tool for advancing foreign policy objectives and promoting international cooperation. However, it also poses challenges and risks, such as privacy issues and cyber threats, and there is potential for miscommunication or misinterpretation (Cassidy, 2018). Governments and diplomats, therefore, need to collaborate and develop more precise strategies and guidelines for how to use digital media technologies as part of diplomatic relations.

Digital diplomacy would not substitute traditional diplomacy, but it can quickly and effectively maintain a government's international relations. Lately, it has become an essential element of foreign policy, as it enables advancing foreign procedure goals, develops transnational alignments, and involves individuals who have never placed themselves in the global embassies (Rashica, 2018). The online environment and algorithmic factors of the communication structure in which it operates have potentially conducted diplomatic assignments via social media is developed by (Spry, 2020). Consequently, many governments have developed the ability to progressively use digital diplomacy via digital campaigns and strategies using specific narratives to interpret world events and international policies and freely present their standpoints and national policies. In some governments, diplomatic actors have utilised social media to retweet and re-share content in international online networks to create more robust signals on a crisis and display their commitment and position on relevant international opinions (Cassidy, 2018). Despite high expectations for social media participation as a chance to conduct new public diplomacy, MFAs have often preferred control and traditionalism in their strategies (Spry, 2020).

Social media amplified the engagement within diplomatic and international matters. Diplomats must remain applicable and robust online and offline players, as they could benefit from digital advancement in all conditions in the increasingly pervasive tendency of social media platforms (Cassidy, 2018). This chapter also outlines how social media's usefulness varies significantly from nation to nation but can be generally considered more beneficial in countries with younger and smaller populations. It examines how social media has impacted normal diplomatic relations between nations, using case studies and highlighting best and worst practices, and indicates how governments, MFAs, diplomats, and other institutions had to adopt digital diplomacy quickly and then become over-enthusiastic about its potential.

## GLOBAL CIVIL SOCIETY AND SOCIAL MEDIA

Civil society must proactively discuss what comprises sufficient online political behaviour and what is not permitted. The discussion is important to know how society can distinguish between public diplomacy and influence processes, political movement and information manipulation, and cyber-hack and online political activism (Gleicher et al., 2021). The straightforward line between genuine and deceitful strategies in this digital environment must still be more apparent. Therefore, society should collectively resolve how to tackle these problems without damaging freedom of speech values and principles of democracy. At the same time, the term global civil society refers to the various networks of civil society organisations (CSOs), non-governmental organisations

(NGOs), and any other groups that work to promote and maintain democracy, social justice, human rights, and sustainable development on a global scale.

Digital and social media have profoundly impacted global civil society, increasingly allowing civil society members to engage with broader, more diverse, international and global stakeholders and providing new opportunities for advocacy, mobilisation and communication (Suwana, 2019). Social media platforms have enabled the rise of new types of online activism (Suwana, 2018, 2019), hashtag campaigns (Baer, 2016; Stornaiuolo & Thomas, 2017) and online petitions (Suwana, 2018), which have helped raise awareness of various social, political, and environmental issues (Gerbaudo, 2017; Joyce, 2010; Suwana, 2018). Previous research has shown that activists utilise online activism they were following on social networks such as Instagram, TikTok, YouTube and Facebook, and above all Twitter, YouTube and Twitch (Munoz, 2021). Social media sites have allowed civil society members to reach wider audiences, build communities, and coordinate activities across geographic boundaries. Civil society has thus become an emerging power that has the capacity to advocate for openness—a vital element of the Internet and digital media (Wijayanto et al., 2022).

One of the key benefits of social media for global civil society is that it enables rapid, ubiquitous and decentralised communication. Social media platforms allow NGOs and social movements to disseminate information, organise events, and mobilise supporters faster than traditional media. Social media also plays an essential part in the work of NGOs and social movements going forward. However, social media's ubiquitous character is often exploited in information-based conflict, and its position may become more significant (Van Niekerk & Maharaj, 2013). For example, social media platforms have generated enormous amounts of data and other relations, posting and forwarding instant messages, uploading photos, and connecting users, enabling live information distribution and extensive contemporary communication media, social networks, and engagement (Lin, 2022). These social media activities have been significant in contexts where traditional media are tightly controlled or censored, especially in authoritarian countries, as social media tends to be less restricted and edited. However, the sheer volume of information and content on social media can also make it difficult for NGOs and social movements to cut through the noise and reach their target audiences. In addition, large organisations often own and control social media platforms, which can limit the ability of NGOs and social movements to maintain their narratives to inform society.

Government agencies must support civil society's understanding of transnational political warfare and educate them regarding the components and safety implications of critical technologies such as AI (Artificial Intelligence) and 5G technology. In Australia, the Digital Industry Group (DIGI) has stated that multiple stakeholders must perform and commit to handling misinformation and disinformation, including public officers, educators, civil society, and media organisations (Carson & Fallon, 2021). This report also stressed the importance of collaboration between these stakeholders and endorsed regulations promoting digital media literacy to secure advanced participation of accountability and responsibility to fight misinformation and disinformation (Carson & Fallon, 2021). Therefore, it would be a regional, national and global multistakeholder initiative and cooperation for tackling the misinformation and disinformation together.

Another significant regional initiative, this time from European countries, has been the development of the European Centre of Excellence for Countering Hybrid Threats, an intergovernmental think-tank to which member states supply funding and governance that transmits a bread of academic and professional perspectives on political warfare trends and the activities of Russia and China (Mansted, 2019). At a global level, there is First Draft, a collaboration of media, academies, online platforms, and civil society bodies that aspire to recognise misinformation established on the virtue of information and disinformation with connection to the activities and manners of those who spread it, and the content's tendency to generate harmful situation (Carson & Fallon, 2021).

Like these organisations, CSOs can contribute to verifying and disseminating accurate information. In several countries, fact-checking initiatives by CSOs and independent journalists have helped to counter misinformation and disinformation campaigns. For example, in the national context, Indonesia has several agencies collaborated nationally and locally on identifying and characterising disinformation campaigns, including the National Indonesian Police, the Ministry of Information Communication and Technology (KOMINFO), the anti-hoax civil society organisation MAFINDO, the Indonesia State Intelligence Agency, and the Indonesia Cyber and Crypto Agency (Carson & Fallon, 2021). In 2018, several instruments established a committed website of Stophoax in collaboration with Indonesian anti hoax civil society organisation (MAFINDO) and the Google News Initiative, which seeks to enlighten Indonesian society about differentiating fake information (Carson & Fallon, 2021). KOMINFO also designated the nationwide digital media literacy programme Siberkreasi in 2017 to educate the public and share awareness about distributing dangerous content online (Suwana, 2021). This programme is essential, as research has shown that 19 of the top 50 active social media profiles can distribute information to counter disinformation meaning that citizens are prominent participants in distributing information. However, they must also grow their critical roles in countering disinformation (Golovchenko et al., 2018).

The Indonesian government's response to misinformation has shown the crucial situation that needs to be addressed, such as the state's use of multistakeholder collaboration programmes and civil society coalition-building to tackle misinformation and increase digital literacy levels in all societies, which are thus worth replicating elsewhere. As public awareness of foreign states' political warfare campaigns can start one to benefit democratic fundamentals by mobilising a broader society to manage security risk and responding to intervention and coercion, civil society itself must become a far more significant part of the national security conversation, not least to ensure that it supports proper judgments and feels the policy process is fair and reasonable (Mansted, 2019). Any meaningful attempt to fight digital disinformation must acknowledge that civil society is a new information curator and creator of narratives and counter-narratives with truth and credibility values and engage with citizens and civil society groups, both to raise awareness and mobilise (Golovchenko et al., 2018) and to educate them about digital media literacy (Suwana, 2021).

## CONCLUSION

Establishing a disinformation campaign and placing out a thousand messages is affordable because one part must work. Academics, professionals and policymakers must comprehend numerous elements and respond from multiple issue angles as efforts must successfully counter disinformation campaigns (Bulger & Davison, 2018). Some recommendations reflect this complexity, calling for collaboration across multistakeholder and multidisciplinary studies while believing the asymmetric recommendation of a digital media literacy response to fake news (Bulger & Davison, 2018).

From the above case, digital media literacy programmes designed to tackle the impacts of cyber warfare need to be expanded, with more efforts made to enhance literacy, including the ability to recognise untruth information and remove harmful content in the digital environment. However, this complex situation still requires involvement and cooperation from multistakeholders nationally and internationally. Innate in the multiplication of the requirement for diverse parties to inform society about what and why they are distributing online fake news (Carson & Fallon, 2021). Governments that address online misinformation and disinformation must also welcome their society's experience and expertise of the conditions under which information warfare occurs, along with those with specific expertise and knowledge, including academics/scholars, policymakers, and professionals. Civil society needs help from national and international organisations and governments to mitigate the impact of information warfare on social media. Therefore, collaborative coalitions between multistakeholders must be designed to improve fact-checking, deliver digital literacy education to the public and monitor national and international issues, along with completing other activities. There is an urgent need to continue a comprehensive effort and multi-pronged approach to tackling information warfare is essential.

## REFERENCES

Al-Rawi, A., & Rahman, A. (2020). Manufacturing Rage: The Russian Internet Research Agency's Political Astroturfing on Social Media. *First Monday*.

Aral, S., Muchnik, L., & Sundararajan, A. (2009). Distinguishing Influence-based Contagion from Homophily-driven Diffusion in Dynamic Networks. *Proceedings of the National Academy of Sciences, 106*(51), 21544–21549.

Aslam, S., Hayat, N., & Ali, A. (2020). Hybrid Warfare and Social Media: Need and Scope of Digital Literacy. *Indian Journal of Science and Technology, 13*(12), 1293–1299.

Azad, T. M., Haider, M. W., & Sadiq, M. (2023). Understanding Gray Zone Warfare from Multiple Perspectives. *World Affairs, 186*(1), 81–104.

Bacio Terracino, J., & Matasick, C. (2022). Disinformation and Russia's War of Aggression against Ukraine: Threats and Governance Responses. *Organization for Economic Co-Operation and Development.* Retrieved May 14, 2023, from https://www.oecd.org/ukraine-hub/policy-responses/disinformation-and-russia-s-war-of-aggression-against-ukraine-37186bde/

Baer, H. (2016). Redoing Feminism: Digital Activism, Body Politics, and Neoliberalism. *Journal Feminist Media Studies, 16*(1), 17–34.

Baulch, E., Matamoros-Fernández, A., & Suwana, F. (2022). Memetic Persuasion and WhatsAppification in Indonesia's 2019 Presidential Election. *New Media & Society*, 14614448221088274.

Bentley, R. A., Horne, B., Borycz, J., Carrignon, S., Shteynberg, G., Vidiella, B., & O'Brien, M. J. (2023). Cultural Evolution, Disinformation, and Social Division. *Adaptive Behavior.* https://doi.org/10.1177/10597123231186432

Bergstrom, C. T., & West, J. D. (2021). *Calling Bullshit: The Art of Skepticism in a Data-Driven World.* Random House Trade Paperbacks.

Bjola, C., & Pamment, J. (2016). Digital Containment: Revisiting Containment Strategy in the Digital Age. *Global Affairs, 2*(2), 131–142.

Bliss, N., Bradley, E., Garland, J., Menczer, F., Ruston, S. W., Starbird, K., & Wiggins, C. (2020). An Agenda for Disinformation Research. arXiv preprint arXiv:2012.08572.

Boyd-Barrett, O. (2019). Fake News and 'RussiaGate' Discourses: Propaganda in the Post-truth Era. *Journalism, 20*(1), 87–91.

Buckingham, D. (2019). Teaching Media in a "Post-truth" Age: Fake News, Media Bias and the Challenge for Media/Digital Literacy Education. *Cultura y Educación, 31*(2), 213–231.

Bulger, M., & Davison, P. (2018). The Promises, Challenges, and Futures of Media Literacy. *Journal of Media Literacy Education, 10*(1), 1–21.

Carson, A., & Fallon, L. (2021). Fighting Fake News: A Study of Online Misinformation Regulation in the Asia Pacific.

Carson, J., & Titcomb, J. (2017). What is Fake News? Its Origins and How It Grew in 2016. *The Telegraph*, January 12. Retreived from http://www.telegraph.co.uk/technology/0/fake-newsorigins-grew-2016/

Cassidy, J. (2018). *Digital Diplomatic Crisis Communication: Reconceptualising Diplomatic. Signalling in an Age of Real Time Governance.* Working Paper No 3. Oxford Digital Diplomacy Research Group. Retrieved from http://www.qeh.ox.ac.uk/sites/www.odid.ox.ac.uk/files/DigDiploROxWP3.pdf

Chin, W. (2019). Technology, War and the State: Past, Present and Future. *International Affairs, 95*(4), 765–783.

Ciglic, K., & Hering, J. (2021). A Multi-stakeholder Foundation for Peace in Cyberspace. *Journal of Cyber Policy, 6*(3), 360–374.

Dawson, A., & Innes, M. (2019). How Russia's Internet Research Agency Built its Disinformation Campaign. *The Political Quarterly, 90*(2), 245–256.

Del Vicario, M., Vivaldo, G., Bessi, A., Zollo, F., Scala, A., Caldarelli, G., & Quattrociocchi, W. (2016, December). Echo Chambers: Emotional Contagion and Group Polarization on Facebook. *Scientific Reports, 6*, 37825. https://doi.org/10.1038/srep37825

Dowse, A., & Bachmann, S. D. (2019). Explainer: What is 'Hybrid Warfare' and What is Meant by the 'Grey Zone'? *The Conversation, 17.*

Francois, C., & Lin, H. (2021). The Strategic Surprise of Russian Information Operations on Social Media in 2016 in the United States: Mapping a Blind Spot. *Journal of Cyber Policy, 6*(1), 9–30.

Gerbaudo, P. (2017). Social Media Teams as Digital Vanguards: The Question of Leadership in the Management of Key Facebook and Twitter Accounts of Occupy Wall Street, Indignados and UK Uncut. *Information, Communication & Society, 20*(2), 185–202. https://doi.org/10.1080/1369118x.2016.1161817

Gleicher, N., Franklin, M., Agranovich, D., Nimmo, B., Belogolova, O., & Torrey, M. (2021). Threat Report. The State of Influence Operations 2017–2020 (May). *Facebook.*

Golovchenko, Y., Hartmann, M., & Adler-Nissen, R. (2018). State, Media and Civil Society in the Information Warfare over Ukraine: Citizen Curators of Digital Disinformation. *International Affairs, 94*(5), 975–994.

Grossman, D., Chase, M. S., & Ma, L. (2017). *Taiwan's 2017 Quadrennial Defense Review in Context.* RAND Corporation.

Haciyakupoglu, G., & Ang, B. (2019). Civilians in the Information Operations Battlefront: China's Information Operations in the Taiwan Straits. In *DRUMS: Distortions, Rumours, Untruths, Misinformation, and Smears* (pp. 83–113).

Jacoby, J. (2018). The Facebook Dilemma EP:1. Frontline, Television Program, PBS, 25th of November.

Jacoby, J., & Zuckerberg, M. (2018). The Facebook Dilemma EP:2. Frontline, Television Program, PBS, 25th of November.

Jakubowski, G. (2019). What's Not to Like? Social Media as Information Operations Force Multiplier. *Joint Force Quarterly, 3*, 8–17.

Jankowicz, N. (2020). *How to Lose the Information War: Russia, Fake News, and the Future of Conflict.* Bloomsbury Publishing.

Jantunen, S. (2018). *Infosõda.* SA Kultuurileht.

Joyce, M. (2010). Introduction: How to Think About Digital Activism. In M. Joyce (Ed.), *Digital Activism Decoded: The New Mechanics of Change* (pp. 1–14). International Debate Education Association.

Kahne, J., & Bowyer, B. (2017). Educating for Democracy in a Partisan Age: Confronting the Challenges of Motivated Reasoning and Misinformation. *American Educational Research Journal, 54*(1), 3–34.

Kahne, J., Lee, N. J., & Feezell, J. T. (2012). Digital Media Literacy Education and Online Civic and Political Participation. *International Journal of Communication, 6*, 24.

Kwok, Y. (2017). Where Memes Could Kill: Indonesia's Worsening Problem of Fake News. Time, January 6, 2017. Retrieved from http://time.com/4620419/indonesia-fake-news-ahok-chinese-christian-islam/

Lin, Y. (2022). Social Media for Collaborative Planning: A Typology of Support Functions and Challenges. *Cities, 125*, 103641.

Manor, I., & Manor, I. (2019). A Discussion of the Digitalization of Public Diplomacy. *The Digitalization of Public Diplomacy*, 323–352.

Manor, I., & Pamment, J. (2019). Towards Prestige Mobility? Diplomatic Prestige and Digital Diplomacy. *Cambridge Review of International Affairs, 32*(2), 93–131.

Mansted, K. (2019). *Activating People Power to Counter Foreign Interference and Coercion.* Policy Options Paper (Australian National University: National Security College).

McCombie, S., Uhlmann, A. J., & Morrison, S. (2020). The US 2016 Presidential Election & Russia's Troll Farms. *Intelligence and National Security, 35*(1), 95–114.

Mejias, U. A., & Vokuev, N. E. (2017). Disinformation and the Media: The Case of Russia and Ukraine. *Media, Culture & Society, 39*(7), 1027–1042.

Ministry of Foreign Affairs of Ukraine, MFAU. (2019). *10 Facts You Should Know About the Russian Military Aggression Against Ukraine.* December 19, viewed June 24 2021. Retrieved from https://mfa.gov.ua/en/10-factsyou-should-know-about-russian-military-aggression-against-ukraine

Munoz, P. (2021). The Birth of the Influencer-Activist, a Case Study from Spain.

Nimmo, B., Eib, C. S., & Ronzaud, L. (2020). Operation Naval Gazing. Facebook Takes Down Inauthentic Chinese Network. Graphika.

Nissen, T. E. (2015). *The Weaponization of Social Media: Characteristics of Contemporary Conflicts.* Royal Danish Defence College.

Ong, J. C., & Tapsell, R. (2020). Mitigating Disinformation in Southeast Asian Elections: Lessons from Indonesia, Philippines and Thailand. *NATO Strategic Communications.* Retrieved from https://www.stratcomcoe.org/mitigating-disinformation-southeast-asianelections

Ottis, R. (2008). Analysis of the 2007 Cyber Attacks Against Estonia from the Information Warfare Perspective. In *Proceedings of the 7th European Conference on Information Warfare* (p. 163). Academic Publishing Limited.

Patrikarakos, D. (2017). *War in 140 Characters: How Social Media is Reshaping Conflict in the Twenty-First Century.* Hachette UK.

Paul, C., & Matthews, M. (2016). *The Russian "Firehose of Falsehood" Propaganda Model: Why It Might Work and Options to Counter It.* RAND Corporation. Retrieved June 1, 2022, from https://www.rand.org/pubs/perspectives/PE198.html

Poornima, B. (2020). *The Shades of Cyberwarfare in the Era of Grey Zone Conflicts.* The Centre for Land Warfare Studies (CLAWS). Retrieved March 6, 2024, from https://www.claws.in/the-shades-of-cyberwarfare-in-the-era-of-grey-zone-conflicts/

Prier, J. (2020). Commanding the Trend: Social Media as Information Warfare. In *Information Warfare in the Age of Cyber Conflict* (pp. 88–113). Routledge.

Rashica, V. (2018). The Benefits and Risks of Digital Diplomacy. *Seeu Review, 13*(1), 75–89.

Robertson, A. (2018). Facebook Suspends 273 Accounts and Pages Linked to Russian Misinformation Agency. The Verge, 3 April. Retrieved June 19, 2021.

Ross, A. R., Vaccari, C., & Chadwick, A. (2022). Russian Meddling in US Elections: How News of Disinformation's Impact can Affect Trust in Electoral Outcomes and Satisfaction with Democracy. *Mass Communication and Society, 25*(6), 786–811.

Sampson, C. (2018). *Putin's Asymmetric Assault on Democracy in Russia and Europe: Implications for US National Security.* Simon and Schuster. Retrieved from https://www.foreign.senate.gov/imo/media/doc/FinalRR.pdf

Sanderson, J. A., & Ecker, U. K. (2020). The Challenge of Misinformation and Ways to Reduce its Impact. In P. Van Meteris, A. List, D. Lombardi, & P. Kendeou (Eds.), *Handbook of Learning from Multiple Representations and Perspectives* (pp. 461–476). Routledge.

Santosa, H. P., Hasfi, N., & Lukmantoro, T. (2018). Digital Media Unequality During the 2014th Indonesian Presidential Election. In *E3S Web of Conferences* (Vol. 73, p. 14006). EDP Sciences.

Sinan, A. (2020). *The Hype Machine: How Social Media Disrupts Our Elections, Our Economy and Our Health—And How we Must Adapt.* HarperCollins Publishers.

Singer, P. W., & Brooking, E. T. (2018). *Like War: The Weaponization of Social Media*. Eamon Dolan Books.

Smith, R., & Perry, M. (2022). Fake News and the Pandemic in Southeast Asia. *Australian Journal of Asian Law, 22*, 131.

Spry, D. (2020). *Winning Hearts and Likes*. Australian Strategic Policy Institute. Retrieved from https://www.aspi.org.au/report/winning-hearts-and-like

Stornaiuolo, A., & Thomas, E. E. (2017). Disrupting Educational Inequalities Through Youth Digital Activism. *Review of Research in Education, 41*(1), 337–357.

Sunstein, C. R. (2002). The Law of Group Polarisation. *Journal of Political Philosophy, 10*(2), 175–195. https://doi.org/10.1111/1467-9760.00148

Suwana, F. (2018). *Digital Media and Indonesian Young People: Building Sustainable Democratic Institutions and Practices* (Doctoral dissertation, Queensland University of Technology).

Suwana, F. (2019). What Motivates Digital Activism? The Case of the Save KPK Movement in Indonesia. *Information, Communication & Society, 23*(9), 1295–1310.

Suwana, F. (2021). Content, Changers, Community and Collaboration: Expanding Digital Media Literacy Initiatives. *Media Practice and Education, 22*(2), 153–170.

Tapsell, R. (2018). *Disinformation and Democracy in Indonesia*. New Mandala. Retrieved from https://www.newmandala.org/disinformation-democracy-indonesia/

Tolmach, M., Trach, Y., Chaikovska, O., Volynets, V., Khrushch, S., & Kotsiubivska, K. (2023). Artificial Intelligence in Countering Disinformation and Enemy Propaganda in the Context of Russia's Armed Aggression Against Ukraine. In *World Conference on Information Systems and Technologies* (pp. 145–152). Springer Nature Singapore.

Van Niekerk, B., & Maharaj, M. (2013). Social Media and Information Conflict. *International Journal of Communication, 7*, 23.

Ventsel, A., Hansson, S., Rickberg, M., & Madisson, M. L. (2023). Building Resilience Against Hostile Information Influence Activities: How a New Media Literacy Learning Platform Was Developed for the Estonian Defense Forces. *Armed Forces & Society*, 0095327X231163265.

Wardle, C., & Derakhshan, H. (2017). *Information Disorder: Toward an Interdisciplinary Framework for Research and Policymaking* (Vol. 27, pp. 1–107). Council of Europe.

Watts, C. (2017). Extremist Content and Russian Disinformation Online: Working with Tech to Find Solutions. *Statement Prepared for the Senate Judiciary Committee, Subcommittee on Crime and Terrorism*. Retrieved from https://www.judiciary.senate.gov/imo/media/doc/Watts%20Responses%20to%20QFRs.pdf

Whyte, C. (2020). Protectors without Prerogative: The Challenge of Military Defense against Information Warfare. *Journal of Advanced Military Studies, 11*(1), 166–184.

Wijayanto, Suwana, F., & Sardini, N. H. (2022). Cyber Terror, the Academic Anti-corruption Movement and Indonesian Democratic Regression. *Contemporary Southeast Asia, 44*(1), 31–55.

Wineburg, S., & Reisman, A. (2015). Disciplinary Literacy in History: A Toolkit for Digital Citizenship. *Journal of Adolescent & Adult Literacy, 58*(8), 636–639.

Zollo, F., Bessi, A., Del Vicario, M., Scala, A., Caldarelli, G., Shekhtman, L., Havlin, S., & Quattrociocchi, W. (2017). Debunking in a World of Tribes. *PLoS One, 12*(7), e0181821. https://doi.org/10.1371/journal.pone.018182

## CHAPTER 9

# The Dark Side of Social Media?

## INTRODUCTION

This chapter considers some of the more persistent and compelling concerns that emerge from the social media paradigm, including the ethical debates of personal privacy and young people online to the democratic and public health concerns associated with political polarisation and conspiracy theories. In doing so, we seek to identify the role of human actors as active participants in social media not only as users but also as creators. We intend to demystify some of the arguments and demonstrate what the evidence shows. We also contextualise this within a longer history of moral panic in the wake of new technologies.

This scepticism is necessary, as when it comes to reactions to new technology, history has a habit of repeating itself. From the emergence of the printing press to the introduction of television and today's social media technologies, innovation is nearly always met with a wave of panic and fearmongering regarding the harmful effects of new technology on society. Many of the fears are the same—will it affect our politics? will it damage the economy? will it corrupt the minds of the youth?

Orben (2020) refers to this pattern as the *Sisyphean cycle of technology panics*, named after the Greek myth about a prince who was doomed by the gods to repeatedly push a boulder up and down a hill for eternity. The metaphor embodies an ongoing habit among scholars, politicians and the public to rehash concerns over new technology but never learn from the inaccurate assumptions made during the last technological crisis. As we acclimatise to new technology, the public's attention is often drawn to the next big thing by which to fret over and debate. Even Socrates criticised the written word as a threat to humanity—though somewhat ironically, he too was prosecuted on the grounds that *he* was damaging the fabric of society (Drew, 2016).

This pattern does not mean technology is not impactful, or that fears should be merely dismissed. Instead, this understanding might be useful for helping to

J. Hutchinson et al., *Social Media in Society*,
https://doi.org/10.1007/978-3-031-66360-4_9

identify which issues are new, and which have been ongoing. We can, and should, look to older debates to better understand those emerging in the present day. Moral panics highlight an asymmetry in the way people evaluate emerging technologies in comparison to established ones. Nobody complains about the social harms of the printing press anymore. Moral panics emerge from social change that is often a disruptive force for the hegemonic powers in society (McRobbie & Thornton, 1995), be it governments, parents, the media, or business interests. In thinking about moral panic or resistance to technological change, we should also reflect upon who is issuing these complaints and what their vested interests might be.

One lesson we can learn, emerges from debates between theories of *technological determinism* and the *social construction of technology*. Technological determinism refers to an assumption made by scholars that technology has a direct effect that determines the way society is organised and the values that people keep. Most notably, Karl Marx and Marshall McLuhan's core arguments hinge on a technological determinist worldview (Hughes, 1994). Drew (2016) contends this worldview is indicative of a bias in scientific thinking to "parse social reality down to causes and effects". One other problem with technological determinist arguments is the tendency to remove the agency of people from these debates by framing humans as passive consumers of technology. Social construction of technology theory, as an alternative, emphasises the role of people and society in both the creation and use of technology (McQuail & Deuze, 2020, p. 133). It also encourages researchers to maintain interpretive flexibility when thinking about new media, recognising that each technology will have a different value and use case for different groups of people. As such, a conflict arising from technology like social media might be reinterpreted as a conflict between social groups that is in part *mediated* by the emerging technology.

In this chapter, we therefore identify technological panics and their debate as part of a larger ongoing process whereby media technology does not inherently create problems or have a direct effect on society. Instead, as emerging media technologies are popularised or imposed upon others, they brush up against existing vulnerabilities and insecurities in our society. As such the problems that emerge are not purely technological but also social and therefore must be addressed at a social level too.

## INFORMATION DISORDER

Of all the worries directed at social media, fake news might be the most widely discussed and debated. Two key historical events have helped solidify fake news as an issue at the forefront of the public imagination: Russian meddling in the 2016 US presidential election and the proliferation of conspiracy theories at the peak of the COVID-19 pandemic. Indeed, the fallout of the 2016 election of Trump was so significant that the phrases 'fake news' and 'post-truth' were named words of the year by Collins and Oxford dictionaries (BBC, 2016;

Flood, 2017). Among scholars, the phenomenon of fake news is often encompassed within the broader term 'information disorder'. This concept is distinct in that fake news specifically refers to the deliberate spread of false stories masquerading as legitimate news whereas information disorder encompasses a range of issues and phenomena that emerge from false information online (Lazer et al., 2018).

Information disorder can be organised into three categories: misinformation, disinformation and mal-information (Wardle & Derakhshan, 2017, 2018). Misinformation refers to when incorrect information is shared without malintent. This might be the most commonly occurring form of fake news, where users online may publish mistaken or misunderstood information. Conspiracy theories and vaccine hesitancy regarding COVID for instance are often thought to emerge from long-held beliefs and distrust regarding government and the medical industry (Jennings et al., 2021). Disinformation is when it is shared with malintent. The proliferation of false information in 2016 by the Russian troll farm, the Internet Research Agency, to try and sway the US presidential election would be considered an example of this. Mal-information is when correct information is shared but with the intent to harm. This tends to be much rarer, but examples might include leaked information about people or organisations with the intent to generate reputational damage.

Part of the perceived problem with information disorder isn't just the presence of false information but also the sheer overwhelming scale of it. In 2020, the World Health Organization coined the term *infodemic* to refer to the overload of false and inaccurate information being disseminated during the early months of the COVID-19 pandemic (Cinelli et al., 2020; Gaeta et al., 2023). How users respond to false information plays an important role in its effect. Early research into misinformation during the pandemic pointed to the critical literacy of the public playing an important role in determining its effect (Barua et al., 2020).

While citizen journalism has been valuable in drawing attention to stories that the mainstream media has overlooked, there are also examples of community fact-finding efforts getting it wrong. For example, a community effort on Reddit to identify culprits for the 2013 Boston Marathon bombing mistakenly identified a missing student from Brown University (BBC, 2013; Suran & Brown, 2017). In another such example, false information was deliberately spread online regarding a vehicle attack at a counter-protest in Charlottesville, Virginia in 2017 (Krafft & Donovan, 2020). Social media platforms are effective for sharing stories quickly, but their openness also creates vulnerabilities in the information system for the proliferation of low-quality research, rumour mongering and disinformation.

Studies have shown that false stories online may begin small in subcommunities on sites such as 4chan but eventually "trade up the chain" to more mainstream platforms like Facebook or Twitter (Krafft & Donovan, 2020). Rumours may begin as small fact-finding efforts that turn into "evidence collages" where users bring together collections of screenshots and pieces of information that help tell a story but may also perpetuate a particular ideology. As these collages move across platforms, they lose the context of the discussions where they were formed, including dissenting voices. This decontextualisation makes verifying facts more difficult and hides the original authorship. As such the need for authentication is not only more important on social platforms but a more challenging task.

Waruwu et al. (2021) emphasise the role of social cohesion as an important influence in meaning-making for online news. Rather than a purely individual and cognitive act, authentication of news online is also shown to be a collective endeavour. Focus groups with Singaporean residents who shared news online found that users will prioritise group harmony and look for social cues when authenticating stories. This in turn can have an effect on how news is disseminated in group settings, as users must prioritise their own beliefs against that of their in-groups.

These examples demonstrate that not only is the creation of misinformation online a community effort, but its authentication and dissemination are also vulnerable to social biases which extend beyond the technology itself. In these instances, technology plays an important role in enabling the speedy collection and spread of information, but it is people who create and share misinformation.

## POLITICAL POLARISATION

Since Britain's decision to exit the European Union and the US election of Donald Trump as President in 2016, significant conjecture has been made about the role of social media and 'filter bubbles' in creating polarised political communities. Nguyen and Vu (2019) provide an account of these claims, with articles from outlets like The Economist, New Statesman and NiemanLab espousing that the algorithms and the proliferation of fake news and misinformation on social media had contributed to voting outcomes. If we were to take these claims at face value, the implications *would* be significant. Can polarised news, misinformation and algorithmic bias polarise the public who use social media? While it is an interesting notion, the empirical evidence suggests otherwise.

In July 2023 a series of landmark studies were published in leading journals *Science* and *Nature* examining political polarisation on Facebook and Instagram (González-Bailón et al., 2023; Guess et al., 2023a, 2023b; Nyhan et al., 2023). The papers examined the links between content sharing, algorithms and ideological segregation during the 2020 US Presidential Election. Their analysis was particularly significant because one of the studies used aggregate data from 208 million Facebook users, conducted in conjunction with a partnership with Meta Platforms (González-Bailón et al., 2023). In others, they used large-scale data donations from users (Guess et al., 2023a, 2023b), and in another a multiwave field experiment (Nyhan et al., 2023). These studies produced several important findings which included:

- Clear evidence of political polarisation on Facebook, which was higher among groups who had direct exposure to news and even higher again if they were engaging with it (González-Bailón et al., 2023).
- An asymmetry among the news ecosystem, which showed that there was a large pocket of news production and consumption that was almost exclusively conservative (González-Bailón et al., 2023).
- Misinformation was significantly more apparent among this conservative corner of the news ecosystem (González-Bailón et al., 2023).
- When compared to algorithmic feeds, chronological feeds significantly decrease the amount of time users spend browsing. At the same time, chronological feeds expose users to more untrustworthy and political content (Guess et al., 2023a).
- Chronological feeds reduce the amount of offensive or hostile content users receive but the feed style doesn't appear to impact polarisation, political knowledge or attitudes.
- Resharing content helps to amplify political content, but it doesn't appear to have an impact on belief or opinion (Guess et al., 2023b).
- Reducing exposure to like-minded content didn't appear to have an effect on polarised political attitudes (Nyhan et al., 2023).

These studies are methodologically significant not only due to their scale but also due to the highly empirical methods used and their large and interconnected research teams. They show that while political polarisation is apparent on Facebook, it doesn't appear to come because of the content that people consume. The findings of their large-scale experiments showed that changing the controls on user feeds to adjust for polarised content has no significant effect on user attitudes. This doesn't mean that there isn't a relationship between polarised content and polarised communities, but the top-down effect of news polarising people is not supported by the data.

These results would likely come as no surprise to proponents of the minimal effects model for political communication—a framework that emerged from studies conducted in the mid-twentieth century which showed that media had minimal direct effect on political attitudes (Bennett & Iyengar, 2008; Klapper, 1960). This also affirms arguments made by eminent social media scholar Axel Bruns (2019) who is critical of claims regarding the existence and effects of echo chambers and filter bubbles. They suggest instead that audiences are more likely organised by factors that are social rather than technological. Furthermore, Bruns (2019) contends that these fears "only divert our attention from the much more critical question of what drives increasing polarisation and hyperpartisanship in many established and emerging democracies".

## MINIMAL EFFECTS

When discussing media systems and content, there is a propensity to inadvertently attribute the media as a causative agent for large-scale social effect. Famously, writers Edward S. Herman and Noam Chomsky (1988) have been notable in their critique of the political economy of mass communication systems for its perceived impact on audiences. Their propaganda model for communication describes news reporting as having editorially distorting filters which are said to influence the shape of content. They indicate that the close relationship between large scale, profit driven, media enterprises and big businesses means that media operators must cater to financial interests to remain profitable or otherwise risk alienating advertisers.

While their book, *Manufacturing Consent*, has been a popular text, the relevance of their analysis is arguably contingent on what are commonly referred to as media effects. If assertions regarding the effect of political economic systems on the media are accurate, the next step would be to consider if this has a flow on effect onto audience beliefs and behaviours. It is Herman and Chomsky's claim that the function of the media is to "amuse, entertain, and inform, and to inculcate individuals with the values, beliefs, and codes of behaviour that will integrate them into the institutional structures of the larger society" (Herman & Chomsky, 1988, p. 1). Within this framework, any controlling effect on the content of news would also be influential in shaping public values, beliefs and behaviour. But is this true?

Since the 1940s there has been significant debate among political communication scholars regarding the effect of the media on voter attitudes and their voting behaviours. A minimal effects model introduced by Klapper (1960) suggests that political communication only has a marginal effect on voter behaviour. More recent debates have seen scholars attempting to both reaffirm (Bennett & Iyengar, 2008) and challenge (Holbert et al., 2010) this idea. Critiques of minimal effects point to the changing media landscape of today which is significantly more complex and more involved in the everyday lives of individuals than it was in the 1940s.

Refinement of persuasive models of communication resulted in the Elaboration Likelihood Model (O'Keefe, 2013; Petty & Cacioppo, 1984). It proposes two main routes to persuasion: a central route and a peripheral route. The central route involves deep, thoughtful consideration of the arguments presented by the media content, leading to long-lasting attitude change. The peripheral route, however, involves less scrutiny and is influenced by superficial cues, resulting in more temporary attitude changes. The model suggests that the likelihood of elaboration, or the extent to which a person carefully considers arguments, depends on their motivation and ability to process messages. This framework has been offered as a counterpoint by scholars challenging the minimal effects model (Holbert et al., 2010). Yet, as other scholars have noted, there are further methodological issues for the Elaboration Likelihood Model that need to be addressed too, such as the rigor of the initial studies, inadequate testing of some of its core constructs and that it too was developed in a different era of mass communication than that which is prevalent today (Kitchen et al., 2014).

As media forms have evolved, and new systems such as social media platforms have emerged, these competing theories have been revisited in the context of the social web. The previously discussed Meta Platforms studies (González-Bailón et al., 2023; Guess et al., 2023a, 2023b) are mostly indicative of the minimal effects hypothesis. Conversely, research by Shi et al. (2018) have been somewhat affirming of the elaboration likelihood model, showing that X influences user posting behaviour. Yet, studies haven't been able to demonstrate social media content or algorithmic recommender systems as having a significant or direct effect on voter behaviour or attitudes off-platform.

## Mental Health, Wellbeing and Youth

An early, but oft-cited systematic review by Best et al. (2014) identified a range of harms associated with social media usage and the wellbeing of young people. These included "increased exposure to harm, social isolation, depression and cyber-bullying" (Best et al., 2014). The results of the studies they reviewed showed mixed outcomes regarding these factors. For example, instant messenger services showed links to depression in one study but were absent from another. Similar mixed results were also found for studies of youth loneliness and blogging practices. Conversely, Best, Manktelow and Taylor's review also found compelling research to show that online social networking provided many social benefits, including "increased self-esteem, perceived social support, increased social capital, safe identity experimentation and increased opportunity for self-disclosure" (Best et al., 2014). The results of this research highlight the pitfalls of a good-versus-bad approach to studying social media. With complex and highly social systems the likelihood of finding consistent results attributable to the technology is unlikely as the researchers are also simultaneously observing the social context in which the participants are situated.

More recent studies have reached more nuanced conclusions. A review by Kross et al. (2021) found that there was compelling evidence to show small, but negative effects from social media use; however, a range of benefits are also observable. They too highlight the issue of taking a reductive approach to a multifaceted phenomenon, but also emphasise the problem with aggregating different social media platforms under one banner. As we highlighted in our first chapter, many of these platforms offer distinctly different content forms and varied network capabilities alongside unique algorithmic controls. As such, a more atomised approach to discussions of wellbeing and harm is needed when it comes to individuals and social media usage.

A lack of nuance has resulted in what is often termed as a jingle-jangle problem among social media research (Kross et al., 2021). As an interdisciplinary exercise, scholars from various fields including psychology, sociology, computer science, political science and communication and media studies have all coalesced as the point of social media studies. These varying traditions bring with them their own definitions and analytical frameworks, and as such a lack of common lexicon creates situations where different works are used interchangeably that might have more nuanced meanings, i.e. social networking sites and social media. Alongside the indiscriminate aggregation of diverse platforms, the jingle-jangle problems mean it isn't always clear whether social media researchers are studying the same or different phenomena.

## DATA ETHICS AND SAFETY

Alongside mass connectivity, we also live in a period of mass surveillance and data collection. The collection of overwhelmingly large archives of data, also known as 'big data', is something that most social media and digital technology companies have in common. Indeed, not only are companies like Meta, Alphabet and Amazon in the business of big data but so too are telecommunication companies, retail chains and governments (Broomfield & Reutter, 2022; Smith et al., 2012).

Social media and technology companies use data for a range of purposes including targeting and inference practices for advertising but also as inputs for recommender systems and other algorithmic decision-making (Zuboff, 2015, 2019). Collecting data is important for technology companies hoping to work on a global scale, but this comes with questions regarding ethics and responsibility. For instance, how much ownership and control should users be able to retain about the data and in what ways is it fair for companies to exploit it for financial gain? Furthermore, if companies are storing large swatches of information about their users, what is their duty of care for personal privacy and data protection?

This extensive collection of user data has been an issue of concern raised by scholars and civil advocacy groups. Big data poses a threat to user privacy and safety for a variety of reasons, including but not limited to:

- The inability of users to remain fully aware of where and when they are being depicted in uploaded media or recorded in databases (Smith et al., 2012).
- The possibility of being microtargeted by advertisers (Papakyriakopoulos et al., 2018).
- Having their content or likeness used to train large language models (LLMs) used by generative artificial intelligence companies.
- Geo-location data being exploited by hackers, cyber-stalkers, abusers or hostile governments.
- Discrimination by recommender systems and other decision-making algorithms (Mittelstadt et al., 2016).
- Digital footprints and the difficulty of leading a fully offline existence.

- The potential for 'chilling effects' whereby users self-censor and stifle their social media use to avoid possible governmental retaliation (Büchi et al., 2022).

Based on these examples we can see that there is a wide range of possible issues which arise from the proliferation of user data. Broadly we might categorise these as psychological, physical, economic and democratic threats.

Research has shown that most users do care about their privacy on social media. Notably the Cambridge Analytica scandal helped draw attention to the potential harm of mishandled data and the lack of transparency by which it is collected. In 2018 it was revealed that the UK-based data analytics company had been collecting data from 87 million Facebook users to create psychographic profiles without their explicit consent. This data was used to provide campaign advice to US presidential candidates, Ted Cruz and Donald Trump. Research has shown that while many users are aware of the scandal most are unsure of what steps they could undertake to protect their data (Hinds et al., 2020).

The collection of big data, while in part a technological phenomenon, should also be recognised as a social phenomenon. While platform companies collect many data points not actively disclosed by the users, such as browsing habits and geolocation data, users also participate in acts of self-disclosure—the practice of freely sharing information about themselves online. A 5-year longitudinal study conducted by Tsay-Vogel et al. (2018) examined the effects of Facebook usage on self-disclosure behaviour and perceptions of privacy. Their results showed increased platform use and relaxed attitudes towards privacy were associated with greater self-disclosure behaviours. What is particularly notable about this finding is that the behaviour persisted even in offline settings. The researchers suggest that being active on platforms may cultivate a social reality where "personal data are freely exchanged and self-disclosure is highly routinised" (Tsay-Vogel et al., 2018). However, the researchers also found that heavy users of the platform tended to show an increased desire for governmental privacy protection as time went on. These results highlight a friction between personal privacy behaviours and attitudes on social media platforms. While users appear to become more likely to divulge information on platforms as they spend more time, they also desire greater protection of that privacy.

While attitudes of global governments towards data regulation differ significantly, there have been promising steps by some countries to better protect users. In 2018 the European Union enacted the General Data Protection Regulation (GDPR)—a set of laws guided by the assertion that "the protection of natural persons in relation to the processing of personal data is a fundamental right". The provisions ensure that users either give consent to the processing of their data, have a contractual relationship with the organisation, or must have another legal obligation by which to collect a person's data. One of the more significant outcomes of the regulation is the inclusion of a right to be forgotten, in which users can request the erasure of their data from platforms. Notably, the social media aggregator quickly Klout ceased its operations because of the EU regulation as the company was not capable of providing its service while conforming to the GDPR framework (Reed, 2018).

## TROLLING, NETWORKED HARASSMENT AND DOXING

Among the very real threats to user well-being on platforms are the practices of trolling, networked harassment and doxing. These practices each refer to different behaviours of harassment committed against a user or group that can be harmful and augmented by platform affordances.

Gabrielle de Seta (2017) describes trolling as a placeholder for a "variety of practices, ranging from mocking or taunting each other for fun to disrupting large online communities, and from engaging in large-scale harassment campaigns to impersonating multiple identities engaging in extremist activities". This wide range of activities highlights the complexity and multifaceted nature of online interactions that can quickly escalate from harmless jokes to serious forms of cyber abuse. In its most modest form, trolling might be considered an extension of online humour, like pranking or being sarcastic, but the label has also been applied to encompass a range of activities constituting cyber abuse (March & Marrington, 2019). Trolling appears to be social media's manifestation of offline behaviours but is further facilitated and augmented by the platform affordances of reach and anonymity. Such affordances have a significant impact on the nature of online harassment, expanding the potential for harm. As a result of these affordances, the ability to be targeted en-masse is a real possibility. Furthermore, belligerents can use digital technologies to enhance their abrasive creativity, including deepfakes and doctored images, impersonating accounts, and memes designed to harass.

Networked harassment has also been described as a form of moral contagion whereby groups of users may target a user due to a perceived violation of community norms (Marwick, 2021). Networked harassment may come in the form of the mass flagging of content, response videos (Lewis et al., 2021) or pile-on activities, where a community floods a specific user's posts with negative messages. The latter of these is commonly referred to as being 'ratioed' on X/Twitter, which reflects the high ratio of comments to the number of likes that a post might receive. While the community may feel like they are righteous in their practice, the users receiving the criticism may also see it as a vehicle for harassment. Instances of witch-hunts being perpetrated against users may differ in terms of motivation by the perpetrator, but the behaviour can be similar. The inability of platforms to address this kind of harassment in real-time has seen recipients of so-called hate raids on Twitch take matters into their own hands and develop community strategies to help mitigate antisocial behaviour (Meisner, 2023).

Doxing, alongside trolling and networked harassment, stands out as one of the more egregious forms of online harassment. Anderson and Wood (2021,

p. 205) define doxing as "the practice of publishing private, proprietary, or personally identifying information on the internet, usually with malicious intent". This could also be understood as a form of information disorder's mal-information, as discussed earlier in this chapter. Like networked harassment, doxing can be perpetrated by vigilante groups hoping to provide moral justice, for example, the exposure of white supremacist groups by hacker collective, Anonymous (Colton et al., 2017). However, the question of what is moral and normative is not consistent between communities. Furthermore, there are numerous examples of vigilante justice being served by unqualified community members to the detriment of innocent individuals—see Reddit's attempt to ascertain the identity of the Boston Bomber in 2013 (Trottier, 2020).

Studies show that journalists are frequently the targets of gendered harassment on social media, with discourse analysis of their X/Twitter pages revealing many interactions to be sexist in nature (Davis Kempton & Connolly-Ahern, 2022). Furthermore, the act of trolling is perceived by users as more often being perpetrated by male, White and conservative groups (Ortiz, 2020).

The disconnect between user expectations and platform policies is another facet of the challenge. User expectations don't always match the community guidelines and content management practices exercised by platforms. Studies conducted with adult Internet users from the US by Schoenebeck et al. (2023) suggests that platform policies aren't capable of fully remedying reputational harm. As such, while banning might help prevent further damage, without recourse for pursuing a public apology or setting the record straight, reputational damage may persist online.

These practices lead to a pressing issue: the challenge of moderating online spaces effectively. Having to rely on algorithms and user reporting to identify antisocial behaviour poses a challenge to the effective moderation of anti-social behaviour. In Australia, persons can report this behaviour to the eSafety commission which can make requests to platforms to remove content or investigate cases of targeted harassment. However, the issue of harassment goes beyond the capability of algorithms and regulatory bodies to control.

One of the issues at the core of harassment on social media platforms is the responsibilities of the platform owners in identifying, preventing and remedying harmful behaviour. Much like the challenges platforms face regarding news and misinformation, the intent of the platforms and the solutions they provide always don't match that of other domains and as such there can be a dissonance between the platform and the communities and governments, they are accountable to. The push to be perceived as a technology company, akin to a telecommunication service provider rather than a media outlet, helps to absolve platforms of extensive content moderation responsibilities.

## YOUNG PEOPLE AND ONLINE SAFETY

In a similar tone to the previous described concerns of political polarisation, data and ethics, and broad online safety, so too is the environment that surrounds young people and their digital and online lives. That is, there are real and serious concerns for their wellbeing as new media technologies emerge and are integrated into their schooling lives, social practices and everydayness in digital spaces. However, it is crucially important that the moral and media panics that surround this group of users are dispelled and the core concerns for their safety are in the first instance identified and then addressed accordingly. Unfortunately, the romanticism of young people outside climbing trees and kicking footballs clouds the reality of how their lives have dramatically changed due to media technologies. The prevalence of media panics about young people has skewed the conversation about what is important and has excluded the voices of those most impacted by these conversations: young people.

Recent empirical research has suggested the scenario is significantly more complex than the common tropes of 'my child spends too much time online'. Humphry, Hutchinson and Boichak (2023) undertook empirical research with young people and their parents and carers to better understand the sorts of issues they are facing in the contemporary digital media environments. The purpose of that work is to better inform policy that protects this sector of our society, and in the context of Australia, provide better resources for the eSafety Commissioner to respond to issues flagged by young people. The following section will draw on that research to broaden our discussion here around the perceived dark sides of social media.

### 'The Kids Are Alright'

Based on two rounds of focus groups –including an appreciative enquiry workshop (Youth Action, 2023)– with young people aged 12–14 and 15–17 and their parents and carers, the research implemented a co-design approach with a focus to create media resources that explain the current environment, highlight the dangers and talked about the strengths of young people. In the early stages of that research, it became clear the concerns of parents and carers and their young people were vastly different. For example, parents and carers were concerned for what Livingstone (2023) often frames as pedestrian concerns—stranger danger, giving out sensitive information, talking with people they don't know online, being exposed to inappropriate content, and a range of other genuine and relative concerns. What became increasingly clear is that young people have developed a range of coping mechanisms to avoid these sorts of issues.

Young people reported that they are not worried about strangers online and have mechanisms such as blocking or starting new accounts, or simply moving the conversation away from so-called strangers online. Young people also were united in that they don't want to be exposed to inappropriate material and will make every effort to avoid content that includes nudity, violence or harm. Young people are also incredibly aware of technological settings such as location services and other personally identifiable settings and will turn those off to avoid some of the issues that their parents and carers often cited as serious concerns for them. Broadly speaking, the young people have developed a range of safety settings in their worlds to avoid the sorts of issues that largely their parents and carers believed to be of significance.

That, however, does not mean their lives are absolutely OK and, in many ways, experience the sorts of issues that have been outlined in this chapter already. The key issues that young people did highlight included having content removed from platforms, retrieving their own personal data, having little to no understanding of what happens to their personal data or that it is being generated while they engage in online spaces, while also feeling safe and unprotected at times on social media platforms. In many of these instances, they rely on the support of their school, friends and family networks to work through these kinds of challenges.

### A Broader Sharing of Responsibility for the Challenges of Young People

While young people have developed skills in how to avoid scams, how to block users and how to deny services such as geolocation, they still rely on a broader group of users for the issues that challenge them. This includes schools, friends, social media platforms and other sources to provide information on how to stay safe online.

There was an overwhelming response from young people and their carers that platforms needed to be increasingly transparent and improve their accountability. Young people feel they have no control over content that others place of them online. This builds on the earlier outlined concerns that the increase in datafication, or big data and its production, is done outside of a user's control, where young people feel especially vulnerable around actions such as others posting images of themselves. If young people attempt to extract data from platforms, they noted it was overly cumbersome and difficult to find and download in the first instance. This is of course ahead of trying to have content removed from online sites.

Beyond the pedestrian online issues, the emergence of data challenges emerged as the key concern for this group of young people. Often, young people were not aware of the sorts of data being extracted from their everyday activities. If they were, they had little understanding of how to approach a platform like Snapchat, Roblox or Instagram and request the content be taken down. This scenario manifested as a significant source of anxiety for this group of online users. Similarly, if young people can navigate the sorts of issues other thought were challenging for them, this represents a significant gap in what we think we know about young people and their social media lives and how that might be better managed.

## *Dark Social Media and Young People?*

So, what does this research highlight about the dark side of social media? While it is focussed on young people and social media, the key takeaway message that can be applied to all our understandings of social media is the sizeable gap in knowledge about what is important and what is deemed to be important. More importantly, it is this gap that is highly mediatised and politicised for broader groups of users to deter our attention from those real challenges of social media. The impact of this gap results in inappropriate policy design, or incomplete policy design, that leaves users un-protected while platform providers exploit these gaps to improve their marketplace strongholds.

The localised and real-world impact of this scenario sees parents and carers focussing on issues that are from several years ago that have in many ways been solved locally by young people themselves, building on the sorts of functionality that have become available in recent years, i.e. blocking functions. This exact scenario has encouraged extensive resources to be prepared and delivered in schools and provided to parents to help their young people makes sense of the worlds around them. This is not a bad thing, and considerably helps in sharing knowledge between young people and their carers. However, it moves the attention away from the emerging issues that young people face right now and need that network of shared responsibility to ensure they are safe online. At the time of writing, the concerns that we uncovered in 2022, while still important, have now also been superseded by the most recent challenges. *Wizz* has since emerged as a 'tinder-style' app for young people, resurfacing the issues around data privacy, body shaming and the associated conversations concerns related to young people and the dating scene. It should also be noted that the idea of sexting can be a positive thing for young people, and researchers have proven this to be an important process for young people to experience as they develop (McKee et al., 2022). However, what aspects of this new platform will provide new challenges for young people, their carers and the policies that protect their online lives?

None of this is new. Media technologies emerge, present challenges and are interpreted by users in ways that work best for their lives. A we highlighted earlier, this process is as old as Aristotle would be today. However, it is the emergence of new challenges and how we identify them, understand them and react to them in helpful and useful ways that matter.

## CONCLUSION

As demonstrated in this chapter, when it comes to the dark sides of social media, speculation and evidence aren't always aligned. Broad claims about the impacts of social media on political polarisation have been challenged by large scale empirical evidence. While polarisation on platforms exists, the direction of causality between public opinion, choices in news content and algorithms are unclear. The evidence shown might suggest that people use content and news more like a sports jersey—something they consume to reflect their personality and opinion, rather than something that directly affects it. Likewise, the harms attributed to social media in terms of self-esteem and mental wellbeing may only have minimal effects on users, with studies showing many inconsistent and conflicting results. Young people and their use of social media reinforce this same argument and highlight the contradictions especially.

Part of the challenge of determining what effect social media has on people stems from the biases in our thinking about the relationship between society and technology. With giant networks of people online, bringing with them their diverse attitudes, beliefs, behaviours and social structures, the attributability of platform technologies to human and democratic harms is difficult to establish. This is reaffirmed by the very much human and social issues that we see on platforms, which have been proven to be difficult to moderate with technological solutions alone. While platforms are responsible for their technology and data extraction practices, to what extent are they responsible for the behaviour of individuals on global platforms with user bases sometimes numbering in the billions? This tension is reflected in the disconnect between user expectations and platform policies. A desire among the public for further government regulation, as seen in the studies mentioned earlier in this chapter.

Alongside concerns regarding democratic and psychological harms is the practices of individuals on these platforms. Antisocial behaviour such as trolling, networked harassment and trolling appear to be frequently encountered by users and sometimes to devastating effect. Research has shown that many of these behaviours are also gendered, with women more likely to be targeted and harassed on platforms. For journalists, this of particular risk as current industry practice encourages more direct engagement between reporters and their audiences.

Privacy and the widespread availability of data is also a real and significant issue…

As the Sisyphean cycle of technology panics re-emerges with the arrival generative artificial intelligence technologies, scholars and practitioners ought to be mindful the panic and fearmongering that has been attributed to social media technology and other prior innovations. No doubt there will be widespread concern regarding the safety of our democracies and psychological wellbeing, but we should also seek to understand both the technological and social elements that are at play. We should also be mindful not to forget that these technologies are also owned and controlled by companies with their own vested interests. One need only look at the recent deals made by Reddit, Tumblr and WordPress to sell user content data to AI projects for north of $60 million dollars (Ohlheiser, 2024; Tong et al., 2024; Wired, 2024).

REFERENCES

Anderson, B., & Wood, M. A. (2021). Doxxing: A Scoping Review and Typology. In *The Emerald International Handbook of Technology-Facilitated Violence and Abuse* (pp. 205–226).

Barua, Z., Barua, S., Aktar, S., Kabir, N., & Li, M. (2020). Effects of Misinformation on COVID-19 Individual Responses and Recommendations for Resilience of Disastrous Consequences of Misinformation. *Progress in Disaster Science, 8,* 100119.

BBC. (2013). Reddit Apologises for Online Boston 'Witch Hunt'. *Technology.* Retrieved from https://www.bbc.com/news/technology-22263020

BBC. (2016). *'Post-truth' Declared Word of the Year by Oxford Dictionaries.* Retrieved from https://www.bbc.com/news/uk-37995600

Bennett, W. L., & Iyengar, S. (2008). A New Era of Minimal Effects? The Changing Foundations of Political Communication. *Journal of Communication, 58*(4), 707–731.

Best, P., Manktelow, R., & Taylor, B. (2014). Online Communication, Social Media and Adolescent Wellbeing: A Systematic Narrative Review. *Children and Youth Services Review, 41,* 27–36.

Broomfield, H., & Reutter, L. (2022). In Search of the Citizen in the Datafication of Public Administration. *Big Data & Society, 9*(1), 20539517221089302. https://doi.org/10.1177/20539517221089302

Bruns, A. (2019). *Are Filter Bubbles Real?* Wiley.

Büchi, M., Festic, N., & Latzer, M. (2022). The Chilling Effects of Digital Dataveillance: A Theoretical Model and an Empirical Research Agenda. *Big Data & Society, 9*(1), 20539517211065368. https://doi.org/10.1177/20539517211065368

Cinelli, M., Quattrociocchi, W., Galeazzi, A., Valensise, C. M., Brugnoli, E., Schmidt, A. L., et al. (2020). The COVID-19 Social Media Infodemic. *Scientific Reports, 10*(1), 1–10.

Colton, J. S., Holmes, S., & Walwema, J. (2017). From NoobGuides to# OpKKK: Ethics of Anonymous' Tactical Technical Communication. *Technical Communication Quarterly, 26*(1), 59–75.

Davis Kempton, S., & Connolly-Ahern, C. (2022). "Who's Going to be a Creep Today?" Understanding the Social Media Experiences of Women Broadcast Journalists. *Social Media + Society, 8*(2), 20563051221108410. https://doi.org/10.1177/20563051221108410

De Seta, G. (2017). Trolling, and Other Problematic Social Media Practices. In *The SAGE Handbook of Social Media* (pp. 390–411).

Drew, R. (2016). Technological Determinism. In *A Companion to Popular Culture* (pp. 165–183).

Flood, A. (2017). *Fake News is 'Very Real' Word of the Year for 2017.* Retrieved from https://www.theguardian.com/books/2017/nov/02/fake-news-is-very-real-word-of-the-year-for-2017

Gaeta, A., Loia, V., Lomasto, L., & Orciuoli, F. (2023). A Novel Approach Based on Rough Set Theory for Analyzing Information Disorder. *Applied Intelligence, 53*(12), 15993–16014.

González-Bailón, S., Lazer, D., Barberá, P., Zhang, M., Allcott, H., Brown, T., et al. (2023). Asymmetric Ideological Segregation in Exposure to Political News on Facebook. *Science, 381*(6656), 392–398.

Guess, A. M., Malhotra, N., Pan, J., Barberá, P., Allcott, H., Brown, T., et al. (2023a). How do Social Media Feed Algorithms Affect Attitudes and Behavior in an Election Campaign? *Science, 381*(6656), 398–404.

Guess, A. M., Malhotra, N., Pan, J., Barberá, P., Allcott, H., Brown, T., et al. (2023b). Reshares on Social Media Amplify Political News but do not Detectably Affect Beliefs or Opinions. *Science, 381*(6656), 404–408.

Herman, E. S., & Chomsky, N. (1988). *Manufacturing Consent: The Political Economy of the Mass Media*. Pantheon.

Hinds, J., Williams, E. J., & Joinson, A. N. (2020). "It Wouldn't Happen to Me": Privacy Concerns and Perspectives Following the Cambridge Analytica Scandal. *International Journal of Human-Computer Studies, 143*, 102498.

Holbert, R. L., Garrett, R. K., & Gleason, L. S. (2010). A New Era of Minimal Effects? A Response to Bennett and Iyengar. *Journal of Communication, 60*(1), 15–34.

Hughes, T. P. (1994). Technological Momentum. In M. R. Smith & L. Marx (Eds.), *Does Technology Drive History?: The Dilemma of Technological Determinism*. The MIT Press.

Humphry, J., Boichak, O., & Hutchinson, J. (2023). Emerging Online Safety Issues: Co-creating Social Media with Young People—Research Report. In *Emerging Online Safety Issues—Co-creating Social Media Education with Young People—Research Report*.

Jennings, W., Stoker, G., Bunting, H., Valgarðsson, V. O., Gaskell, J., Devine, D., et al. (2021). Lack of Trust, Conspiracy Beliefs, and Social Media Use Predict COVID-19 Vaccine Hesitancy. *Vaccines, 9*(6), 593. Retrieved from https://www.mdpi.com/2076-393X/9/6/593

Kitchen, P. J., Kerr, G., Schultz, D. E., McColl, R., & Pals, H. (2014). The Elaboration Likelihood Model: Review, Critique and Research Agenda. *European Journal of Marketing, 48*(11/12), 2033–2050.

Klapper, J. T. (1960). *The Effects of Mass Communication*. French Press.

Krafft, P. M., & Donovan, J. (2020). Disinformation by Design: The Use of Evidence Collages and Platform Filtering in a Media Manipulation Campaign. *Political Communication, 37*(2), 194–214.

Kross, E., Verduyn, P., Sheppes, G., Costello, C. K., Jonides, J., & Ybarra, O. (2021). Social Media and Well-being: Pitfalls, Progress, and Next Steps. *Trends in Cognitive Sciences, 25*(1), 55–66.

Lazer, D. M., Baum, M. A., Benkler, Y., Berinsky, A. J., Greenhill, K. M., Menczer, F., et al. (2018). The Science of Fake News. *Science, 359*(6380), 1094–1096.

Lewis, R., Marwick, A. E., & Partin, W. C. (2021). "We Dissect Stupidity and Respond to It": Response Videos and Networked Harassment on YouTube. *American Behavioral Scientist, 65*(5), 735–756.

March, E., & Marrington, J. (2019). A Qualitative Analysis of Internet Trolling. *Cyberpsychology, Behavior, and Social Networking, 22*(3), 192–197.

Marwick, A. E. (2021). Morally Motivated Networked Harassment as Normative Reinforcement. *Social Media + Society, 7*(2), 20563051211021378. https://doi.org/10.1177/20563051211021378

McKee, A., Ingham, R., Byron, P., & Litsou, K. (2022). Fifty Years of Academic Research on Pornography. In A. McKee, R. Ingham, P. Byron, & K. Litsou (Eds.), *What Do We Know About the Effects of Pornography After Fifty Years of Academic Research?* (pp. 1–17). Routledge.

McQuail, D., & Deuze, M. (2020). In D. McQuail & M. Deuze (Eds.), *McQuail's Media & Mass Communication Theory* (7th ed.). Sage Publications.

McRobbie, A., & Thornton, S. L. (1995). Rethinking 'Moral Panic' for Multi-mediated Social Worlds. *British Journal of Sociology, 46,* 559–574.

Meisner, C. (2023). Networked Responses to Networked Harassment? Creators' Coordinated Management of "Hate Raids" on Twitch. *Social Media + Society, 9*(2), 20563051231179696. https://doi.org/10.1177/20563051231179696

Mittelstadt, B. D., Allo, P., Taddeo, M., Wachter, S., & Floridi, L. (2016). The Ethics of Algorithms: Mapping the Debate. *Big Data & Society, 3*(2), 2053951716679679. https://doi.org/10.1177/2053951716679679

Nguyen, A., & Vu, H. T. (2019). Testing Popular News Discourse on the "Echo Chamber" Effect: Does Political Polarisation Occur Among Those Relying on Social Media as Their Primary Politics News Source? *First Monday, 24*(5).

Nyhan, B., Settle, J., Thorson, E., Wojcieszak, M., Barberá, P., Chen, A. Y., et al. (2023). Like-Minded Sources on Facebook are Prevalent but not Polarizing. *Nature, 620*(7972), 137–144.

O'Keefe, D. J. (2013). The Elaboration Likelihood Model. In *The SAGE Handbook of Persuasion: Developments in Theory and Practice* (pp. 137–149).

Ohlheiser, A. W. (2024). *A Poster's Guide to Who's Selling Your Data to Train AI.* Retrieved from https://www.vox.com/technology/24086039/reddit-tumblr-wordpress-whos-selling-your-data-to-train-ai

Orben, A. (2020). The Sisyphean Cycle of Technology Panics. *Perspectives on Psychological Science, 15*(5), 1143–1157. https://doi.org/10.1177/1745691620919372

Ortiz, S. M. (2020). Trolling as a Collective Form of Harassment: An Inductive Study of How Online Users Understand Trolling. *Social Media + Society, 6*(2), 2056305120928512. https://doi.org/10.1177/2056305120928512

Papakyriakopoulos, O., Hegelich, S., Shahrezaye, M., & Serrano, J. C. M. (2018). Social Media and Microtargeting: Political Data Processing and the Consequences for Germany. *Big Data & Society, 5*(2), 205395171881184.

Petty, R. E., & Cacioppo, J. T. (1984). Source Factors and the Elaboration Likelihood Model of Persuasion. *Advances in Consumer Research, 11*(1), 668–672.

Reed, J. (2018). *Klout Throws in the Towel on Whatever They were Trying to Accomplish—Long Live GDPR!* Retrieved from https://diginomica.com/klout-throws-in-the-towel-on-whatever-they-were-trying-to-accomplish-long-live-gdpr

Schoenebeck, S., Lampe, C., & Triệu, P. (2023). Online Harassment: Assessing Harms and Remedies. *Social Media + Society, 9*(1), 20563051231157297. https://doi.org/10.1177/20563051231157297

Shi, J., Hu, P., Lai, K. K., & Chen, G. (2018). Determinants of Users' Information Dissemination Behavior on Social Networking Sites: An Elaboration Likelihood Model Perspective. *Internet Research, 28*(2), 393–418.

Smith, M., Szongott, C., Henne, B., & Von Voigt, G. (2012). *Big Data Privacy Issues in Public Social Media.* Paper presented at the 2012 6th IEEE International Conference on Digital Ecosystems and Technologies (DEST).

Suran, M., & Brown, D. K. (2017). Freedom from the Press? How Anonymous Gatekeepers on Reddit Covered the Boston Marathon Bombing. *Journalism Studies, 18*(8), 1035–1051.

Tong, A., Wang, E., & Coulter, M. (2024). *Exclusive: Reddit in AI Content Licensing Deal with Google*. Retrieved from https://www.reuters.com/technology/reddit-ai-content-licensing-deal-with-google-sources-say-2024-02-22/

Trottier, D. (2020). Denunciation and Doxing: Towards a Conceptual Model of Digital Vigilantism. *Global Crime, 21*(3–4), 196–212.

Tsay-Vogel, M., Shanahan, J., & Signorielli, N. (2018). Social Media Cultivating Perceptions of Privacy: A 5-Year Analysis of Privacy Attitudes and Self-Disclosure Behaviors Among Facebook Users. *New Media & Society, 20*(1), 141–161. https://doi.org/10.1177/1461444816660731

Wardle, C., & Derakhshan, H. (2017). *Information Disorder: Toward an Interdisciplinary Framework for Research and Policymaking* (Vol. 27). Council of Europe Strasbourg.

Wardle, C., & Derakhshan, H. (2018). Thinking About 'Information Disorder': Formats of Misinformation, Disinformation, and Mal-information. In *Journalism, 'Fake News' & Disinformation* (pp. 43–54).

Waruwu, B. K., Tandoc, E. C., Jr., Duffy, A., Kim, N., & Ling, R. (2021). Telling Lies Together? Sharing News as a Form of Social Authentication. *New Media & Society, 23*(9), 2516–2533.

Wired. (2024). *Reddit's Sale of User Data for AI Training Draws FTC Inquiry*. Retrieved from https://www.wired.com/story/reddits-sale-user-data-ai-training-draws-ftc-investigation/

Zuboff, S. (2015). Big Other: Surveillance Capitalism and the Prospects of an Information Civilization. *Journal of Information Technology, 30*(1), 75–89.

Zuboff, S. (2019). In S. Zuboff (Ed.), *The Age of Surveillance Capitalism: The Fight for the Future at the New Frontier of Power*. Profile Books.

## CHAPTER 10

# Conclusion: The Case for Hope, the Path Forward

## SOCIAL MEDIA FOR SOCIAL GOOD

Over the course of this book, we have looked at a large amount of scholarly work and empirical examples of social media. In many ways, this book has painted a negative picture of the impact social media is having on individuals and the broader society those users take part in. This is true in many ways, but it's important to not understate the positive effects social media has also had on our lives. Having a longitudinal view, and empirical experience, of social media and the changes it has had on family, friends and communities, we are well placed to adequately highlight the opportunities and challenges of its use.

Friends sharing moments with other friends or catching up with family moments while in different countries, or even video calling one's grandma have just been some of the most amazing benefits of social media in recent times. Finding your community of like-minded flute players, or joining a group of dining enthusiasts, or finding a group of people who are excited by thrills on the weekend has secured the role of social media at the forefront for most people. It is the breadth of gratification that makes social media shine through as one of the most successful forms of media in history. But one of its key benefits is the way in which communities mobilise in a variety of ways.

One of those key benefits of social media is its contribution to citizen mobilisation and participation. Activism and campaigning have become more accessible and affordable, expanding activists' capacity for managing, communicating and mobilising information and society. Characteristics of this new type of connective action include personal expression and voluntary coordination without organisational infrastructure or leadership. It is through affordances such as these that social media maintains a moment of hope—a future that uses its infrastructures and communication capacities to engage people, mobilise them for a variety of reasons, include their voices in major decisions, and improve how we might live. The early visions of a digital utopian have all but

J. Hutchinson et al., *Social Media in Society*,
https://doi.org/10.1007/978-3-031-66360-4_10

disappeared under the weight of scandals, political scams, deceit and misinformation. However, the central tenets of social media still provide a glimmer of hope as we transition out of updating your status on Facebook/TikTok/X and towards a more automated, and generated artificially, communication epoch.

To unpack this as the final arena of enquiry of this book, this chapter introduces research from diverse communities in the Global South, noting the diversity of political and cultural contexts that impact social media activism and seeking, to some extent, to address the relative paucity of research into and discussion of social media campaigns outside of North America and Europe. The research in some areas of the Global South, for example, indicates, *among other things*, how individuals who trust that social media activity allows them to influence transformations at the community level have more potential to have effective change at national and international levels. In other words, social media can be empowering. Examples of promoting, establishing, and supporting campaigns from local to national include the ForBALI movement (the Balinese People's Forum to Reject Reclamation in Bali Island), the School Strike 4 Climate campaign, and local include the Black Lives Matter movement. Moreover, global to local (glocalisation), including the #MeToo movement.

This chapter also points to prospects for an improved digital experience for future generations. It considers how social media users are, for good or ill, more digitally immersed and grow up with more access to information and connections. In principle and practice, it considers social media literacy as a strategy for addressing concerns and promoting social media's productive and critically reflexive uses—in whatever communication forms take hold in the coming decade.

## The Advantage of Social Media

Social issues often produce emotive reactions that are fundamental to supporting collaborative efforts to reach governments, politicians, industry people and other actors. Resource mobilisation theory research argues that grievances are essential emotions (Golhasani & Hosseinirad, 2017) because they stimulate collective action (Curti, 2008). Spontaneous participation in social movements is usually related to the activation of grievances (Jasper & Poulsen, 1995; Stewart et al., 2015) because they provide a shared focus that substitutes for leadership and formal organisation (Bray et al., 2018). Social media platforms are tools that enable individuals to express personal and emotive narratives around grievances that motivate others to act (Suwana, 2019). Personalised expression via social media also enables individuals to connect flexibly, adapting activism to suit their ideology, lifestyles and purposes.

One of the defining features of crowd-enabled connective action is its emphasis on personal expression, online communication and voluntary coordination without organisational infrastructure or leadership (Bennett & Segerberg, 2012; Castells, 2012; Earl & Kimport, 2011; Mason, 2013;

Papacharissi & Trevey, 2018; Penney & Dadas, 2014; Pickerill & Krinsky, 2012). Social media activism arises because of a convergence between connective action and the struggle against oppression; when personal expression supports a shared struggle and leads to an early point of change, social media becomes a restorative space. Social media provides an organisational infrastructure for activism and mobilisation and serves as the backbone of communication for the moment. Moreover, they provide expressive forms of networking that are created and shared online.

The collective action logic highlights the importance of goal orientation, the high costs of group formation and the organisational power of groups compared to individuals (Papacharissi & Trevey, 2018). Nevertheless, the capabilities of digital media reduce the cost of coordinating political actions (Berg & Hofmann, 2021). The effect of digital media on activism has been debated for years, and it is essential to remember that despite some scholars arguing that digital media can weaken socio and political actions (Juris, 2012; Keen, 2015; Morozov, 2011), However, there are some scholars who argue that digital media is a powerful tool for creating positive change, connecting, coordinating, sharing information, mobilising people/content, and managing socio-political movements effectively (Gerbaudo, 2012; George & Leidner, 2019; Suwana, 2019; Toepfl, 2018).

The rise of connective action in social movements has been global, regional, and national, exemplified by the Arab Spring and Occupy Wall Street (Greene & Kuswa, 2012; Bennett & Segerberg, 2013), the Save KPK (Corruption Eradication Commission) movement in 2015 (Suwana, 2018, 2019) and the ForBALI (Forum Rakyat Bali Tolak Reklamasi) movement (Bräuchler, 2020; Suwana, 2020). The latest logic of connective action complements, rather than replaces, collective action. It identifies how social media provides new ways for individuals to participate in civic and political activities. The first type of network, the crowd-enabled, is the progressive form of connective action in which people's authentic expressions function as a coordination mechanism that builds up engagement in collective action (Bennett & Segerberg, 2013). Crowd-enabled networks in social media platforms can sustain long-term protests by unaffiliated crowds.

A movement's success or failure depends on its ability to mobilise resources and exploit political chances to achieve its purposes (Martin, 2015), and its achievements rely on the effectiveness of its information production and distribution. Social movements need to be aware of how political, organisational, and strategic situations can affect their impact (Maher et al., 2019); while a protest cycle develops, the organiser should modify their social media platform strategies to adapt to the changing environment (Martin, 2015), which, in turn, will influence external factors. For example, movement actors might adopt a more political logic to negotiate with people in authority or power at the same time as the movement itself encourages society to participate via social media, with the online strategies positively influencing the effectiveness of the movement and resulting in the campaign being embraced by the formal political system like in the case of Taiwan that we unpacked in Chap. 8.

## SOCIAL MEDIA FOR SOCIAL AND POLITICAL MOVEMENTS

We have already unpacked and explored several political movements that used social media to mobilise individuals and make an impact on the broader societal environment in which individuals live. The following two examples build on those case studies, but extend them to highlight the positive aspects, or the case for hope, of social media. As we begin to see the sunset on what we currently understand to be social media communication, the following case studies enable us to identify the positive aspects of social media that might be integrated to the next media technology.

### *School Strike 4 Climate*

Greta Thunberg, a 16-year-old girl from Sweden, founded and led the School Strike 4 Climate (SS4C) movement and operated #SchoolStrike4Climate in 2018. This movement began as a local protest but grew into a global movement led by younger generations who oppose older generations' improper actions towards the environment (Boulianne et al., 2020; Catanzaro & Collin, 2021; Hee et al., 2022). Greta Thunberg's school strike initiative has inspired many young individuals to form and participate within the activist group *Fridays for Future*. This movement advocates striking and demonstrating every Friday, and this strike has earned global recognition (Almlund, 2020; Hee et al., 2022). It has also given rise to numerous worldwide demonstrations to support this movement. It is worth noting that the first two international school strikes took place on March 15 and May 24, 2019, with a remarkable 1.8 million participants across 133 countries in over 130 countries (Almlund, 2020; Irfan, 2019; Boulianne et al., 2020). This condition highlights the growing awareness and concern for the environment among the younger generation—an idea shared and mobilised across social media. It serves as a call to action for individuals and governments to take more proactive steps to address climate change.

SS4C builds on contemporary digital activism by using unique images, particularly of protestors and transnational marches, disseminated extensively on social media platforms (Boulianne et al., 2020; Catanzaro & Collin, 2021). For example, some images describe Greta Thunberg's first solo school strike to demand action for global climate justice from the Swedish Parliament in which Thunberg poses beside a simple hand-painted sign declaring "Skolstrejk For Klimatet", went global due the power of social media. Building from this moment, alongside the global protest marches in 2019, creative online strategy through social media platforms distributed information, organised actions, and mobilised participation locally and globally. Graphic content like sign posters, memes, and images are part of its digital strategy by SS4C (Hee et al., 2022);

this strategy is to share their political demands, standpoints, and motivations as part of young people's shared expression.

Numerous photos of Thunberg and the placard of the SS4C movement have been disseminated via social media, building transnational solidarity and communicating the movement's narrative and political actions (Boulianne et al., 2020; Moran, 2019). Moreover, Thunberg has used X as a social media platform to oppose older generations' past and current actions on the environment, with her tweets being shared, liked, and commented upon by young people (Boulianne et al., 2020). This movement shows how social media offers possibilities for activists and protestors to communicate opinions about the strike, mobilise youth leaders, and discuss climate change as an environmental policy issue.

Social media enabled Thunberg's local action to become a global discussion about environmental policy issues. The placards carried at SS4C marches illustrated the protestors' ideas, beliefs and expectations about climate change and the extent of the powerful emotions experienced by young people due to political action. However, they were also recurrently disseminated online via social media platforms (Catanzaro & Collin, 2021). Many SS4C tweets targeted US President Donald Trump's Twitter efforts as they mentioned the size of the event that are not pro-environment (Boulianne et al., 2020), while in Australia, pictures and cards about the image of Prime Minister Scott Morrison were displayed (Catanzaro & Collin, 2021). Activists utilise social media platforms to communicate their standpoints and to reach global leaders about the importance of climate change, as emotive online expressions are a fundamental way to support collaborative efforts and appeal to governments, politicians, industry people, and other actors.

The power of social media is reflected in its role of extending the development of the SS4C's local and national actions to become global actions. The ecological movement has effectively used social media platforms to connect disparate local events and bring them together under a giant global activism umbrella. This social media movement has helped fill the gaps in power structures between society and government, providing a platform for civil society to share their standpoint and to connect with global leaders who have more resources and mechanisms to act on supporting the environment and addressing climate change issues.

### The ForBALI Movement

ForBALI is a short name for Forum Rakyat Bali Tolak Reklamasi, and this is an alliance of Balinese society regarding the environmental movement established in 2003. It is a civil society-run advocacy movement that has been fighting against Presidential Regulation No. 51 since 2013. It is also another example of a positive affordance that emerged from social media, again to mobile citizens around their politics. This regulation, an authorised amendment to Presidential Decree No. 45 of 2011, removes the conservation status of Benoa

Bay, South Bali and designates it as a commercial zone. Consequently, it allows land reclamation in Benoa Bay. Balinese civil society has opposed land reclamation on their island and refused to allow a commercial area in the conservation area. The information about ForBALI's history and efforts is on their official website, ForBali.org.

The movement was initiated and supported by activists, artists, civil society, musicians, members of non-governmental organisations, public figures, reporters, solicitors, young people, and community leaders (Bräuchler, 2020; Suwana, 2021). This movement has attracted national and international participants (Bräuchler, 2020; Freedom House, 2016). Social media has developed extended coalition groups in crowd-enabled networks that coordinate and promote action, information and people. It has become a longer-term movement that has been active for eight years as of 2021.

The ForBALI coalition groups operate using different online strategies for managing websites, email and instant messaging, and using social media platforms, for example, Facebook, Instagram, YouTube and Twitter, to target potential supporters, including youth, art lovers, civil society, and community groups (Bräuchler, 2020; Suwana, 2021). They have also utilised hashtags to disseminate proper information, to help promote alternative narratives, and connect citizens to their activism. Online participants in digital activism have also undertaken different types of action, including digital storytelling (Canella, 2017; Bakardjieva, 2012), operating hashtags to support and maintain activism (Baer, 2018; Stornaiuolo & Thomas, 2017), and to counter authoritarianism (Amgott, 2018). Therefore, the ForBALI movement has also utilised creative content distributed through social media (Fig. 10.1). Their work reveals the strength of connective action by social media for digital activism.

**Fig. 10.1**  The creative posters of the ForBALI movement (Sources: Inside Indonesia/Alit Ambara)

The ForBALI movement has demonstrated the benefit of social media in rallying society and disseminating information. The initial small group has grown into an extensive network with members from diverse social backgrounds and levels of digital media literacy. They have harnessed their online experiences and expertise to support activism, disseminate information and coerce the government for change. The volunteers joined from various societies and organisations. They became united via social media platforms to produce, manage, disseminate, circulate and mobilise information, using numerous online tactics and social media platforms to support and sustain the anti-reclamation movement. Thus, their digital activism has also shaped society, and they have become agents of change on the issue of land reclamation in Bali.

## SOCIAL MEDIA FOR MOBILISING INFORMATION AND SOCIETY

A key aspect of each of these case studies is to highlight the local to global phenomena. As explained in the SS4C case study, the idea of one individual in Sweden utilised a targeted social media campaign to reach millions of young people around the world. This local to global connection is common through a number of these positive social media experiences. To draw this out further we cast the lens on the #BlackLivesMatter protests.

### Local to Global: The Black Lives Matter Movement

The Black Lives Matter (BLM) movement is a global movement initiated in the African American society that campaigned against brutality and systemic racism towards black people. This movement began online when co-founder Alicia Garzia shared a post following the murder of a young Black boy with the hashtag' #blacklivesmatter' in 2012 (Brown & Mourão, 2021). As the movement gathered momentum, it aimed to sustain national actions that facilitate vigorous opposition against police cruelty targeting Black Americans in the USA, and its efforts included rallies following the deaths of some individuals, negotiation with policymakers, outreach and digital activism (Freelon et al., 2016). Although many non-governmental organisations have emerged from this movement, such as the BLM Global Network, the hashtag' #blacklivesmatter' remains un-trademarked by any group or organisation, meaning the movement's actions can be broader and extended further.

The support for Black Lives Matter or BLM, emerged in reaction to the acquittal of George Zimmerman for the shooting and killing of Trayvon Martin in July 2013, and police officer Darren Wilson for the killing of 18-year-old Michael Brown (Leach & Allen, 2017; Brown & Mourão, 2021). The Black Lives Matter movement has effectively utilised social media platforms like Facebook and X to amplify its political message and agenda. This movement highlights the crucial role that social media plays in organising and mobilising collective action for social justice causes. In recent times, social media has emerged as a collection of platforms where people can connect and collaborate to effect change, form mobilisation, disseminate resources, challenge dominant narratives, and adapt their activism to suit their goals (Bennett & Segerberg, 2012; Cammaerts, 2015; Castells, 2015; Tufekci, 2014; Harlow et al., 2017; Suwana, 2018).

The effectiveness of BLM's content, which includes hashtags, images, memes and videos, supports the notion that social media platforms and features have become critical to the effectiveness of digital activism. The effectiveness of BLM's social media content, including hashtags, images, memes and videos, highlights the crucial role of social media in effective digital activism. News stories about BLM street protests on social media are more likely to receive higher engagement when accompanied by visual content (Brown & Mourão, 2021; Mourão & Brown, 2022). Data from the Pew Research Centre stated that in 2020 there were 47.8 million uses of the #BLM Twitter hashtags, while the average of hashtags used daily was just under 3.7 million times (Anderson et al., 2020). Other data also showed TikTok has 12 billion views for the hashtag #BlackLivesMatter, while Instagram has 24 million #BlackoutTuesday views and #sharethemicnow reached 300 million followers on Instagram (Maqbool, 2020). The influence of social media on the level of support for BLM's actions has been significant, as it has influenced the spread of related content across various social media networks and became news in mainstream media.

BLM represents a movement within the Black community that aims to terminate police brutality and improve the criminal justice system; it is not just a network of specific communities at local, national and global levels (Coles & Saleem, 2021). Social media allow movements such as BLM to convey their messages to a broader audience without the filtering and gate-keeping that occur in the traditional media system (Coles & Saleem, 2021; Brown & Mourão, 2021). This movement also played a critical role in establishing and facilitating the movement. It facilitated digital activists to accumulate evidence of the cause and BLM to grow from a national to a global human rights stand.

## The Key to Overcoming the Disadvantages of Social Media

Social media has increased awareness among its users of its potential to sustain social and political actions. Political parties, mass organisations and non-governmental organisations now use websites and social media accounts as valuable tools for achieving social and political change. The development of digital activism is one of the critical keys to supporting democracy. Online content and data have recently gained importance, and they have the potential to become one of the strengths of social media. Young people, educated, urban middle-class society, have increasingly used social media to support political participation. This trend could be a significant evolutionary step in widespread online socio-political activism. However, it also highlights the need to improve digital media literacy.

Developing social and digital media literacy is a long-term solution that requires continuous education and advocacy efforts beyond sporadic and voluntary movements. To achieve this, we must understand how social media contributes to public spaces and impacts our social, political and economic lives. Achieving this requires the collaboration of multiple stakeholders, such as government officials, civil society, private industry, education organisations, the media industry and the technology sector, who can work together and support each other to contextualise social media usage in everyday lives.

Digital media platforms are transforming the proportion between spectatorship and participation (Araya, 2015; Gee, 2010), as people can participate and not only oversee. Individuals can create news, audio, audio visual and video games, whereas previously, these abilities were restricted to media or creative professionals (Bennett, 2008; Flew, 2014). The power of social media has enabled the voiceless to become creators so they can express themselves and allow audiences to become empowered (Wilding et al., 2018). In the digital era, individuals can play the dual role of consumers and producers of content, referred to as produsers (Bruns, 2018; Papacharissi, 2010; Napoli, 2011). Evolving both as a source and as a receiver of social media is complex and determined by distinct characteristics, which includes social media literacy skills to manage it well.

Digital capabilities are essential and critical for socio and political life in the online environment. There are some digital capabilities like information access and retrieval, analysis and evaluation, communication and creation, reflection and acts that have been identified by scholars as crucial components of effective and efficient learning (Hobbs, 2010; Kahne et al., 2012; Van Laar et al., 2020). At the same time, they include the capability to utilise new media platforms to critically read online texts in various methods, to analyse online media, questions, problem-solving mindset, and to produce content (Leu et al., 2013). Society must, therefore, advance its digital media literacy skills so that individuals can not only consume online content but also create and distribute it and actively participate in socio-political life. Multiple stakeholders need to assist individuals in developing critical thinking skills about digital media and information to navigate valuable usage in the online environment. In other words, digital media literacy is a lens for developing critical ability and practising digital activism (Amgott, 2018). The competencies required for critical thinking about online media content include analysing information integrity, credibility, and angle and its potential effects or consequences—skills that broad audiences typically do not have.

Online information is more easily circulated by social media platforms compared with more traditional forms of media, and as these platforms have shortened the gatekeeping process of traditional media news and allowed information to circulate directly from one person to another (Bruns, 2018; Buckingham, 2017). However, the distribution of misinformation and disinformation via social media has been growing as we pointed out in Chap. 9, and how to obtain correct information for the public is becoming a crucial condition. The circulation of misinformation and disinformation is a complex process and introduces considerable chance to harm democracy (Bradshaw et al., 2021; Carson & Titcomb, 2018; Kahne & Bowyer, 2017). The high levels of Internet exposure in a population are contribute to the promotion, creation and distribution of disinformation and misinformation (Naeem & Kamel, 2021; Nadzir et al., 2019; Wibowo et al., 2019). If lower levels of digital media literacy are present, this is a potential recipe for disaster (Irawanto, 2019; Tapsell, 2018). Therefore, individuals must possess and improve digital media literacy skills to evaluate online information and produce factual content critically.

To combat all these issues and maintain a healthy democratic society, it is crucial to ensure exposure to diverse perspectives. Unfortunately, there is an alarming rise in concerns about the prevalence of biased information in civic and political discussions at national, regional and global levels (Kahne et al., 2012; Vasist et al., 2023). Furthermore, it is urgent that civil society takes commitment and produces online content solely based on facts, correct values, ethics and trust. Right now, the onus is place on individuals to be responsible for ensuring that their online content exhibits the correct values, prevents disinformation, and does not create misinformation—an incredibly difficult task when placed alongside digital literacy. Therefore, civil society must have the capacity to increase digital media literacy to create and distribute online content that effectively supports positive living, including activism. The framework for developing digital media literacy skills focuses on four key elements: content, changers, community, and collaboration; this framework expands existing initiatives and supports new programmes and online activities (Suwana, 2021) that will empower everyone to participate in democratic cultures and practices (Fig. 10.2).

Building on the work of Suwana (2021), the framework consists of several elements, the first one being content. With the advent of digital media, there is now more excellent proximity, volume and variety of content available to engage with daily. This advantage has significantly changed the online media environment and transformed how we consume and produce content. Therefore, creating content creation skills among young people demonstrates beneficial improvement in helping them to overcome their fears and enabling them to disseminate their views, understanding and culture online as active citizens in democratic countries.

The second component of the digital media literacy movement framework is the concept of changers or agents of change. The framework suggests that some groups of people have the potential to become agents of change.

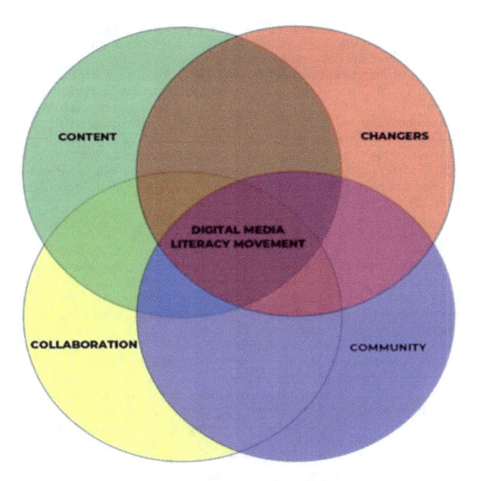

**Fig. 10.2** The digital media literacy movement framework

However, these young people need opportunities to enhance their digital media literacy skills and receive help in utilising people to build connection and to partake in digital activism. The role of change agents who can also support the digital media literacy movement is more extensive than that of young people alone. Activists, parents, teachers and lecturers, academics, influencers, civil workers, police, library keepers, professional workers, digital technology experts, government and lawmakers can all be agents of change for digital media literacy.

The third important aspect of improving digital media literacy is the community. The community-based learning technique is critical in providing access to digital media literacy education for individuals unable to obtain formal education. Some individuals often depend on their peer groups or communities to informally learn digital media literacy skills. Thus, it is essential to involve digital media literacy communities in developing and supporting literacy skills agendas and curriculums. This community will ensure that individuals have the required support and opportunities to understand and enhance these skills with the help of their communities and civil society.

The final element in the digital media literacy movement framework is collaboration. The many stakeholders involved in digital media literacy movements must collaborate to create and support the changes, content and communities that will improve every member of society's digital literacy skills and knowledge. Collaboration on digital media literacy initiatives that are data driven is essential for fostering active citizenship in democratic nations. The digital media literacy is important to equip members of societies to participate in social and political issues and create digital strategies to improve social and political movements in the digital era.

## Conclusion

This book has examined social media from its early inception post Web 2.0, through to the current moments that sees the rise of TikTok, the pushback against influencers and the imminent implosion of X as one of the key platforms of our time. During this almost 20-year period, there has been the rise of its popularity which brought with it the insatiable datafication of all aspects of social media that enable its use to be stored, sorted, sold and manipulated. Specific individuals emerged as thought leaders and influencers, entire industries were formed and flourished, and existing institutions and industries incorporated social media in ways that elevated their *raison d'être*. The opportunities that have surfaced has been unlike any other media technology and communication moment in the past, making the focus of social media research one of the most sought-after fields for humanities and social science researchers.

That scholarship has also followed a path that examined the awe of the tools, through to the critical examination of its use and implementation, followed by the current lens that explores the vast impact of misinformation. During that process, journalism studies, political science, marketing and business schools, cultural studies, economics and a range of other fields developed and incorporated their own perspectives on social media into their scholarship. Social media emerged and evolved to become one of the biggest events of our modern times, bringing with it promises of utopian futures: informed citizens, truly democratic societies with rich public spheres, equality and diversity. And while it did deliver on some of these aspects, it also brought with it a host of issues that are at the centre of our current societal makeup.

We've outlined these opportunities and challenges throughout this book to prompt scholars and students to implement on future communication technologies that are emerging on the horizon. That is to say, with change and opportunity, the process remains the same: egalitarian opportunities emerge, fringe users and groups implement these to provide voice to those who have less, these opportunities are gamed for political and commercial benefit, and the system overall becomes a place of class and inequality. If we look at the current social media environment, we are certainly experiencing a place of inequality, challenged safety, misinformation and hatred. This is the time to step away from social media and work towards the next communication giant: generative artificial intelligence.

While we are appreciative of the affordances that emerged through the social media epoch, it is crucial that we understand what worked and what was exploited for personal gain of a few individuals. As we commence our path down the next era, it is crucial that we take these learnings and establish safe environments form the get go for the users who will make creative industries, new communication possibilities, markets and industries, cultural experiences, art, music and the like. The worst mistake we could make is to ignore the revelations of the last 20 years and repeat the same path again and again as new media technologies emerge.

Thanks, social media. You were excellent for a time, and you certainly showed us what was possible. It's time for humanity to extract the best parts and move on to the next communication era.

## REFERENCES

Almlund, P. (2020, June 22). *Greta Thunberg—A climate activist.* Nordics Info, Aarhus University. Retrieved from https://nordics.info/show/artikel/greta-thunberg

Amgott, N. (2018). Critical Literacy in# Digital Activism: Collaborative Choice and Action. *The International Journal of Information and Learning Technology, 35*(5), 329–341.

Anderson, M., Barthel, M., Perrin, A., & Vogels, E. A. (2020). #BlackLivesMatter surges on Twitter after George Floyd's death. *Pew Research Centre.* Retrieved from https://www.pewresearch.org/short-reads/2020/06/10/blacklivesmatter-surges-on-twitter-after-george-floyds-death/

Araya, D. (2015). *Rethinking US Education Policy: Paradigms of the Knowledge Economy.*

Baer, H. (2018). Redoing Feminism: Digital Activism, Body Politics, and Neoliberalism. In *Digital Feminisms* (pp. 25–42). Routledge.

Bakardjieva, M. (2012). Reconfiguring the Mediapolis: New Media and Civic Agency. *New Media & Society, 14*(1), 63–79.

Bennett, W. L. (2008). *Changing Citizenship in the Digital Age.*

Bennett, W. L., & Segerberg, A. (2012). The Logic of Connective Action: Digital Media and the Personalization of Contentious Politics. *Information, Communication & Society, 15*(5), 739–768. https://doi.org/10.1080/1369118X.2012.670661

Bennett, W. L., & Segerberg, A. (2013). *The Logic of Connective Action: Digital Media and the Personalization of Contentious Politics.* Cambridge University Press.

Berg, S., & Hofmann, J. (2021). Digital Democracy. *Internet Policy Review, 10*(4).

Boulianne, S., Lalancette, M., & Ilkiw, D. (2020). "School Strike 4 Climate": Social Media and the International Youth Protest on Climate Change. *Media and Communication, 8*(2), 208–218. https://doi.org/10.17645/mac.v8i2.2768

Bradshaw, S., Bailey, H., & Howard, P. N. (2021). *Industrialised disinformation: 2020 global inventory of organised social media manipulation.* Computational Propaganda Project at the Oxford Internet Institute.

Bräuchler, B. (2020). Bali Tolak Reklamasi: The local adoption of global protest. *Convergence*. Online First. https://doi.org/10.1177/2F1354856518806695

Bray, L. A., Shriver, T. E., & Adams, A. E. (2018). Mobilizing Grievances in an Authoritarian Setting: Threat and Emotion in the 1953 Plzeň Uprising. *Sociological Perspectives, 62*(1), 77–95.

Brown, D. K., & Mourão, R. R. (2021). Protest Coverage Matters: How Media Framing and Visual Communication Affects Support for Black Civil Rights Protests. *Mass Communication and Society, 24*(4), 576–596.

Bruns, A. (2018). *Gatewatching and News Curation: Journalism, Social Media, and the Public Sphere*. Peter Lang.

Buckingham, D. (2017). Media Theory 101: AGENCY. *Journal of Media Literacy, 64*(1), 12–16.

Cammaerts, B. (2015). Social Media and Activism. In R. Mansell & A. P. Hwa (Eds.), *The International Encyclopaedia of Digital Communication and Society* (pp. 1027–1034). Wiley-Blackwell.

Canella, G. (2017). Social Movement Documentary Practices: Digital Storytelling, Social Media and Organising. *Digital Creativity, 28*(1), 24–23.

Carson, J., & Titcomb, J. (2018, January 29). Fake news: What exactly is it—And how can you spot it. *The Telegraph*. Retrieved from http://www.telegraph.co.uk/technology/0/fake-news-exactly-has-really-had-influence/

Castells, M. (2012). *Networks of Outrage and Hope: Social Movements in the Internet Age*. Wiley.

Castells, M. (2015). *Networks of Outrage and Hope: Social Movements in the Internet Age* (2nd ed.). Wiley.

Catanzaro, M., & Collin, P. (2021). Kids Communicating Climate Change: Learning from the Visual Language of the SchoolStrike4Climate Protests. *Educational Review, 75*, 9. https://doi.org/10.1080/00131911.2021.1925875

Coles, S. M., & Saleem, M. (2021). Social media expression and user predispositions: Applying the differential susceptibility to media effects model to the study of issue polarization. *Social Media + Society*. https://doi.org/10.1177/2F20563051211052907

Curti, G. H. (2008). From a Wall of Bodies to a Body of Walls. *Emotion, Space and Society, 1*(2), 106–118. https://doi.org/10.1016/j.emospa.2009.02.002

Earl, J., & Kimport, K. (2011). *Digitally Enabled Social Change: Activism in the Internet Age*. MIT Press.

Flew, T. (2014). *New Media: An Introduction*. Oxford University Press.

Freedom House. Freedom in the World 2016 - Indonesia, 7 June 2016, https://www.refworld.org/reference/annualreport/freehou/2016/en/110485, Accessed 12 October 2024.

Freelon, D., McIlwain, C. D., & Clark, M. (2016). *Beyond the hashtags: # Ferguson, # BlackLivesMatter, and the online struggle for offline justice*. Centre for Media & Social Impact, American University, Forthcoming. https://doi.org/10.2139/ssrn.2747066

Gee, J. P. (2010). A Situated-sociocultural Approach to Literacy and Technology. *The New Literacies: Multiple Perspectives on Research and Practice, 165*, 193.

George, J. J., & Leidner, D. E. (2019). From Clicktivism to Hacktivism: Understanding Digital Activism. *Information and Organization, 29*(3), 100249. https://doi.org/10.1016/j.infoandorg.2019.04.001

Gerbaudo, P. (2012). *Tweets and the Streets: Social Media and Contemporary Activism.* Pluto Press.

Golhasani, A., & Hosseinirad, A. (2017). The Role of Resource Mobilization Theory in Social Movement. *International Journal of Multicultural and Multireligious Understanding, 3*(6), 1–5. https://doi.org/10.18415/ijmmu.v3i6.58

González-Bailón, S., Borge-Holthoefer, J., Rivero, A., & Moreno, Y. (2011). The Dynamics of Protest Recruitment Through an Online Network. *Scientific Reports, 1*(1), 1–7.

Greene, R. W., & Kuswa, K. D. (2012). "From the Arab Spring to Athens, from Occupy Wall Street to Moscow": Regional Accents and the Rhetorical Cartography of Power. *Rhetoric Society Quarterly, 42*(3), 271–288.

Harlow, S., Salaverría, R., Kilgo, D. K., & García-Perdomo, V. (2017). Protest Paradigm in Multimedia: Social Media Sharing of Coverage about the Crime of Ayotzinapa, Mexico. *Journal of Communication, 67*(3), 328–349. https://doi.org/10.1111/jcom.12296

Hee, M., Jürgens, A. S., Fiadotava, A., Judd, K., & Feldman, H. R. (2022). Communicating Urgency Through Humor: School Strike 4 Climate Protest Placards. *Journal of Science Communication, 21*(5), A02.

Ho, M. S. (2018). From Mobilization to Improvisation: The Lessons from Taiwan's 2014 Sunflower Movement. *Social Movement Studies, 17*(2), 189–202.

Hobbs, R. (2010). Digital and Media Literacy: A Plan of Action. A White Paper on the Digital and Media Literacy Recommendations of the Knight Commission on the Information Needs of Communities in a Democracy.

Irawanto, B. (2019). Making it Personal: The Campaign Battle on Social Media in Indonesia's 2019 Presidential Election. *ISEAS Yusof Ishak Institute, 28*, 1–11.

Irfan, U. (2019). One of the largest environmental protests ever is underway. It's led by children. *Vox-Understand the News. May, 24.*

Jasper, J. M., & Poulsen, J. D. (1995). Recruiting Strangers and Friends: Moral Shocks and Social Networks in Animal Rights and Anti-nuclear Protests. *Social Problems, 42*(4), 493–512.

Juris, J. S. (2012). Reflections on# Occupy Everywhere: Social Media, Public Space, and Emerging Logics of Aggregation. *American Ethnologist, 39*(2), 259–279. https://doi.org/10.1111/j.1548-1425.2012.01362.x

Kahne, J., & Bowyer, B. (2017). Educating for Democracy in a Partisan Age: Confronting the Challenges of Motivated Reasoning and Misinformation. *American Educational Research Journal, 54*(1), 3–34.

Kahne, J., Lee, N. J., & Feezell, J. T. (2012). Digital Media Literacy Education and Online Civic and Political Participation. *International Journal of Communication, 6*, 24.

Kahne, J., Middaugh, E., Lee, N. J., & Feezell, J. T. (2012). Youth Online Activity and Exposure to Diverse Perspectives. *New Media & Society, 14*(3), 492–512.

Keen, A. (2015). *The Internet is not the Answer.* Atlantic Monthly Press.

Leach, C., & Allen, A. (2017). The Social Psychology of the Black Lives Matter Meme and Movement. *Current Directions in Psychological Science, 16*(6), 543–547. https://doi.org/10.1177/2F0963721417719319

Leu, D. J., Forzani, E., Burlingame, C., Kulikowich, J., Sedransk, N., Coiro, J., & Kennedy, C. (2013). The New Literacies of Online Research and Comprehension: Assessing and Preparing Students for the 21st Century with Common Core

State Standards. *Quality Reading Instruction in the Age of Common Core Standards, 219,* 236.

Maher, T. V., Martin, A., McCarthy, J. D., & Moorhead, L. (2019). Assessing the Explanatory Power of Social Movement Theories Across the Life Course of the Civil Rights Movement. *Social Currents, 6*(5), 399–421. https://doi.org/10.1177/2F2329496519850846

Maqbool, A. (2020). *Black Liver Matter social media—digital impact and beyond,* Mediakix. Retrieved from https://mediakix.com/blog/black-lives-matter-social-media/

Martin, G. (2015). *Understanding Social Movements.* Routledge.

Mason, D. (2013). *Voluntary Nonprofit Enterprise Management.* Springer Science & Business Media.

Moran, L. (2019, September 23). *Incredibly moving' photo of Greta Thunberg's first climate strike goes viral.* Huffpost. September 23, 2019. Retrieved from https://www.huffpost.com/entry/greta-thunberg-photo-viral-again_n_5d85f07ae4b070d468cd3bb7?ri18n=true

Morozov, E. (2011). *The Net Delusion: How not to Liberate the World.* Penguin.

Mourão, R. R., & Brown, D. K. (2022). Black Lives Matter Coverage: How Protest News Frames and Attitudinal Change Affect Social Media Engagement. *Digital Journalism, 10*(4), 626–646.

Nadzir, I., Sari Seftiani, S., & Yogi Setya Permana, Y. S. (2019). Hoax and Misinformation in Indonesia: Insights from a Nationwide Survey. *Perspective, 92.* Retrieved from https://www.iseas.edu.sg/images/pdf/ISEAS_Perspective_2019_92.pdf

Naeem, S. B., & Kamel, M. N. B. (2021). COVID-19 Misinformation Online and Health Literacy: A Brief Overview. *International journal of environmental research and public health, 18*(15), 8091.

Napoli, P. M. (2011). *Audience Evolution: New Technologies and the Transformation of Media Audiences.* Columbia University Press.

Papacharissi, Z. (2010). *A Private Sphere: Democracy in a Digital Age.* Polity.

Papacharissi, Z. (2015). *Affective Publics: Sentiment, Technology, and Politics.* Oxford University Press.

Papacharissi, Z., & Trevey, M. T. (2018). Affective Publics and Windows of Opportunity: Social Media and the Potential for Social Change. In G. Meikle (Ed.), *The Routledge Companion to Media and Activism* (pp. 87–96). Routledge.

Penney, J., & Dadas, C. (2014). (Re)Tweeting in the Service of Protest: Digital Composition and Circulation in the Occupy Wall Street Movement. *New Media & Society, 16*(1), 74–90. https://doi.org/10.1177/1461444813479593

Pickerill, J., & Krinsky, J. (2012). Why does Occupy Matter? *Social Movement Studies, 11*(3–4), 279–287. https://doi.org/10.1080/14742837.2012.708923

Stewart, J., Enciso Bendall, M., & Morgan, C. V. (2015). Jobs, Flags, and Laws: How Interests, Culture, and Values Explain Recruitment into the Utah Minuteman Project. *Sociological Perspectives, 58*(4), 627–648.

Stornaiuolo, A., & Thomas, E. E. (2017). Disrupting Educational Inequalities Through Youth Digital Activism. *Review of Research in Education, 41*(1), 337–357.

Suwana, F. (2018). *Digital media and Indonesian young people: Building sustainable democratic institutions and practices* [Doctoral dissertation, Queensland University of Technology, 2018].

Suwana, F. (2019). What Motivates Digital Activism? The Case of the Save KPK Movement in Indonesia. *Information, Communication & Society, 23*(9), 1295–1310. https://doi.org/10.1080/1369118X.2018.1563205

Suwana, F. (2020). Digital Activism in Bali: The ForBALI Movement. In A. Vandenberg & N. Zuryani (Eds.), *Security, Democracy, and Society in Bali: Trouble with Protection* (pp. 253–284).

Suwana, F. (2021). Content, Changers, Community and Collaboration: Expanding Digital Media Literacy Initiatives. *Media Practice and Education, 22*(2), 153–170. https://doi.org/10.1080/25741136.2021.1888192

Tapsell, R. (2018). Disinformation and democracy in Indonesia. *New Mandala*. Retrieved from https://www.newmandala.org/disinformation-democracy-indonesia/

Toepfl, F. (2018). From Connective to Collective Action: Internet Elections as a Digital Tool to Centralize and Formalize Protest in Russia. *Information, Communication & Society, 21*(4), 531–547. https://doi.org/10.1080/1369118x.2017.1290127

Tufekci, Z. (2014). Social Movements and Governments in the Digital Age: Evaluating a Complex Landscape. *Journal of International Affairs, 68*(1).

Van Laar, E., Van Deursen, A. J., Van Dijk, J. A., & De Haan, J. (2020). Determinants of 21st-Century Skills and 21st-Century Digital Skills for Workers: A Systematic Literature Review. *Sage Open, 10*(1), 2158244019900176.

Vasist, P. N., Chatterjee, D., & Krishnan, S. (2023). The Polarising Impact of Political Disinformation and Hate Speech: A Cross-Country Configural Narrative. *Information Systems Frontiers, 26*, 1–26.

Wibowo, K. A., Rahmawan, D., & Maryani, E. (2019). In Indonesia, young and old share fake news on social media. *The Conversation*. Retrieved from https://theconversation.com/in-indonesia-young-and-old-share-fake-news-on-social-media-111433

Wilding, D., Fray, P., Molitorisz, S., & McKewon, E. (2018). *The Impact of Digital Platforms on News and Journalistic Content*. University of Technology Sydney.

# INDEX

GPSR Compliance
The European Union's (EU) General Product Safety Regulation (GPSR) is a set
of rules that requires consumer products to be safe and our obligations to
ensure this.

If you have any concerns about our products, you can contact us on

ProductSafety@springernature.com

In case Publisher is established outside the EU, the EU authorized
representative is:

Springer Nature Customer Service Center GmbH
Europaplatz 3
69115 Heidelberg, Germany